HOW TO BE A GEEK

D1594031

HOW TO BE A GEEK

Essays on the Culture of Software

Matthew Fuller

polity

This collection © Polity Press 2017
Introduction & Chapters 3, 6, 10, 11 & 12 © Matthew Fuller
Chapter 1 © Matthew Fuller & Andrew Goffey
Chapter 2 © Matthew Fuller & Graham Harwood
Chapter 4 © Matthew Fuller, Andrew Goffey, Adrian Mackenzie, Richard Mills & Stuart Sharples
Chapter 5 © Matthew Fuller, Nikita Mazurov & Dan McQuillan
Chapter 7 © Matthew Fuller & M. Beatrice Fazi
Chapter 8 © Matthew Fuller & Olga Goriunova
Chapter 9 © Matthew Fuller & Sónia Matos

The right of Matthew Fuller to be identified as Author of this Work has been asserted in accordance with the UK Copyright, Designs and Patents Act 1988.

First published in 2017 by Polity Press

Polity Press
65 Bridge Street
Cambridge CB2 1UR, UK

Polity Press
350 Main Street
Malden, MA 02148, USA

All rights reserved. Except for the quotation of short passages for the purpose of criticism and review, no part of this publication may be reproduced, stored in a retrieval system or transmitted, in any form or by any means, electronic, mechanical, photocopying, recording or otherwise, without the prior permission of the publisher.

ISBN-13: 978-1-5095-1715-2
ISBN-13: 978-1-5095-1716-9 (pb)

A catalogue record for this book is available from the British Library.

Library of Congress Cataloging-in-Publication Data

Names: Fuller, Matthew, editor.
Title: How to be a geek : essays on the culture of software / [compiled by] Matthew Fuller.
Description: Cambridge, UK ; Malden, MA, USA : Polity, 2017. | Includes bibliographical references and index.
Identifiers: LCCN 2016042587 (print) | LCCN 2016058649 (ebook) | ISBN 9781509517152 (hardback) | ISBN 9781509517169 (pbk.) | ISBN 9781509517183 (Mobi) | ISBN 9781509517190 (Epub)
Subjects: LCSH: Software engineering–Psychological aspects. | Software engineering–Social aspects.
Classification: LCC QA76.76.H85 H69 2017 (print) | LCC QA76.76.H85 (ebook) | DDC 005.1–dc23
LC record available at https://lccn.loc.gov/2016042587

Typeset in 10.5 on 12 pt Sabon by Toppan Best-set Premedia Limited
Printed and bound in Great Britain by CPI Group (UK) Ltd, Croydon

The publisher has used its best endeavours to ensure that the URLs for external websites referred to in this book are correct and active at the time of going to press. However, the publisher has no responsibility for the websites and can make no guarantee that a site will remain live or that the content is or will remain appropriate.

Every effort has been made to trace all copyright holders, but if any have been inadvertently overlooked the publisher will be pleased to include any necessary credits in any subsequent reprint or edition.

For further information on Polity, visit our website: politybooks.com

CONTENTS

ACKNOWLEDGEMENTS

'The Obscure Objects of Object Orientation' (with Andrew Goffey) was previously published in Penny Harvey, Eleanor Conlin Casella, Gillian Evans, Hannah Knox, Christine McLean, Elizabeth B. Silva, Nicholas Thoburn and Kath Woodward, eds., *The Routledge Companion to Objects and Materials*, Routledge, London, 2013, and in a variant form in *Zeitschrift für Medienwissenschaft*. With thanks to Claus Pias, Elizabeth B. Silva and Nicholas Thoburn.

'Abstract Urbanism' (with Graham Harwood) was previously published in Rob Kitchin and Sung Yueh Perng, eds., *Code and the City*, Routledge, London, 2016, and presented at the Programmable City workshop at Nirsa in Maynooth the previous year. Thanks to all at the Programmable City project.

'Software Studies Methods' was previously published in Jentery Sayers, ed., *The Routledge Companion to Media Studies and Digital Humanities*, Routledge, New York, 2016. With thanks to Wendy Hui Kyong Chun and Jentery Sayers.

'Big Diff, Granularity, Incoherence and Production in the Github Software Repository' (with Andrew Goffey, Adrian Mackenzie, Richard Mills and Stuart Sharples) was previously published in Ina Blom, Trond Lundemo and Eivind Røssaak, eds., *Memory in Motion: Archives, Technology and the Social*, Amsterdam University Press, Amsterdam, 2016. It follows research with the co-authors in the ESRC-funded Metacommunities of Code project, led by Adrian Mackenzie.

'The Author Field' (with Nikita Mazurov and Dan McQuillan) follows from work on the *London Cryptofestival* in November 2013. With thanks to Yuk Hui.

'Always One Bit More: Computing and the Experience of Ambiguity' was previously published in Olga Goriunova, ed., *Fun and Software: Pleasure, Pain and Paradox in Computing*, Bloomsbury, New York, 2015. With thanks to Olga Goriunova, Annet Dekker and Anette Weinberger.

'Computational Aesthetics' (with M. Beatrice Fazi) was previously published in Christiane Paul, ed., *A Companion to Digital Art*, Wiley-Blackwell, Oxford, 2016. With thanks to Christian Paul and Beatrice Fazi.

'Phrase' (with Olga Goriunova), was previously published in Celia Lury and Nina Wakeford, eds., *Inventive Methods*, Routledge, London, 2013. With thanks to Olga Goriunova, Celia Lury and Nina Wakeford.

'Feral Computing: From Ubiquitous Calculation to Wild Interactions' (with Sónia Matos) was previously published in *Fibreculture Journal*, Sydney, 2011. With thanks to Sónia Matos and Andrew Murphie.

'Just Fun Enough To Go Completely Mad About: On Games, Procedures and Amusement' was previously presented as a paper at the St Petersburg Centre for Media Philosophy; a workshop organized by the ARITHMUS research project at Goldsmiths; and C-Dare at Coventry University. Thanks to Alina Latypova, Evelyn Ruppert, Baki Cakici, Hetty Blades and Scott de la Hunta.

An early version of 'Black Sites and Transparency Layers' was given as a talk organized by Robin McKay of Urbanomic at Thomas Dane Gallery, London, March 2015. With thanks to John Gerrard. A later version was presented at the Academy of Fine Arts Nuremburg, with thanks to Kerstin Stakemeier; at the Interface Politics conference, Barcelona, April 2016, with thanks to Jaron Rowan and Pau Alsina; and as an inaugural lecture at Goldsmiths, with thanks to everyone there.

Thanks to Femke Snelting and Sarah Magnan of Open Source Publishing for the cover design, and to John Thompson and George Owers at Polity for an easy and affable collaboration. Many thanks to Fiona Sewell for brilliant diagnoses and surgery of the text.

BIOGRAPHIES OF CO-AUTHORS

M. Beatrice Fazi is a Research Fellow at the Humanities Lab, Sussex University, where she works on the cultural theory and philosophy of computing.

Andrew Goffey is co-author, with Matthew Fuller, of *Evil Media* and translator of books by Félix Guattari and Isabelle Stengers amongst others. He is Associate Professor in Critical Theory and Cultural Studies at the University of Nottingham.

Olga Goriunova is Senior Lecturer in the Department of Media Arts, Royal Holloway, University of London, and is editor and curator of many projects, and author of *Art Platforms and Cultural Production on the Internet*.

Graham Harwood is a member of the artist group YoHa and Senior Lecturer at Goldsmiths, University of London.

Adrian Mackenzie is Professor of Sociology at Lancaster University and author of numerous books including *Wirelessness: Radical Empiricism in Network Cultures*.

Sónia Matos is a designer, Lecturer in the Department of Design, University of Edinburgh, and a Research Fellow at the Madeira Interactive Technologies Institute.

Nikita Mazurov is a security and forensics researcher and Postdoctoral Researcher at the Living Archives Project, University of Malmö.

Dan McQuillan is Lecturer in Creative and Social Computing at Goldsmiths, University of London, and science and technical lead for Science for Change Kosovo.

Richard Mills is a Research Associate at the Psychometrics Centre, University of Cambridge, and a researcher in the statistical analysis of online data.

Stuart Sharples is a Senior Research Associate in the Department of Sociology, University of Lancaster.

INTRODUCTION

The mode of knowing software is not yet established. We are still at a point where a critical language to understand the wider domain of computational culture is only beginning to ferment. There is a lot of writing about software, a lot of writing in and as software, and a lot of conjuration of alphanumeric strings that is done by and as software. Writing on software which works through a critical or speculative mode is not especially different from these things; it inhabits some of the same modes, idioms and intellectual habitats. It works, at one scale or another, with the same logical aggregates. Writing on software is thus at least partially inside software, even when presented as a paper book. The point in this collection of texts is to work into a few places within that condition.

Due to the complexity and variety of entities and processes that produce computational cultures, and the multiplicity of ways in which they can be understood, experienced, put into play, there is a movement between modes of writing here. Some of the texts are musings, almost dazed, gazing into the screen, across a slither of cable, or into the genealogies of logics in an attempt to discern a murmuring between registers. Others are more programmatic essays that attempt to find the intersections between certain combinations of parabola of enquiry and to draw some locations, speeds and movements out from them. Concatenations of numbers drawn from systems are arrayed and compared, alongside ideas about what numbers are.

To write about software cultures, then, is not to attempt to stamp an order on it, but to draw out some conditions that are particular to the way in which computational systems, and the different scales of their articulation, from minor aspects of interface to globally oriented mechanisms, can be brought into resonant communication

1

with ideas and questions that extend them beyond the private con-versations of technical experts into wider conjugations of ways of asking questions and making problems. Equally, much of the work here operates with the concepts of computer science as fundamentally cultural and political, as something core to contemporary forms of life and thus as open to theoretical cultural exploration as much as architecture, sexuality or economics might be. Indeed, a proposition of this book is that computing is aligned with all three of these, and other factors, in numerous ways and that tracing these conjugations can give us some information about contemporary life that would be unavailable otherwise. This is to say, too, that whilst the work to address software as culture is currently taking many forms, to reduce it solely to the stable sets of categories and objects known to existing disciplines is to miss the historical moment.

Geek

To be a geek is, in one way or another, to be over-enthused, over-informed, over-excited, over-detailed. There is an awkwardness born out of a superfluity of an extraneous kind of desire that becomes a febrile quiver in the face of an interesting problem. To be geeky is to have too much interest in something to the detriment of comport-ment, code spilling over into a gabble, a liveliness found in something that a more reserved protocol would keep under wraps or avoid. To be a geek is to be a bit too public with your enthusiasms, to be slightly unaware in turn that these thrills may, to others, rightly be dull as dust dehydrated with a special process of your own invention. Its mixture of juiciness and dryness, being able to get juiced on dryness, perhaps gets to the core of the problem. Frankly, it's a ludicrous position to be in – it is after all a bit bewildering to find this stuff so fascinating – but it is one whose perversity puts it in a strange relation of proximity to fundamental dynamics in contemporary life.

Such a condition leads many geeks into precariously powerful positions. Companies founded and staffed by geeks rule the world in many ways. They fill institutions and create commercial entities. One can be both ludicrous and lucrative, a maniac for certain details that remake the cosmos by their syntax, or that found a new grammar of relation between things. Geeks created the internet and fight over its meaning. They govern and subvert governance, or keep it ticking over with regular incremental upgrades. Geeks produce extravagant con-traptions that cement their positions in the most comedically venal ways, but they also make machines with panache that auto-destruct in deserts and car parks and servers; sometimes intentionally. They make games that provide the grounds of individuation for millions, and then find the wealth it occasionally brings depressingly pointless but irresistible.

Given this, geeks may often mute themselves, try and pass as underwhelming. This is probably an adequate survival strategy in many circumstances. An alternative to it is a form of intellectual cosplay: learn to grow and stretch out your membranes to generate new kinds of sensitivity to the present. In the growth of such tender surfaces and depths, become slightly perturbing (as in the Dutch word *gek*, which shares a common etymological root with *geek*, meaning mad, or crazy), develop the capacity to feel the interaction of electromagnetic waves with your anorak of ideas. Work their ordering via logic into concatenations of circuits that then propitiate further ordering. Sense on into their interaction with other forces arrayed as fields and intensities at the scales of the social, the aesthetic, the ideational or economic. Learn to trace, cajole and heighten the fatal and illuminating crossings of wires and desires.

Such an unfolding and an invention of sensitivities means also some reflection on the figure of the geek, as something both powerful and flawed. The geek tragedy improves on the traditional mixture of these two qualities by adding the factor of technology. This variant of the tragedy is there since that of Icarus, who flew too close to the sun and melted his wings. If the traditional reading of Icarus is a warning about the hubris of knowledge in relation to nature and the inviolable space of the gods, technology folds in both violation and knowledge as constitutional factors. Any attempt to 'White Box' technology as a simple Good that needs no examination misses this fundamental transformative characteristic. But contemporary technology is not simply an extension of a man – like wings of wood, wax and feather – which would be a purely mechanical effect. (At the very least, the physics of the nineteenth century, which was radically changed by the fields and waves of electromagnetism, should have curtailed that conjecture.) It is one whose characteristics are also profoundly mathematical and logical, bringing the force of abstractions into combination with materialities as diverse as labour, the primitive accumulation economies of extraction (for making metal-hungry devices), and into the complexities of contemporary cultural geopolitics that move from the interpersonal to the international with unaccustomed rapidity. The powers of electronics, and the ability to couple and intensify those with logical descriptions that create processes that traverse the

3

social, economic and cultural, intensify in turn the powers of fascination and the ability to invent that are characteristic of geeks. We have yet to find ways to think through the full combination of these forces and scales of articulation. As luck, which begins every tragedy, would have it, however, we are in the midst of all this and have at least the capacity to geek out on the problematic. The texts collected here are different kinds of attempts to do just this.

Collaborators

But talking of geeks: crucial to many of the texts brought together in this book is that they are collaboratively written. My companions in their writing are a designer, programmers, computer scientists, security researchers, statisticians, social scientists, philosophers, cultural theorists, a reluctant artist, and combinations of these. Such collaborations bring and induce capacities, ideas, combinations and indeed data that would otherwise not come into communication with each other. Key to software studies approaches is that of engaging with texts, ideas, objects and systems from computer science and digital technologies in dialogue with those of cultural theory, digital media cultures, art, hacking and elsewhere. People who embody and enliven this dialogue in different ways are fundamental to this book and provide the corrugation necessary to make these papers stand up.

As a field, software studies has so far successfully remained minor in an era of the consolidation of disciplines – which survive, and strengthen, primarily as buttresses against institutional attrition. This 'success' of course is presided over by the irony that, since it emerges to address some of the key features of the last decades, these features are sometimes more or less attended to by other approaches, more disciplinary in nature, that then stand in for a more fundamentally inter- or anti-disciplinary form of knowledge. Here, elements of computational cultures operate as metonyms for what then is magically imaginable as a resolvable whole; or are addressed solely in terms of the categories, tools and formats of such disciplines without taking the risk of their transformation. It is the tendency towards the whole-hearted embrace of the contact zone that characterizes software studies.

This is not a fully accomplished, uncomplicated or universalizable proposition, however. Each of the collaborations here has its own texture rather than a generalized or un-preworked wide-openness. The patterns that each essay brings together create resonances across distributions of knowledge and skill that create different tensions and confluences. The allocation of terminology or inference, or in the discussions and iterative decisions as to what constitutes a useful fulcrum for levering up and analysing the entity or processes under discussion, provide forces around which the text aggregates. Indeed, in some cases here, the operation of programs and scripts, their relations to systems and data, or the use of forensic techniques, provide another set of collaborators that in turn generate the texts here.

Overview

Collectively, this book presents an assembly of explorations of some of the fundamental infrastructures of contemporary life: computational structures, entities and processes that undergird, found and articulate economies, entertainment and warfare, to name simply their interactions with the ascendant holy trinity. This is to say that software is considered to be fundamentally cultural. Working with the objects and ideas of computer science as part of culture is to say that they take part fully in numerous ways of life; that they are inscribed by ideas and produce feelings and relations through and incidentally to these; and, as a scientific and technically generative set of fields, that it has numerous consistencies and textures within it that are both 'internally' significant within those fields, with their own codes, powers and sources of fascination, and, in these more or less abstract or autonomous conditions, able to create alliances with and patterns of excitement, disequilibria and amplification for other aspects of culture, asymmetrically ranging in their iterative acuity in relation to things as disparate as alphabets and institutions, as caresses and contracts. It is the interplay and development of the internal formulations that in many senses excites geeks. But it is their interleaving with these other aspects of software as culture that also changes the position of geeks today. Geeks are not only a 'people to come' – inhabiting a world ahead of its realization in ideas or in artefacts, or in selves, by means of what might retrospectively become their precursors – but are also brought into being as entities that inherently entail a kind of spasm of parody, of silliness. This, alongside the way in which the logical foundations of computing render it unstable at different scales, and are therefore often scaffolded, corralled, against this logical unfinishedness at others, is part of what initiates the figure of the geek, and the processes of computing open to their outsides at different scales.

5

But these logical foundations are also what allows for a remarkable continuity of form – through the generality of the abstract machine, a metamachine that computing puts into place – that sets up much of the tension and generativity in computing. Between abstraction and control, between replicability and translation, between generality and precision, computing forges and sometimes enforces new conjunctures, tensions and orderings. That is why software is both experiential and political, both iterated through the human yet markedly posthuman, as well as being multiply tied into the political mechanisms that seem only able to offer themselves in terms of a charade of humanism (as its mirror, as its tools, as its better self, as its means of knowledge and communication, as something that will iteratively deduce its secrets and its ailments, and so on). At the same time these political mechanisms curtail the humanism they claim to enhance, enforce seriality, tie it ever more closely into transactional mechanisms that translate to capital as a twinned and increasingly informational abstract machine where the individual, whom it ostensibly lauds, is merely figured as a nexus of contracts and flows of credit units and data. The essays collected in this book are aimed in different ways at prising open this condition.

They are published in thematic clusters: Histories, Entities, Aesthetics, Powers. The *Histories* section develops accounts of two key objects in computing history, object orientation and agent-based modelling. The chapter entitled 'The Obscure Objects of Object Orientation' charts a cultural and critical history of this fundamental form of programming through the development of object-oriented programming in educational psychology and social democratic forms of workplace governance to its present dominance in both the conceptual modelling and the development of software to its position in the global software authoring economy.

'Abstract Urbanism' provides a genealogy of key projects and thinking in the domain of urban modelling from the 1960s onwards, developing an account of the way in which it embodied critical and speculative approaches to mathematics, logic and city and social processes, with sometimes dubious and often creative significance. Modelling as a form of thought, as a means of experimentation with parameters and actions, has become one of the most subtle and advantageous computational operations. Its actual and ostensive power authorizes and encourages decisions. Understanding the computational part and the evidential grounding of such decisions, as well as the way they are socially located and conceptually and technically delimited, is crucial in developing the capacity of modelling

6

for thinking through cities as condensers of social and technical forces.

The *Entities* section presents ways of addressing analyses of software cultures at different scales and via the different kinds of objects or entities that they entail. It starts with a chapter outlining a brief survey of 'Software Studies Methods'. Since software is so heterogeneous and so multi-scalar, this chapter is necessarily incomplete as a survey, but it points towards a range of different ways for engagement, analysis and reflection that are being developed. Around these are numerous clusters of researchers, more or less in communication about what come into being as mutual or distinct modes and points of enquiry. Shared amongst them is the sense that, whilst software is not absolutely distinct from other factors, such as, most obviously, hardware, it has sufficient specificity and significance in its own terms to demand enquiry and speculative development. Whilst terms, such as algorithm, code, or infrastructure and others, may move in and out of focus of different kinds of collective attention over time, numerous kinds of continuity are also developed by the field.

The section then goes on to two chapters that describe and analyse two exemplary kinds of object in contemporary software culture. 'Big Diff' takes as its object a large-scale distributed software repository, Github. Merging data science techniques with a theoretically grounded analysis, this essay provides both a reading of this major part of contemporary software development infrastructure and what is a hopefully methodologically interesting work in between the two approaches. Github, which is built on the file-management system Git, developed by Linus Torvalds, is particularly interesting as a site of production because it is symptomatic of the way in which some of the conditions of software culture, derived both from computational forms and from cultural tendencies that are manifest as conventions realized in software, drive forms of work, communication and value-creation in ways that are articulated through software's work on itself. The way in which Git and Github re-order the question of the nature of the archive is particularly symptomatic here. Like much on the internet today, Github is an architecture that centralizes the distributed structure of Git – a file structure that dramatically inverted a social taboo (that against forking, duplicating and varying, code) as a means of establishing a collective resource. In turn, the site also provides the grounds for what this article suggests is a Post-FLOSS (free, libre and open source software) form of code. But software's work on itself is something that also figures as a subtext of the book as a whole, indicating both the developing complexity and maturity of aspects of software cultures and the degree to which it also becomes something reflexive.

The following chapter, 'The Author Field', takes a more microscopic object as its approach, developing a genealogy of a specific piece of metadata, as named in the title. Forensic and counter-forensic literature and techniques are used to examine the modulation between apotheosis and disappearance this term is subjected to by the technical operations of mundane technologies such as word processors. What are the ways in which forms of writing are produced, stabilized, repeated, transducted in such processing – and how does this articulate the figure of the user, author or other such category? In this sense, like some of the other texts gathered here, this chapter develops a line of enquiry also present in a previous book of mine which shares this one's subtitle, *Behind the Blip: Essays on the Culture of Software*, with which there is a strong sense not only of continuity of topic, but also of the widely expanding nature of the grounds of enquiry.

Shared also with that book is a set of attempts to address the aesthetic dimension of contemporary software cultures. Aesthetics is meant in the broad sense here, of addressing the means by which sensation and perception are involved, at deep levels, with the technical. As a field, software studies draws heavily from art, including the early software art movement, for some of its sensibility. Both are heavily involved in working through the different scales and modes of circulation of software as sites saturated in machinings of various kinds: interpretation which conjoins knowing and transforming, perceiving and doing; interaction with its fusing of experience and technique; hacking with its bringing together of cultural invention and mischief as a mode of subjectivation. Here, art is founded on the capacity of invention that relies on multiplicities of meaning and the absence of any final vindicating authority as the grounds for creation. Reflection on technological experience via technological means as they weave into and interfere with those of other scales is a means of taking them beyond the question of their intents or their purposes, to explore them as conditions of possibility.

The *Aesthetics* section therefore develops accounts of computational aesthetics, understood in the broad sense of involving both perception and composition. It proposes software aesthetics as something with specific idiomatic qualities and as something that mixes with and recomposes other cultural forms, and that in turn may condense through the powers of art at a scale that disrupts other forces of aggregation and conformity. But this is a difficult question, one that has to be taken as it comes; and with a dose of precision, whilst understanding that the modality of that precision itself interacts with what it works in the midst of.

The first chapter in this section, 'Always One Bit More', is a reading of theories of the experience of mathematical calculation, particularly found in the Intuitionist movement, an influence on the work of Alan Turing, as a means of reading computational artefacts and games such as Minecraft. Brouwer, a key theorist of Intuitionism, and, in certain texts, an advocate of mathematics as a mode of cosmic understanding more broadly, argues for calculation as an experiential form of life. This chapter argues that some of the ways in which computer games have been taken up and reworked by players echoes this thick involvement in numerical transitions. Like other texts in this book, one of the underlying arguments is that technical, and mathematical, documents, ideas and movements have notions of culture baked into them. Part of the work of culture is to draw these out and to see how they exceed themselves.

Building on such work, the chapter entitled 'Computational Aesthetics' is a somewhat programmatic statement of the impact and significance of the qualities of computation as a set of aesthetic principles. Whilst ineluctably unfinished as a statement of such a vast set of things, the mode of analysis offered in this chapter proposes grounds for critical work with computing in a way that may encourage taking its specificity into consideration. The chapter proposes a subset of characteristic attributes of computing that have particular significance in establishing its aesthetic valences. Setting out the propositions for such a set of traits implies neither the re-description of the contents page of a basic manual of computer science in more lofty terms, nor simply the correlating of existing and established entities in aesthetic theory with those that establish the circuits of computing, but instead seeing what might pass through and change such a set of terms from both computing and aesthetics and in doing so establish their translation and reconstitution.

This specificity also of course involves complications of scales of experience and analysis, and their conjunction with a massive array of movements and dynamics moving across and as them. The following chapter, 'Phrase', develops such concerns in relation to the way in which computational forms interweave with other aspects of material life, ranging from dance to voting systems. How, in turn, might we think through these conjunctions as temporary or enduring aggregates that form themselves as, in a term taken from dance, phrases of movement that cross between things as movements of movement? Such transitions that aggregate then dissipate as a phrasal entity are particularly articulated in technological forms that thrive on conjunction.

Following such an approach, 'Feral Computing' elaborates an argument drawing on the question of ubiquitous and distributed computing in relation to the implications of recent developments in cognitive science, specifically those of the enactive, embodied, ecological and extended mind. Aesthetics is founded exactly where one is at this moment, but it also starts in the transitions across the gap between such a position and the movements and reflections that it takes to realize this state as a condition, and that therefore ungrounds itself. As computing moves into distributed forms that draw in spatial characteristics and conditions, and also starts to integrate with things that are more characteristically described in relation to thinking processes, it becomes wilder, begins to leak out of its boxes in ways that are similarly ungrounded. But calculation, experience and thought begin to have spatial characteristics. It is their particular texture as such that they gain the capacity to move from a model of computing as merely a closed mechanism of calculation to one that grounds itself in interaction. It is interactivity as an undergirding drive in the history of computing that, in this text, provides the means for computing to go beyond itself and into a further stage.

The condition of interaction has numerous modes. It also involves some that are more lackadaisical, networks of dawdling, skiving, goofing off, mass enactments of parodies of productivity staged via purposefully pointless protocols. This condition is explored in 'Just Fun Enough To Go Completely Mad About', which develops an account of recent debates in software studies by a reflection of the role of algorithms and processes in games. By contrast to the common argument for theorization of games by militantly enthusiastic gamers (whom I admire but can't keep up with), it adopts a more spaced-out, daydreamy approach, one that takes pleasure in phenomena where logic, procedure and paradox are enacted by myriads of users. The two games discussed in this chapter are Agar.io and Twitch Plays Pokemon. Both embody, in different ways, an approach to the intercalation of rules, spaces, movement and interaction, amongst other things, that take them at a tangent. The latter game, or more properly, an event within the conjunction of two gaming systems, was remarkable in playing out some of the more recondite pleasures of play. The embrace of the ludicrous, indeed a founding of logical relations under the fullness of its moon, are what define and drive such games.

The pair of texts under the title *Powers* addresses the way in which computational forms establish new grammars and forces of power, but also work to revise and reconstitute prior imaginaries of virtue. Such virtues may be found in conditions not only of communication, of direct manipulation of and access to data, of clarity of design and structure, but also of the reinvention of a broader sense of relation between the ideal user, or subject, and the world at large.

'Black Sites and Transparency Layers' analyses the formations of transparency, openness and their manifestation in recent 'flat design' interfaces and the changed human–computer interaction (HCI) of the smartphone and tablet, the new architecture of Silicon Valley company HQs, and the relation of these forms to the black sites of surveillance centres, server farms and related places. The chapter proposes that each grammar of transparency set in place by such systems and imaginaries also installs certain conditions of opacity that, whilst not inevitable, are unreflected upon or disavowed. No system of transparency-formation is identical to any other, each bringing its own intentional and incidental plays of shadow and light that are also not immediately parseable into a calculus of black and white. The essay proposes some diagnostic means to find the ways in which contemporary design, at the level of interface, architecture and process, articulates what becomes transparent, to what or to whom and how, and in what ways the pleasures and reasons of transparency are enforced or avowed. At present, Silicon Valley is in a moment of its pomp. The ways, after the revelations of Edward Snowden (that follow on those of the preceding years of the Five Eyes and Echelon systems), in which it inscribes transparency as an official good, in devices ranging from its operating systems to its palaces, are therefore instructive.

Following this, 'Algorithmic Tumult and the Brilliance of Chelsea Manning' attempts to map the political-computational condition of the present in relation to the themes of posthumanism, related to the feminist work of Rosi Braidotti, and in particular to the kinds of agency, understanding and skill deployed and embodied by Chelsea Manning. The article proposes that there is a particular conjuncture between two universal systems of equivalence: the Turing Machine – which integrates all symbol-based processes and media, whilst re-composing them in ways that are peculiar to networked and computational digital media – and capital, which providentially allows for the imaginary transduction of all entities, states and processes into numerical and tradeable equivalents. The particular conditions of this conjuncture are primary drivers of contemporary life in which new means of action and subjectivation are both possible and urgently needed.

Part of the aim of this book then is to show that if computing is going to saturate everything, which seems tendentially, if by no means absolutely, to be one traceable trajectory for its unfolding, then as a field, as a science and as a manifold set of practices of numerous kinds, it can either be thought to reduce everything to its own terms and conditions, or generate a sufficiently complex relation to what it meshes with to recognize that it is, in turn, going to be mutated. One of the fields of such mutations is culture, something not reducible to the mere rubric of 'digitization'. As a young science with, so far, only a few basic tenets, but with an enormous complexity of things arising from them, computing has much more to go through. This book attempts to map some of the ways this conjugation of culture and computing is underway.

HISTORIES

THE OBSCURE OBJECTS OF OBJECT ORIENTATION

Matthew Fuller and Andrew Goffey

Object orientation names an approach to computing that views programs in terms of the interactions between programmatically defined objects – computational objects – rather than as an organized sequence of tasks embodied in a strictly defined ordering of routines and subroutines. Objects, in object orientation, are groupings of data and the methods that can be executed on that data, or *stateful abstractions*. In the calculus of object-oriented programming, anything can be a computational object, and anything to be computed must so be, or must be a property of such. Object-oriented programming is typically distinguished from earlier procedural and functional programming (embodied in languages such as C and Lisp respectively), declarative programming (Prolog) and more recently component-based programming. Some of today's most widely used programming languages – Java, Ruby, C# – have a decidedly object-oriented flavour or are explicitly designed as such, and whilst as a practice of programming it has some detractors it is deeply sedimented in both the thinking of many computer scientists and software engineers and in the multiple, digital-material strata of contemporary social relations.

This essay explores some aspects of the turn towards objects in the world of computer programming (a generic term that incorporates elements of both computer science and software engineering). It asks what powers computational objects have, what effects they produce and, more importantly perhaps, how they produce them. Seeking to situate the technical world of computer programming in the broader context of the changing composition of power within contemporary societies, it suggests a view of programming as a recursive figuring out of and with digital materials, compressing and abstracting relations operative at different scales of reality, composing new forms of agency and the scales on which they operate and create through the formalism of algorithmic operations. This essay thus seeks to make perceptible what might be called the territorializing powers of computational objects, a set of powers that work to model and re-model relations, processes and practices in a paradoxically abstract material space.[1]

Computation has seen broad and varied service as a metaphor for cognitive processes (witness the ongoing search for artificial intelligence), on the one hand, and as a synecdoche of a mechanized, dehumanized and alienated industrial society on the other – flip sides of the same epistemic coin. As such it might appear somewhat divorced from the rich material textures of culture and a concern with the ontological dimension of 'things'. Indeed, with its conceptual background in the formalist revolution in mathematics initiated by David Hilbert, computing may not seem destined to tell us a great deal about the nature of things or objects at all. In the precise manner of its general pretension (insofar as one can talk about formalism 'in general') to universality, to be valid for all objects (for any entity whatever, in actual fact), formalism is by definition without any real object, offering instead a symbolic anticipation of that which, in order to be, must be of the order of a variable. Objects and things, the variety of their material textures, their facticity, tend to transmogrify here into the formal calculus of signs.

Little consideration has been given to the details of the transformative operations that computer programming – always something a bit more sophisticated than simple 'symbol manipulation' – is supposed to accomplish, or to the agency of computational objects themselves in these transformations. In this article, we take up this question through a brief consideration of object-oriented programming and its transformative effects. We read computational formalism through the techniques and technologies of computing science and software engineering, to address object orientation as a sociotechnical practice. As such a practice, one that bears a more than passing resemblance to the kinds of means of disciplining experimental objects and processes that are described by Andrew Pickering, the effective resolution of a problem of computation is a matter of the successful creation, through programming, of a more or less stable set of material processes – within, but also without, the skin of the machine.[2]

Languages of Objects and Events

To understand the transformative capacities of computational objects entails, in the first instance, a consideration of the development of

16

programming languages, for it is with the invention of programming languages that the broad parameters of how a machine can talk to the outside world – to itself, to other machines, to humans, to the environment and so on – are initially established. Languages for programming computers, intermediating grammars for writing sets of statements (the algorithms and data structures) that get translated or compiled into machine-coded instructions that can then be executed on a computer, are unlike what are by contrast designated as natural languages. They are different not only in the sense that they have different grammars, but also in being designed, in a specific context, as a focused part of a particular set of sociotechnical arrangements, a constellation of forces – machines, techniques, institutional and economic arrangements and so on. A programming language is a carefully and precisely constructed set of protocols established in view of historically, technically, organizationally etc. specific problems. Usually designed with a variety of explicit considerations – mostly technical but sometimes aesthetic – in mind, programming languages themselves nevertheless register the specific configuration of assemblages out of which they emerge and the claims and pressures that these generate, even as they make possible the creation of new assemblages themselves. The computer scientist, it might be said, 'invents assemblages starting from assemblages which have invented him [sic] in turn'.[3]

The project of object orientation in programming first arises with the development of the SIMULA language. SIMULA was developed by Kristen Nygaard and Ole-Johan Dahl at the Norwegian Computing Centre in the early 1960s.[4] As its name suggests, it aimed at providing a means both to describe – that is, program – a flow of work, and to simulate it. The aim of such simulation was to bring the capacity to design work systems – despite their relative technical complexity – into the purview of those who made up a workplace. As such, the project had much in common with other contemporaneous developments in higher-level computing languages and database management systems, which aimed to bring technical processes closer to non-specialist understanding.[5] Equally, they were a way of bringing formal description of the world out from under the skin of the computer. SIMULA aimed to bring the expert knowledge of the programmer into alliance with the decision-making systems of the workplace in which a social democratic version of workers' councils[6] guided the construction of the staging of work. This tendency arose from what would later become known as participatory design, but it also had its roots in a version of operational research,[7] in which the analysis of work was carried out in order to reduce stressful labour.[8]

The first version of SIMULA, SIMULA 1, was developed not with a view to establishing object orientation as a new format for programming languages per se but rather as an efficacious way of modelling the operation of complex systems. Simulation of work processes becomes desirable as systems develop to a level of complexity that makes understanding them a non-trivial task, and in SIMULA, it was a task that was initially understood as a series of 'discrete event networks'[9] in which inventory, queuing, work and materials processes could be modelled, and in which there would be a clear correlation between the features of the work process and the way in which it was modelled as an ensemble of computational objects. To produce such epistemically adequate models of complex processes, the tacit ontology of discrete event networks utilized by SIMULA (the 'network' was eventually dropped) was one in which real-world processes were understood in terms of events – or actions – taking place between entities, rather than as permanent sets of relationships between them. The language was supposed itself to force the researcher using it to pay attention to all aspects of the processes being considered, directing such attention in appropriate ways.

Initially the language had little impact for general programming; indeed, it wasn't until SIMULA67 was developed that the technical feature that has since been so important to object-oriented programming – the capacity to write programs in which entities combine data and procedures and retain 'state'[10] – was first sketched out, in terms of the possibility of specifying 'classes' and 'subclasses', each of which would be able to initiate or carry out particular kinds of actions. SIMULA itself did not really see full service as a programming language, because the computing resources required to enable it to do the work required of it meant that it was not especially effective. At such an early stage in the history of programming and programming languages, the possibility of having a language that would be materially adapted to describing real-world processes inevitably rubbed up against the practical obstacle of writing efficient programs.

However, the innovations of SIMULA in the matter of providing for structured blocks of code – called classes – that would eventually be instantiated as objects – were taken up a decade and a half later in the development of C++, a language developed in part to deal with running UNIX-based computational processes across networks,[11] something which later also became a driver in the development of a further object-oriented programming language, Java. Its

18

tacit ontology of the world as sequences of events (or actions), the design principles built into it, its links with a different imaginary and enaction of the organization of labour, are indicative of a possibility of a programming that is yet to come.

A variant history of object orientation can be told through the development of the Smalltalk language at Xerox PARC, Palo Alto, in the 1970s and 1980s, under the leadership of Alan Kay.[12] Smalltalk frames the nature of objects through the primary question of messaging between the entities or objects in a system. In fact, it is the relations *between* things that Kay ultimately sees as being fundamental to the ontology of Smalltalk.[13] Objects are generated as instances of ideal types or classes, but their actual behaviour is something that arises from the messages passed from other objects, and it is the messages (or events; the distinction is relatively unimportant from the computational point of view) that are actually of most importance. Here, although the effective ordering in which computational events are executed is essentially linear, such an ordering is not rigidly prescribed and there is an overall sense of a polyphony of events and entities in dynamic relation. Kay adduces a rationale for the dynamic relations that Smalltalk sought to construct between computational objects by referring to the extreme rigidity and inflexibility of the user interfaces that were available on the mainframe computers of the time: an approach organized around computational objects allows for a more flexible relationship between the user and the machine, a relationship that would later be glossed by one of Kay's colleagues as allowing for the creative spirit of the individual to be tapped into.[14] This flexible relationship to dynamically connecting objects is part and parcel of a utopian vision of computing – eventually materializing in the PC – in which control is portrayed as being wrested from the institutions in which computers (typically mainframe machines) exist in favour of a new form of 'personal mastery'.

Critically, for Smalltalk, it is the interactive quality of computation that comes to the fore; a major advance on the rigidly prescriptive order of task execution in extant languages. More specifically, the computational object in Smalltalk is viewed in terms of its capacity to be integrated into a system of learning – one that, following Piaget, Vygotsky and others, is essentially constructivist.[15] As such, the operational brief of the object is not just to function well within the domain of the program, but also to interface with, prompt and sustain – but not, perhaps, to shape (at least, not knowingly) – the learning processes of the user. As with the emphasis on messaging between many lightly but precisely defined objects as the basic structure of the program, Smalltalk emphasizes such interaction, the relations between objects, and between objects' messages and users.

The historical point to be made here is that the link between Smalltalk and interaction-based learning marks something of a shift from the attempts at simulating workplace knowledge evident in the early version of SIMULA, but it is a shift in which there are continuities and discontinuities. Whilst the purposes to which programming is directed are different, the ambivalence that SIMULA hinted at – a program as an epistemically adequate model of some process or set of processes, and a program as a materially effective set of processes in its own right, which might be glossed as the *analytic* and *synthetic* functions of computation – remained in place with Smalltalk. A brief explanation is thus in order.

Discussing the development of Smalltalk, Kay says: 'object-oriented design is a successful attempt to qualitatively improve the efficiency of modelling the ever more complex dynamic systems and user relationships made possible by the silicon explosion'.[16] Modelling here cannot really be understood as a simple representation, because when the complex dynamic systems and user relationships that object-oriented design models are those that are *made possible* by the silicon explosion, we are moving into a zone of ontological artifice: not simply the acquisition of a knowledge of the world through artefacts (as in economist and artificial intelligence theorist Herbert Simon's conception of the sciences of the artificial and as exemplified in the initial project of SIMULA), but rather a matter of creating models of things that don't otherwise exist. The distinction is important although often ignored, because it points towards the limitations of exploring computational objects in the epistemological terms of representation. Understanding computation from the latter point of view is rather widespread; indeed, Kay himself suggests: 'everything we can describe can be represented by the recursive composition of a single kind of behavioural building block that hides its combination of state and process inside itself and can be dealt with only through the exchange of messages'.[17] On this count, a computer program written in an object-oriented programming language develops a kind of intensional logic, in the sense that each of the objects that the program comprises has an internal conceptual structure that determines its relationship to what it 'refers' to, suggesting that objects are, in fact concepts, concepts that represent objects in a machinic materialization of a logical calculus.[18] As concepts materialized in the physical space/time of effective computational processes, but referring to objects outside machine space, Smalltalk objects clearly indicate the 'analytic' function of computation, but insofar as the Smalltalk software is designed as something to be interacted with in its own right, its 'synthetic' function is equally evident.

So, on the one hand, we have the manner in which object-oriented programming purports to enable the decomposition of the processes that it seeks to model into computationally adequate 'representations' of entities (=objects). On the other, the simple fact that a computational object is an entity in its own right; an entity with a specific, material form, which comes into composition with other entities – whether computational or not – that may or may not find some 'representation' materially in that software. It is, we would suggest, this second aspect of computational objects – modelling behaviour *with* objects, as opposed to modelling behaviour *of* objects – that needs to be understood more precisely.[19]

Abstraction, Errors and the Capture of Agency

It is often argued that with the development of object-oriented programming, a new era of *interaction* between humans and machines was made possible. There is some truth in this, not least because of the way that the architecture of relations between objects obviates the need to have a program structure in which the order of actions is rigidly prescribed. However, the notion of interaction, as descriptive of a *reciprocal* relation between two independent entities, is sometimes insufficient when trying to understand the historical genesis and the peculiar entanglement of relations between computers and humans. It would be more appropriate to consider these relations in terms of a series of forms of the abstractive creation and *capture* and codification of agency: a click of the mouse, a tap of the key, data input, affective investments etc. By referring to the creation and capture of agency we seek to underline two things: firstly, that computational objects do not simply or straightforwardly tap into pre-formed capacities or abilities, but instead generate new kinds of agency, kinds of agency which may be similar to what went before but which are nevertheless different (a typewriter, a keyboard and a keypad, for example, capture the agency of fingers in subtly different ways); secondly, that the agency that is created is so as part of an asymmetric relation between human and computer, a kind of cultivation or inculcation of a *machinic habitus*, a set of dispositions that is inseparable from the technologies that codify it and give it expression. It would take too long a diversion to examine in detail how and why this asymmetry exists, but it is crucial to developing an appropriately concrete understanding of the sociotechnical quality of contemporary relations of power.

Part of the rhetoric of interactive computing insists on the 'intelligent', 'responsive' nature of computational devices, but this obscures the dynamics of software development and the partial, additive quality of the development of interactive possibilities. Computers too, are not very good at *repairing* interactions. They tend, in use, to be considerably more intransigent than their users, bluntly refusing to save a file or open a webpage, or even closing down altogether. Whilst system crashes may not be as common now as they once were, the everyday experience of the development of human–computer interactions has been one in which humans have been obliged to spend considerable amounts of time learning to think more like computers, developing workarounds, negotiating with and adapting to computational prescription. 'Bugs' have, in this sense, played an important role in setting up the asymmetric relations between humans and machines. Relatively speaking, humans will adapt to – or at least learn not to notice – the stupidities of the computer much more quickly than the computer will to humans, in part simply because the time between software releases (with bug fixes) is much greater than that between individual interactions with an application. This asymmetry suggests that there is something of a strategic value to the stupidity of machines, a stupidity that gives machines a crucial role in *modelling* the user with which they interact.[20]

In any case, and *pace* Kay, a computational object is a *partial* object: the properties and methods that define it are a necessarily selective and creative abstraction of particular capacities from the thing it models, and which specify the ways that it can be interacted with. The objects – text boxes, lists, hyperlinks and so on – that populate a webpage, for example, define more or less exactly what a user can do with them. This is a function not just of how the site has been designed and built but, more importantly, of a range of previously defined sets of coded functionality. There is a history to each of these objects and their development,[21] which means that the parameters for interaction are determined by a series of more or less successful *abstractions* of a peculiarly composite, multi-layered and stratified kind.

It is important to note here, though, that abstraction is a contingent, *real* process. The taken-for-granted ways in which humans now interact with machines is the product of material arrangements that do not always obtain.[22] More pointedly, these real abstractions are concretely and endlessly re-actualized by the interactions between and with the computational. Such processes of abstraction might be better understood as forms of *deterritorialization* – in Deleuze and Guattari's sense – a process which always involves 'at least two terms' in which 'each of the two terms reterritorializes on the other. Reterritorialization must not be confused with a return to a primitive or older territoriality: it necessarily implies a set of artifices by which one element, itself deterritorialized, serves as a new territoriality for another.'[23]

Considered in these terms, the capture of agency links the formal structuring of computational objects to the broader processes of which they are a part, allowing us in turn (1) to specify more precisely that the formal structuring and composition of objects has a vector-like quality; and (2) to attend more directly to the correlative feature of reterritorialization. Abstracting *from*, in this sense of a real process, is equally an abstracting *to*: an abstraction is only effective on condition that it forms part of another, broader set of relations, in which and by which it can be stabilized and fortified.

We now turn to a more direct consideration of these issues.

Stabilizing the Environment

In theory, anything that can be computed in one programming language can also be computed in another: this is one of the lessons of Turing's conception of the universal machine. What that means more prosaically for the case in hand is that an object-oriented programming language provides a set of *design* constraints on the engineers working with it, favouring specific kinds of programmatic constructs, particular ways of addressing technical problems, over others. The existence of such design constraints is particularly important when trying to consider the dynamics governing the material texture of software culture. The question then becomes this: given the way in which the asymmetries in human–machine relations enable the capture of agency, is there a way in which the propagation and extension of those relations can be accounted for? Can something in the practices of working with computational objects be uncovered that might help understand this dynamic?

One feature that is associated in particular with object-oriented programming is the way that it is argued to facilitate the *re-use* of code. Rather than writing the same or similar sets of code over and over again for different programs, it saves time and effort to be able to write the code once and re-use it in different programs. Re-usability is not unique to object-oriented programming: it is implied in the features of any kind of programming language, in the mundane sense, for example, that whenever one initializes a variable of a given sort within a routine (say a floating point number), the compiling of the code will allocate a value to an address in memory. That is not something the programmer has to do himself or herself; the routinization and automation of computational tasks imply it as a basic feature of operation. But object-oriented programming favours the re-usability of code for computationally abstract kinds of entity and operation – in other words, for entities and operations that are more directly referent to the interfacing of the computer with the world outside. *Class libraries* are typical of this. Although not unique to object-oriented programming languages, they provide sets of objects, with predefined sets of methods, properties and so on, that find broad use in programming situations: in the Java programming language, for example, the Java.io library contains a '*File*' object, which a programmer would utilize when a program needs to carry out standard operations on a file external to the program (reading data from it, writing to it and so on). Code re-use in general suggests that the contexts in which it is situated, the purposes to which it is put, the interactions to which it gives rise and the behaviours it calls forth are relatively regularized and stable. In other words, it suggests that typical forms of software have found and taken part in the making of their ecological *niches*.

The possibility of re-usability here must thus be understood from two angles simultaneously: (1) as something given specific affordance within the structure of an object-oriented language; and (2) as something that finds in its context the opportunity to take root, to gain stability, to acquire a territory. It was suggested in the previous section that the simple dynamics of adaptation or habituation might account for the latter. The former can be located in the technical features of object-oriented programming languages. We will address this issue first before moving on to a broader consideration of stabilizing practices.

One of the main features of object-oriented programming, distinguishing it from others, is the use of *inheritance*. A computational object in the object-oriented sense is an instantiation of a *class*, a programmatically defined construct endowed with specific properties and methods enabling it to accomplish specific tasks. These properties and methods are creative abstractions. Inheritance is a feature that is often – albeit erroneously – characterized semantically as an

24

'is a' relationship: a Persian or a Siamese *is a* cat, a savings account *is an* account etc. The relation of inheritance defines a hierarchy of objects, often referred to in terms of classes and subclasses. How that hierarchy should be understood is itself a complex question (despite attempts to formalize the relation of inheritance by computer scientists). Critically, though, the relation of inheritance allows programmers to build on existing computational objects with relatively well-known behaviour by extending that behaviour with the addition of new methods and properties.

The relation of inheritance implies a situation in which objects extend and expand their purview, their territory, through small variations, incremental additions, that confirm rather than disrupt expectations about how objects should behave. To put it crudely, it is easier to inherit and extend, to *assume* that small differences are deviations from a norm, than it is to consider that such variations might be indices of a different situation, a different world. Modelling behaviour through the technical constraint of inheritance stabilizes the relations and practices captured in software.

Design patterns extend this logic of code re-usability to the situation of a more complex set of algorithms designed to address a broader problem. The notion of the design pattern is borrowed from architect Christopher Alexander, for whom such patterns are the description of problems that 'occur over and over again in our environment'.[24] A design pattern in software provides a reusable solution to the problem posed by a computational context (we will give an example of this shortly), and whilst such a pattern is obviously a technical entity, it is also a partial translation of a problem that will not originally be computational in nature. This is what makes it interesting, because its very existence is evidence of the increasing complexity that computational abstractions are required to address. A business information system that is designed to keep track of stock, for example, based on a 'just-in-time' model of stock control will create design problems entailing a set of relations among computational objects that are rather different to a system based on more traditional models of stock control (such as amassing large amounts of uniform items at lower unit cost), because the system needs to do rather different things. It implies a variant set of relations between software and users, perhaps entailing an automated set of links between one company and companies further up the supply chain.

In one respect, design patterns respond to the core difficulty of object-oriented software development: the analysis, decomposition and modelling of what a program has to do into a set of objects

25

with well-defined properties. Indeed, that is traditionally how design patterns are understood by software engineers. But their very existence itself is interesting because they provide evidence not just of the growing complexity of the computational environment, but also of its stability and regularity – qualities that such patterns in turn produce. Such material presuppositions are not normally considered in discussions of object-oriented programming (or indeed any programming at all), where the self-evident value and common-sense obviousness of thinking in object-oriented terms are generally shored up in textbooks by analogy to the obviousness of objects themselves; for instance, listing all the rather stable objects – tables, chairs, papers, books and the shelves they sit on – in the author's office.[25] And yet the stability of an environment is absolutely critical to enabling computational objects to exert their powers effectively.[26] However, the pedagogical emphasis on the relatively simple – and the consequent attention accorded to the primacy of the epistemological dimensions of computational objects – does not, as we have argued, really do justice to the processes at work in the historical development of software culture. In particular, it does little to help us understand the ways in which agency is not only captured but also configured and stabilized in predictable, routine patterns. It would be more appropriate, perhaps, to view the stable, simple and self-evidently given quality of computational objects as the outcome of a complex sociotechnical genesis.

Encapsulation, Exceptions and Unknowability

Thus far we have sought to address material aspects of the complex processes of abstraction that are at work in object-oriented programming. We need nevertheless to insist that computational objects do have a cognitive role. However, this is a role that is fulfilled primarily through the – often blind and groping – ways in which they give shape to non-computational processes.

The world in which computational objects operate is one to which they relate through precisely defined contractual interfaces that specify the interplay between their private inner workings and their public façades. One doesn't interact with a machine any old how but with a latitude for freedom, a room for manoeuvre, that is very precisely, programmatically, specified. *Encapsulation*, often held to be one of the primary features of object-oriented programming, enforces – along with the *exception* construct – a strict demarcation of inside and outside that is only bridged through the careful design of inter-faces, making 'not-knowing' into a key design principle. The term 'encapsulation' refers to the way in which object-oriented program-ming languages facilitate the hiding of both the data that describes the state of the objects that make up a program, and the details of the operations that the object performs.[27] In order to access or modify the data descriptive of the state of an object one typically uses a 'get' or a 'set' 'method', rendering the nature of the interaction being accomplished explicitly visible. Encapsulation offers a variant, – at the level of the formal constructs of a programming language, – of a more general principle observed by programmers, which is that when writing an interface to some element of a program, one should always hide the 'implementation details', so that users do not know about and are not tempted to manipulate data critical to its function-ing. 'User' here is a term relative to the objects under consideration: programmers don't allow users of websites to play around with the code that sets the terms on which a web browser operates, and one group of programmers may hide the implementation details of a set of computational objects from any other programmers who may want to use it, and so on.

In addition to promoting code re-use, it is said, encapsulation minimizes the risk of errors that might be created by incompetent programmers getting access to and manipulating data that might lead the object to behave in unexpected ways. A key maxim for programmers is that one should always code 'defensively', always write 'secure' code, and even accept that input – at whatever scale one wishes to define this – is always 'evil'.[28] A highly regulated interplay between the inner workings and the outer functioning of objects makes it possible to ensure the stable operations of software. Arguably this is part of an historical tendency and proprietary trend to distance users from the inner workings of machines, effecting a complex sociotechnical knot of intellectual property, risk manage-ment and the division of labour,[29] the outcome of which is to restrict the programmer's ability to gain access to lower levels of operation (whilst theoretically making it easier to write code).

As a principle and as a technical constraint, encapsulation and the hiding of data at the very least gives shape to a technico-economic hierarchy in which the producers of programming languages can control the direction of innovation and change, by promoting 'lock-in' and structuring a division of work that encourages programmers to use proprietary class libraries rather than take the time to develop their own. By facilitating a particular – and now global – division of labour, the development of new forms of knowing through machines is in turn inhibited through the promotion of technically constrained, normative assumptions about what programming should be.

Whilst there are obviously many other factors that intervene to shape the way in which programming practices operate, the deeply sedimented habit of using class libraries is clearly something that has resulted from the technical affordances of encapsulation. A far more finely grained division of the work of software development is made possible when the system or application to be built can be divided into discrete 'chunks'. Each class or class library (from which objects are derived) may be produced by a different programmer or group of programmers, with the details of the operations of the classes safely ignored by other teams working on the project. The contemporary trend towards the globalization of software development, with its delocalizing metrics for productivity, would not have acquired its present levels of intensity without the chunking of work that encapsulation facilitates.[30]

Finally, let us look briefly at *exception handling*. Where encapsulation works to create stabilized abstractions by closely regulating the interplay between the inside and the outside of computational objects, defining what objects can know of one another, exception handling shapes the way in which computational objects respond to anything that exceeds their expectations. A program and the objects that make it up are only ever operative within a specified set of parameters, defining the relations it can have with its environment and embodying assumptions that are made about what the program should expect to encounter within it. If those assumptions are not met (your browser is missing a plug-in, say, or you deleted a vital.dll file when removing an unwanted application), the program will not operate as expected. Exception handling provides a way to ensure that the flow of control through a program can be maintained despite the failure to fulfil expectations, ensuring that an application or system need not crash simply because some unforeseen problem has occurred. And in object-oriented programming, an exception is an object like any other: one can create subtypes of it, extend its functionality and so on.[31]

Technically, the rationale for exceptions is well understood and their treatment as objects, with everything that entails, facilitates their programmatic handling. What is less recognized, though, is the way that practices of exception handling give material shape to the kinds of relations computational objects have with the outside. From the point of view of computational objects, the world in general is a vast and largely unknown ensemble of events, *to* which such objects can only have access under highly restricted conditions, but also *in* which those objects only have a very limited range of interest – the role of the programmer being to specify this range of pertinences as precisely as possible. This is something that can be achieved in many ways: the practice of 'validating' user input, for example (by checking that the structure of that input conforms to some previously specified 'regular expression', say), ensures that the computational objects that process that input do not encounter any surprises that they won't understand (such as a date entered in the wrong format).

Because the use of exception handling in a program makes it possible for computational objects to continue to go about their work without there being too much disruption, and because their status as computational objects in their own right allows them to be programmatically worked with in the same way as other objects,[32] the need to pay closer attention to what causes the problems giving rise to the exceptions in the first place (systems analysis and design decisions, the framing of the specification of the software and so on) is minimized. The common practice of programmatically 'writing' information about the problems that give rise to exceptions to a log file – because this enables software developers to identify difficulties in program design, the routine causes of problems and so on – mitigates this ignorance to a point. However, it must be understood that the information thus derived presumes the terms in which the software defined the problem in the first place. As a result, one can only make conjectures about the underlying causes of that problem (a log file on a web application that repeatedly logs information indicating that a database server at another location is not responding cannot tell us if the server has been switched off or broken down, for example).

The point is that because exception handling facilitates the smooth running of software, it helps to stabilize not only the software itself but also the programming practices that gave rise to it. Exceptions work to preserve the framing of technical problems *as* technical problems, allowing errors to be defined, typically, as problems that the user creates through not understanding the software (rather than the other way round). In this way, exception handling obviates the need to develop a closer consideration of the relationship between computational objects and their environment. Whilst such stabilization allows software to gain a certain unobtrusiveness, this 'grey' quality makes it difficult to get a better sense of the differences that its abstract materiality produces.[33]

Conclusion: Ontological Modelling and the Matter of the Unknown

In the course of this chapter we have endeavoured to sketch out some of the reasons for developing an account of object-oriented programming which considers computation not from an epistemic but from an ontological point of view. It is true that there is an historically well-sedimented association between computation and discourses about knowledge, that computer programming seeks to model reality, that there are links between programming languages and formal logic, and so on. But this is not enough to make understanding computer programming as a science, in the way that, say, physics, chemistry or even the social sciences (sometimes) are understood, a legitimate move. On the contrary, this chapter has tried to suggest, through its examination of some of the features of object-oriented programming, that the abstractive capture and manipulation of agency through software in the calculus of computational objects are better understood as an ensemble of techniques engaged in a practice of *ontological modelling*. In other words, computer programming involves a creative working with the properties, capacities and tendencies offered to it by its environment which is obscurely productive of new kinds of entities, about which it may know very little. Such entities make up the fabric of what we have called here 'abstract materiality', a term we have used to gesture towards the consistency and autonomy of the zones or territories in which computational objects interface with other kinds of entity.

Despite the common connection that is made between computers and knowledge, a connection that is particularly evident in discussions of object-oriented programming and the modelling it accomplishes, a certain kind of unknowability is produced through the technically facilitated processes of abstraction that object orientation yields. This is not simply because encapsulation yields black boxes that parcel out and separate off knowledge or capacities for action – even amongst those that might be technically capable of knowing and working with the innards of such objects – but also because the epistemic valences of object orientation tend to obscure an aspect of computing most often associated with the circulation and refinement of meaning: that of the manipulation and evaluation of symbols. Object orientation draws from interpretation, via abstraction, in order to make things in the world. In this we can remember its genesis in two forms of constructivism: the psychologically derived approach of Kay and others at the Palo Alto Research Center; and that of the technosocial assembled in Scandinavia. That the capacity of objects finds itself in other kinds of alliance at other points, drawing out its acquired ability to hide, rather than to reveal relations, shows its exemplarily paradoxical double agency. Object orientation might be approached from many points of view: the angle taken here is one which insists, in a manner analogous to that of Michel Foucault discussing power, that the problem is not that the sociotechnical practice of programming doesn't know what it is doing. Rather, the techniques and technologies of object orientation produce a situation in which one doesn't know what one does.

NOTES

1   We borrow the notion of territorialization and its cognate terms – de- and re-territorialization – from Gilles Deleuze and Félix Guattari. They are discussed in further detail later.
2   Andrew Pickering, *The Mangle of Practice: Time, Agency and Science*, University of Chicago Press, Chicago, 1995.
3   Gilles Deleuze and Claire Parnet, *Dialogues*, Athlone, London, 1987, p. 52. Translation slightly modified.
4   Kristen Nygaard and Ole-Johan Dahl, 'The Development of the SIMULA Languages', *ACM SIGPLAN Notices*, 13:8 (1978), pp. 245–72; Jaroslav Sklenar, 'Introduction to OOP in SIMULA', based on the 30 Years of Object Oriented Programming seminar, University of Malta, 1997, http://staff.um.edu.mt/jskl1/talk. html; Jan Rune Holmvik, 'Compiling SIMULA: A Historical Study of Technological Genesis', *IEEE Annals of the History of Computing*, 16:4 (1994), pp. 25–37.
5   As in the work of Edgar Codd, for example. Edgar F. Codd, *The Relational Model for Database Management*, 2nd edn, Addison-Wesley, Reading, 1990.
6   A full description of workers' councils is not possible here. But for a historically precedent and advanced strand of work see that of Jacques Camatte and Anton Pannekoek. See Jacques Camatte, *LIP and the Self-Managed Counter-Revolution*, trans. Peter Rachleff and Alan Wallach, Black & Red, Detroit, 1975; Anton Pannekoek, *Workers' Councils*, J. A. Dawson, Melbourne, 1950, https://www.marxists.org/archive/pannekoe/1947/workers-councils.htm.
7   Operational research, or operations research in the USA, is a field arising out of wartime logistics, in which, for instance, the

whole process of managing a supply or chain was thought of as including all levels of production and use, aiming to integrate them in ways that would maximize certain sorts of efficiency.

8   Participatory design itself is a changing domain, involving numerous conflicting tendencies, becoming in some cases simply one of a number of available techniques for effective knowledge management and decision-making within a project and the systematic garnering of relevant human factors without any attempt to stage a critical analysis of work. At the same time, it remains as a persistent demand and exemplar for reasoned relations between the objects and processes of work and those that work with them. See, for instance, Keld Bødker, Finn Kensing and Jesper Simonsen, *Participatory IT Design: Designing for Business and Workplace Realities*, MIT Press, Cambridge, MA, 2004.

9   See Nygaard and Dahl, 'Development of the SIMULA Languages'.

10 In other words, to have a memory of the settings of all their variables. Imagine an object called 'bank account' which kept on forgetting things like 'bank balance', 'account holder' etc.

11 See Bjarne Stroustrop, *A History of C++: 1979–1991*, AT&T Bell Laboratories, Murray Hill, n.d.

12 Kay is a researcher with an intellectual trajectory stretching back to Ivan Sutherland and the invention of Sketchpad, the first CAD (computer-aided design) machine, a system that itself had an understanding of a certain kind of digital object at its core. One only has to survey contemporary computing culture to see the extent of the influence, by more or less direct means of the work groups of which he was part. See, for a contemporary overview of Smalltalk the special issue of *BYTE*, 6:8 (1981).

13 Alan Kay, 'Prototypes Versus Classes', *Squeak Developers' Mailing List*, 10 October 1998, http://lists.squeakfoundation. org/pipermail/squeak-dev/1998-October/017019.html.

14 See Daniel Inglis, 'Design Principles behind Smalltalk', *BYTE*, 6:8 (1981), pp. 286–302.

15 An interesting comparison is to the work of Seymour Papert, developer of the LOGO programming language designed specifically for education, in that both languages were designed with an explicit attention to their epistemic consequences. Both languages, in various different incarnations, are maintained by active user communities.

16 Alan Kay, 'The Early History of Smalltalk', http://gagne. homedns.org/%7etgagne/contrib/EarlyHistoryST.html.

17 Kay 'The Early History of Smalltalk'.

18 On this point, Kay invokes Carnap, whose 1947 essay *Meaning and Necessity* offered a sophisticated development of the notions of intension and extension in logic.

19 A philosophical reference might make this clearer. The notion of synthesis we are pointing to should not be understood along the lines of the syntheses outlined by Kant in his *Critique of Pure Reason*, which still revolve around representation and place a human subject at their centre. The relevant reference instead is Whitehead, whose prehensions offer a principle of synthesis that doesn't depend on representational presuppositions, and allow subjects to 'emerge' as part of the 'concrescent' process of which any prehension is a part. See the third part of Alfred North Whitehead, *Process and Reality*, on the theory of prehensions. Technically, the computational capture of agency involves both prehension *and* ingression, in the sense that a computational object gives a (coded) form of determinateness to whatever it captures. Whiteheadian ingression is not unlike 'recording' in the early work of Deleuze and Guattari. See Alfred North Whitehead, *Process and Reality*, ed. David Ray Griffin and Donald W. Sherburne, Macmillan, New York, 1979. See also Steven Shaviro, *Without Criteria: Kant, Whitehead, Deleuze and Aesthetics*, MIT Press, Cambridge, MA, 2009.

20 Such modelling might be qualified as ontological here because of the way that it works on the mode of existence of users, giving shape to their habits, their expectations and anticipations. This is something that is difficult to 'see' if thought in terms of an epistemological problematic of representation. We return to this question in the conclusion.

21 To borrow from biology, we might say that that history is both onto- and phylo-genetic.

22 The notion of *real abstraction* is one associated with Marx and Marxism. See in particular Alfred Sohn-Rethel's work on intellectual and manual labour and the discussion of it by Alberto Toscano. Alfred Sohn-Rethel, *Intellectual and Manual Labour: A Critique of Epistemology*, Humanities Press, Atlantic Highlands, 1977; Alberto Toscano, 'The Open Secret of Real Abstraction', *Rethinking Marxism*, 20:2 (2008), pp. 273–87. Whitehead and Deleuze and Guattari enable us to develop a precise understanding of this process.

23 Gilles Deleuze and Félix Guattari, *A Thousand Plateaus*, trans. Brian Massumi, University of Minnesota Press, Minneapolis, 1987, p. 193.

24 Christopher Alexander, quoted in Erich Gamma, Richard Helm, Ralph Johnson and John Vlissides, *Design Patterns: Elements of Reusable Object-Oriented Software*, Addison-Wesley, Indianapolis, 1995, p. 2.

25 Stephen J. Goldsack and Stuart J. H. Kent (eds.), *Formal Methods and Object Technology*, FACIT Series, Springer, Vienna, 1996.

26 This is a theme explored in Isabelle Stengers, *Thinking with Whitehead: A Free and Wild Creation of Concepts*, trans. Michael Chase, Harvard University Press, Cambridge MA, 2011. The 'patience' of the environment is what allows the infectious dynamics of power to operate effectively.

27 Not all computer scientists or software engineers agree that encapsulation is the same thing as information or data hiding. The details of the disagreement need not concern us here.

28 See Alfred Tarski, 'Truth and Proof', *Scientific American*, June (1969); reprinted in R. I. G. Hughes (ed.), *A Philosophical Companion to First-Order Logic*, Hackett, Cambridge, MA, 1993. For further discussion see Matthew Fuller and Andrew Goffey, *Evil Media*, MIT Press, Cambridge, MA, 2012.

29 This is one way in which to read the rather deterministic argument proposed by Friedrich Kittler in his essay 'Protected Mode', in Kittler, *Literature, Media, Information Systems*, ed. and trans. John Johnston, G&B Arts, Amsterdam, 1997.

30 The global division of programming labour is discussed in Audris Mockus and David M. Weiss, 'Globalization by Chunking: A Quantitative Approach', *IEEE Software*, 18:2 (2001), pp. 30–7. Notwithstanding the tensions implied by the technosocial genesis of the object, in this present context, it is a subject worth a study in its own right. It is particularly instructive in this regard to compare the distribution and use of code modules for the scripting language Perl with the proprietary class libraries associated with a language like Microsoft's C#. It is also worth noting that one of the criticisms made of object-oriented programming is that it doesn't require any skill to program in, a criticism that can clearly be read in the light of the trend pointed towards here.

31 One might, for example, refer to Microsoft's documentation of the System. Exception class for details of the complex structure of inheritance relations, the properties and methods of exception objects in the C# language, its subclasses and so on.

32 See our earlier comments on inheritance.

33 That techniques and technologies of software culture are bound up in a logic of 'the same' which precludes a deeper understand-

ing of the transformations that they accomplish here finds some elements of an explanation. On the logic of the same and technology, see Isabelle Stengers, *La vierge et le neutrino: les scientifiques dans la tourmente*, Empecheurs de Penser en Rond, Paris, 2006. On the unobtrusiveness of software, see Rob Kitchin and Martin Dodge, *Code/Space. Software and Everyday Life*, MIT Press, Cambridge, MA, 2011.

REFERENCES

Keld Bødker, Finn Kensing and Jesper Simonsen, *Participatory IT Design: Designing for Business and Workplace Realities*, MIT Press, Cambridge, MA, 2004.

Jacques Camatte, *LIP and the Self-Managed Counter-Revolution*, trans. Peter Rachleff and Alan Wallach, Black & Red, Detroit, 1975.

Edgar F. Codd, *The Relational Model for Database Management*, 2nd edn, Addison-Wesley, Reading, 1990.

Gilles Deleuze and Félix Guattari, *A Thousand Plateaus*, trans. Brian Massumi, University of Minnesota Press, Minneapolis, 1987.

Gilles Deleuze and Claire Parnet, *Dialogues*, Athlone, London, 1987.

Matthew Fuller and Andrew Goffey, *Evil Media*, MIT Press, Cambridge, MA, 2012.

Erich Gamma, Richard Helm, Ralph Johnson and John Vlissides, *Design Patterns: Elements of Reusable Object-Oriented Software*, Addison-Wesley, Indianapolis, 1995.

Stephen J. Goldsack and Stuart J. H. Kent (eds.), *Formal Methods and Object Technology*, FACIT Series, Springer, Vienna, 1996.

Jan Rune Holmvik, 'Compiling SIMULA: A Historical Study of Technological Genesis', *IEEE Annals of the History of Computing*, 16:4 (1994), pp. 25–37.

Daniel Inglis, 'Design Principles Behind Smalltalk', *BYTE*, 6:8 (1981), pp. 286–302.

Alan Kay, 'The Early History of Smalltalk', http://gagne.homedns.org/%7etgagne/contrib/EarlyHistoryST.html.

Alan Kay, 'Prototypes Versus Classes', *Squeak Developers' Mailing List*, 10 October 1998, http://lists.squeakfoundation.org/pipermail/squeak-dev/1998-October/017019.html

Rob Kitchin and Martin Dodge, *Code/Space. Software and Everyday Life*, MIT Press, Cambridge, MA, 2011.

Friedrich Kittler, 'Protected Mode', in Kittler, *Literature, Media, Information Systems*, ed. and trans. John Johnston, G&B Arts, Amsterdam, 1997.

Audris Mockus and David M. Weiss, 'Globalization by Chunking: A Quantitative Approach', *IEEE Software*, 18:2 (2001), pp. 30–7.

Kristen Nygaard and Ole-Johan Dahl, 'The Development of the SIMULA Languages', *ACM SIGPLAN Notices*, 13:8 (1978), pp. 245–72.

Anton Pannekoek, *Workers' Councils*, J. A. Dawson, Melbourne, 1950, https://www.marxists.org/archive/pannekoe/1947/workers-councils.htm

Andrew Pickering, *The Mangle of Practice: Time, Agency and Science*, University of Chicago Press, Chicago, 1995.

Steven Shaviro, *Without Criteria: Kant, Whitehead, Deleuze and Aesthetics*, MIT Press, Cambridge, MA, 2009.

Jaroslav Sklenar, 'Introduction to OOP in SIMULA', based on the 30 Years of Object Oriented Programming seminar, University of Malta, 1997, http://staff.um.edu.mt/jskl1/talk.html

Alfred Sohn-Rethel, *Intellectual and Manual Labour: A Critique of Epistemology*, Humanities Press, Atlantic Highlands, 1977.

Isabelle Stengers, *La vierge et le neutrino: les scientifiques dans la tourmente*, Empecheurs de Penser en Rond, Paris, 2006.

Isabelle Stengers, *Thinking with Whitehead: A Free and Wild Creation of Concepts*, trans. Michael Chase, Harvard University Press, Cambridge MA, 2011.

Bjarne Stroustrop, *A History of C++: 1979–1991*, AT&T Bell Laboratories, Murray Hill, n.d.

Alfred Tarski, 'Truth and Proof', *Scientific American*, June (1969); reprinted in R. I. G. Hughes (ed.), *A Philosophical Companion to First-Order Logic*, Hackett, Cambridge, MA, 1993.

Alberto Toscano, 'The Open Secret of Real Abstraction', *Rethinking Marxism*, 20:2 (2008), pp. 273–87.

Alfred North Whitehead, *Process and Reality*, ed. David Ray Griffin and Donald W. Sherburne, Macmillan, New York, 1979.

2

ABSTRACT URBANISM

Matthew Fuller and Graham Harwood

One of the first computational models of a city was set out in Thomas Schelling's 'Models of Segregation'.[1] In this and related papers he attempted to provide a logical model of the dynamics of racial segregation in North American cities and laid the groundwork for what later became agent-based modelling.[2] Although 'Models of Segregation' did not at first use a computer, it sets up some of the basic characteristics and problems of the field. Such work is expressed contemporarily, for instance, in the work of Joshua M. Epstein and others in the area of computational social modelling.[3] We use this work as a starting point to think about the relationship between urban morphologies and the politics of models and – with the increasing and multiform kinds of merger between computational systems, models and city forms – what it means to inhabit different scales of abstract structure. It is in this juncture that abstract urbanism arises.

This chapter examines the ways logical forms are positioned in relation to urban life as a means of discussing the relations between the city and software, and will develop a discussion of such logics in relation to questions of abstraction, reduction and empiricism. By working with the materiality of computational systems, especially as they unfold into the urban – and the urban in a full sense, as something involving complex comings into being of desire, imagination, technologies and forms of power – we can at the same time recognize an art of working with the tendency to reductionism through which modes of abstraction may operate and also work with the highly and complexly empirical. As social simulations are increasingly embedded in, or cleave close to, lived social forms, the texture and reality-forming capacities of these logics and the fantasies they inspire and live by need to be examined.

Development of Simulation as a Scientific Practice

One attractive aspect of modelling as a means of experimental under-standing is that it offers a science of behaviours rather than of essences. It is peculiar, therefore, that one of the earliest examples of social simu-lation derives from a highly essentialist ontology. Perhaps this might be seen as an example of a new epistemic form emerging out of a prior set of commitments that it has yet to break. 'Models of Segregation' builds on the game theory established by Morgenstern and von Neumann.[4] Schelling's earlier game-theoretic book, *The Strategy of Conflict*,[5] can be seen as a presiding spirit in 'Models of Segregation's attempt to map and rationalize options in the decisions around actions in the schematized space of non-zero-sum conflict. The opening stages of the paper set up segregation as a fundamental axiom of great applicability. Schelling mentions men and women, Catholics and Protestants, boys and girls, officers and enlisted men in an army. Not all of them nec-essarily tend towards dichotomous formation. People are also sorted by 'sex, age, income, language, colour, taste, comparative advantage and the accidents of historical location', amongst other factors. It is assumed that the sorting behaviour for each of these is the same.

In the model, a two-dimensional line is drawn (it is important that this is a line, not a grid) with equal divisions of space along its axis. The line is populated with an equal number of blacks and whites. Whilst the distribution looks even on the macro level, at the micro level it is uneven. Maybe three blacks are conjunct with one white, then a black and then three whites. If the whites and blacks are content with a 50 per cent split between the colour of their neighbours, then those who have a white neighbour on one side and a black neighbour on the other reach the contentment threshold and stand still if the neighbourhood to be considered has a radius of one. Those with 'too many' black neighbours or white neighbours will move in order to achieve contentment. In a neighbourhood with a radius of one, the line BBBWBWWW would, several iterations later, become BWBWBWBW. If the neighbourhood extends to two houses then the B and W in the middle of BBBWBWWW would be looking for new neighbourhoods. To summarize, in Schelling's model, each agent is black or white and aims to reside in a neighbourhood where the fraction of blacks/whites is above a predefined tolerance. Schelling's algorithm for determining the pattern of residence creates either complete integration or complete segregation.

Curiously, there is no reflection on the constitution of racial sorting even in excusatory fig-leaf terms. Like the stories of house-hunting amongst 'professors and their wives' that Schelling describes else-where,[6] the specific categories upon and through which segregation operates are described as if natural, not even worthy of equivocation as to their relation to social structure. The racism of the work is both that it operates by means of racial demarcation as an autocatalytic ideological given and, secondly, that it provides a means of organizing racial division at a higher level of abstraction. To say that Schelling operates within an ideologically racialized frame is not to claim either way whether Schelling as a person is or was consciously racist, but to state that, in these papers, racial division is an uncontested, 'obvious' social phenomenon that can be *reduced* in terms of its operation to a precise set of identifiers and operations. Goldberg's formulation of the problem of racism is useful here:

> The mark of racist expression or belief, then, is not simply the claim of inferiority of the racially different. It is more broadly that racial difference warrants exclusion of those so characterized from elevation into the realm of protection, privilege, property, or profit. Racism, in short, is about exclusion through depreciation, intrinsic or instrumental, timeless or time-bound.[7]

The naturalization of such a situation of depreciation by at-a-distance means in which entities kindly self-organize into ghettos out of their own otherwise unlimited choice must have been a marvellous boon to someone. What these papers offer is the construction of a machine for the operation of binary categorization that in turn becomes an engine for spatial organization, of preference-based segregation, as if the provision of housing in the form of a market is entirely smooth and demand driven, as if there are no variations in housing kinds and qualities, geographic features, or cultural variations in population, of wealth, and so on.

What Schelling's work allows for is for an operation of governance beyond that of direct sorting and selection, the direct command and control of populations; rather, it operates by eliciting and installing an action grammar in which people 'spontaneously' recognize, in the words of Nina Simone's song 'Mississippi Goddam', 'I don't belong here, I don't belong there.'[8]

Schelling offers the image of urban form being operated upon by an 'invisible hand', emerging at a higher level in social and material channelling. There is a tension, then, between the figure of this invisible hand and the view of the agent. The hand operates in an ostensibly emergent or natural way, arising out of the conditions of the situation as they are, beyond how they are seen by individual actants.

Abstraction as Urbanism

Schelling's abstract machine is one for the bipolar reduction of variation. One of the advantages of such an abstraction is that it requires no specific material form, simply logical equivalence. As recounted in a glowing festschrift chapter, Schelling initially used pennies, heads or tails up, on a draughts board to simulate 'what sort of segregation patterns develop given various types of preferences and alternative definitions of neighbourhood'.[9] The scale of the board becomes the limit factor of the diagrams published in a later paper, 'Dynamic Models of Segregation'. One can imagine a media-archaeological analysis of the history of simulation starting with such boards. John Conway, in developing the Game of Life, famously extended his to cover most surfaces of his office.[10] Equally, only having four significant neighbours, termed 'Neumann neighbours',[11] draws a simplifying factor from the board, the constraints of which may in turn be surpassed by the volume of processing offered by electronic computing.

Indeed, a media analysis of the field can divulge a number of aspects of its material practice that are often rendered conceptually and procedurally invisible. One such is that models tend to be bound by the temporal constraints of 'turns' in which all agents shift at the same time. Most models need to have all variables change at the same time; but models of sociality need to vary the periodicity of change for individual agents. Equally, in the model's interaction with hardware, the need to represent data to human users renders the allocation of central processing unit (CPU) cycles to drawing graphical representations something of an interference when compared with how many agents could be processed instead.

Some years after Schelling's work was published, Ted Nelson stated in the second edition of *Computer Lib*[12] that 'All simulation is political.' Computers as an abstract machine for the integration of all symbol systems – those operated upon by discrete values, or that can be rendered as digital – provide a great degree of plasticity in the social forms they might potentiate: hence the significance of Nelson's formulation. But the specific kind of politics simulated is also articulated by the qualities of the mathematical structures they come into composition with (rule sets; systems of four or eight neighbours; bounded, unlimited or wrapping grids; and so on). It is a rare case in which there is a direct correlation between the various scales of model, media, mathematics, the social form modelled, the ideological commitments specified as politics in such simulations, and the actual politics of the material operations of such systems in use. Each of these scales is active.

Diagram City

Epstein and Axtell's 1994 book *Growing Artificial Societies: Social Science from the Bottom Up*[13] drew on 'Models of Segregation' and from Conway's Game of Life. In Conway's cellular automata and Schelling's space of segregation, the environment has no active properties, something that has consequences when these models carry over into urban planning and modelling cityscapes. Epstein and Axtell's innovation was to place agents in an active environment with agents programmed to explore for simple codifications of basic resources to keep their metabolism alive. Agents and environment have internal states and behavioural rules that are fixed at the start or that can inherit change in interaction with each other. This is a model as a form of regression analysis, or rather of using regression as a form of proposition-making mechanism, where the relations between entities are fixed but variable. The environment is a lattice of resource-bearing sites in a medium that is separate from the agents, but on which they operate and with which they interact.[14]

Epstein has produced a body of work discussing the ethics around agent-based modelling that seek to affect US governmental policy by creating explicit models that can be used to explain social phenomena; something he is careful to distinguish from prediction. In 'Why Model?' Epstein challenges the assumption that scientific theories are created from the study of data.[15] He asserts that without a good theory, it is not clear what data should be collected. Modelling requires theorization and so creates enquiring habits of mind that he posits as essential to freedom.

By contrast, agent-based models have been eagerly taken up as objective explanations of conflictual social forms. The capacity to express forms of emergence, with the invisible hand effectively rationalizing commonsensical observations of the inevitability of such phenomena as racial segregation, excites dreams of implementation. As such, this aspect of this work evinces a fascination with finding fundamental laws of social aggregation, rhetorically building on those found in natural sciences, in turn afforded by those historically associated with mathematics. Such kinds of model and associated discourse still act in a representational mode rather than one of enquiry.

Simulations now operate in a wide range of cases and kinds. They act as a form of prognosis and forecasting, of pre-emption and the maintenance of irresolvability as well as having the ability to formulate an explanation with empirical traction without having to be true. Simulations also develop specific kinds of techniques and vocabularies, as well as the software to handle and interpret them, object-oriented programming being one such example. Object-oriented programming is fundamental to how agent-based modelling conceives of itself, as it allows objects to hold data and functions in internal states. The object exports a limited set of methods with which to interact with it, and the data, rather than being globally accessible, is held privately to the object. This is why the behaviour of objects comes to the surface, rather than the data that underlies them. Functions or methods are the agents' rules of behaviour.

One novelty in this kind of work is the way particular forms of computational abstraction themselves become operative elements in social and urban formations. Computation becomes folded into the operations of societies, and social forms become computational problems. As the programmable city begins to incorporate models, such systems become more than representational. Here, there is a correlation between formulations such as those of Epstein and Schelling (and those that followed in developing simulated societies) and the social sorting by software described by Steven Graham in his noted article 'Software-Sorted Geographies'.[16] In agent-based modelling, by contrast, there is an interplay between the schema of sorting and the actions of individuals and social formations, without engaging with the level of implementation. Where there is a difference is that Graham describes a disciplinary sorting *on* the social. There are kinds of sorting occurring, but these are more adequately expressed as a multi-scalar, multi-variable sorting enacted by agents bearing seemingly lucid and operable preference lists, arrayed in relation to the behaviour and imagined preferences of others, apparently reducible to hard-and-fast organization. A particularly interesting moment to watch for is when modelling and implementation merge to some extent, either in actual implementation, or in the seductive idea that such reductions are fully adequate explanations of specific slices of reality.

In the case of the racism of Schelling's 'Models of Segregation', the categories pre-exist the machine. The machine is there to sort them, to anticipate their actualization, to provide a degree of abstraction in which they can be reckoned, and by which the abstraction too can be worked up into an actor of a kind in itself. This operation of abstraction is crucial to understanding software as a cultural, city-making force.

Logics

The use of computers implies the interrelation of different forms of logic, at the levels, for instance, of programming the machine to perform calculations and of regulating the behaviour of users in pushing around mice and navigating menu systems to produce desired results. One way to think about how the mass adoption of these forms of logic affects society is in the mode Foucault described as discipline, one that analyses and breaks down a phenomenon through modelling it to produce a kind of remote control. Computation disciplines the way a phenomenon is approached and analysed so that when the phenomenon becomes visible again from within the computer it is made materially available for comparison and modification. As users participate in the flows of power created by the comparison of information and the systems of feedback that these entail, there is a tendency for them to become normalized to its process and are themselves enrolled in the interrelation of logics.

Computational forms of normalization establish the configuration of logics needed to make the materiality of the phenomenon available for modification via abstraction, verification and reward. The repeated construction and use of these forms of logic provide a form of progressive training for those that model, feed, collect, process and react to such logics, as well as those objects that are the subject of its calculations. Logics decompose processes and the entities, including people, that are aggregate with them. The routine processing/interaction with such models provides a collective logic to be applied to all areas of society and the natural world. The move beyond discipline, however, is characterized by the absence, further withdrawal or multiplicity and duplicity of the ultimately reliable, central control that discipline implies as a structuring principle.

Logic Gates

Part of the legacy of Schelling's and Epstein's work is in the police, academic and intelligence projects aiming to predict riots via sentiment analysis. 'Negative words', 'hate speech', 'positivity' and expressions of anger stand in for a population of shifting emotional registers, moving from stable states to those that can be used to require the maintenance of policing budgets, harsher policy and sudden rashes of inflamed and excited research budgets. The operators of such machines sell their technical fixes as providing a neutral oversight, in which the free expression of populations and individuals can be mapped and cross-checked for 'naughtiness'. What happens is rather more complex social forms are interwoven with those of the state, which itself attempts to follow too many filiations and clusterings. In the meantime, academic chancers position themselves as dubious mediators, able to appear to delve into the firehose of text produced by a population mapped according to weightings assigned to strings of characters. We enter into a condition of a generalized politics of experimental control without controlled experiment.

Claus Pias suggests that recent theories such as actor network theory and radical constructivism come from the same stock of ideas as simulation, since for both:

> Their knowledge is consciously – and as a matter of course – furnished with a hypothetical index, they admit to their fictional components, they position themselves within their conceptual frame of reference, they thematize their performance, they are aware of their problematic genesis, and they specify their limited application.[17]

A useful provocation following such a proposition is to be found in Latour and Lépinay's reading of Tarde: 'If you really want to quantify – which is after all the foundation of all sciences – you should try to find all the available types of quantum, instead of just using one to analyse all the others.'[18] This premise underlies some of the enthusiasm for big data analysis at present. It also perhaps implies that social reality is a simplified model of more adequately complex modelling schema. But we can also suggest that radical geographer William Bunge's later mode of maximalist empiricism coupled with high degrees of statistical abstraction is of great relevance here.[19] The proposition here is that to study is to become actively involved, to observe is to change, but also to recognize that, though such change may be reciprocal, it may not be symmetrical and equivalent. These are the stakes now of watching and participating, since in the city understood as a platform for self-organization, algorithms, rule sets, data structures, interfaces and procedures have highly and perhaps questionably promising agency.[20] The recent scandal of researchers from Facebook and the Universities of California and Cornell using Facebook's news feed to operate an experiment on whether people responded to the filtering of what appeared in their news feed on the basis of whether it was associated with emotional 'negativity' or 'positivity' should be seen as a part of this tendency. The researchers note that Facebook constantly experiments with the algorithm to fine tune this aspect of their 'product'.[21] It is this state of perpetual experiment, linking different scales of realities, that is characteristic of the condition of abstract urbanism and the kinds of operations that the integration of modelling with cities encourages.

This operation of the city as open experiment is of course one subject to the analysis of power. For Epstein and Axtell, agent-based modelling enforces habits of mind that are essential to intellectual and democratic freedom. An agent-based model must be explicit and open and be able to be examined and doubted, reconfigured and rerun. Epstein aligns agent-based modelling with scientific modes of enquiry that he sees as antithetical to established discursive intellectual systems. Agent-based modelling provides a freedom to doubt large monolithic and deductive forms of knowledge. Epstein and Axtell propose that we are on the edge of a new enlightenment based on the ubiquity of computing; one in which, for Epstein, '[i]ntellectuals have a solemn duty to doubt, and to teach doubt. Education, in its truest sense, is not about "a saleable skill set". It's about freedom, from inherited prejudice and argument by authority.'[22] The question of whether the enlightenment can be fully called upon in this way is in turn open to doubt, but there is something here that suggests some possibilities in that it is a science that explicitly calls subjects into being.

This proposed new mode of science of active abstractions involves cities and social forms in what Stuart Kauffman calls 'the physics of semantics',[23] logics that have effects in the organization of conjunction, calculation, control and communication. Such a physics of semantics can be seen, at other scales, in the way that the agent-based model is involved in the specific forms of hardware and software development that conjoin both meaning-making scaffolds and physical properties. Object orientation in programming is seen as a cogent worldview capable of answering difficult questions about behaviour that emerge from complex subjects in the social or in economics, where, '[it] facilitates essentially any interaction structure (social network) and activation regime'.[24] In contemporary accounts, agent-based modelling also links its ambition to the rapid growth of CPU processing and the availability of hard disk space and network processors assumed under Moore's Law. The 'promising' nature of abstract cities is thus also woven into multiple scales of their materiality.

This suggests that there is the possibility of a mode of experimentation, and of experimental politics and urban living, that moves from the logics of theorems or axioms to an abstract empiricism. Historically, software-based simulations essentially replaced the kinds of hardware-based simulations or analogues of biological, cognitive and social systems developed in places such as Heinz von Foerster's Biological Computer Laboratory (BCL) in Illinois.[25] The questions posed change in this transition, becoming allied less with the philosophical concerns characteristic of the BCL, with its emphasis on epistemology and the question of abstraction and reduction from material empirical conditions. We are now well into another similar transition, where instead of moving from hardware to software (with hardware becoming less experimental and idiosyncratic as it is rendered in the form of commodity electronics), social and urban forms become places of computational inter-operation and experiment.

Urban space is increasingly produced in the production, circulation and analysis of large volumes of structured and unstructured data. Models and processes of modelization, or making susceptible to modelling, are being integrated into the design of spatial forms such as stadia, streets and stations at conceptual and pre-emptive stages for the purposes of safety, transit design and revenue protection. In such cases, agents become active as urban entities installed in the symbolic and material orders of the city.

Just as computational forms structure reality, so do other kinds of model. Abstract urbanism is hypothetical, fictional, maximally empirical, and of course abstract. This means that the way in which abstractions become materially operative has to operate through these conditions, and also – under certain regimes of rhetoric – to shield them, as simply fact-based extrapolations. To recognize that they are imaginary, as models, without being either merely false or simple reifications, is part of the art of abstract urbanism. To see agent-based modelling in such a way is to recognize that models are also partial cities operating like partial objects, formalized slivers of an urban configuration taken for a whole and working their drives into active diagrams. Such a condition, in which the possibilities of social fractures being triggered in the models and then implemented are manifest, cannot but add an ambiguous potency to the operations such an art promises. To work abstract urbanism, then, in the condition of models becoming cities is also to open the possibility of operating with a maximalist empiricism. It is to operate with delicacy and attentiveness not only in the design of models, but also to the arguments, spaces and politics that they bear, that they determine and into which they are smuggled, driven and suffused, and which in turn they rely on to sustain themselves. It is to saturate models with variables, and to open abstraction to social disruption rather than to prepare the abstract retrenchment of urban injustice.

But to recognize abstract urbanism is not solely to postulate an interesting set of potential political practices, but more to come to terms with a fundamental change in the consistency of cities today: they are suffused with logics. This is to say not simply that streets are data structures, people are variables and the city is a grid laced with numerical nutrients, which in their interaction produce an adequate if simplified mimicry of urban life; but that the city, the exemplary space of modernity in all its complexity of desire, violence, multi-scalar layering, imagination, invention and struggle, is also a place of experiment with modes of composition and of self-emergence at multiple scales of abstraction. Such a space is one where fantasies of control, of understanding, of ordering, of establishing implicit and explicit co-ordination and pre-emption co-exist with their enactment, their failure, their use as excuse, and as a space where logic co-exists with the surprise of the unforeseen.

Agent-based modelling provides a means not only for the fan-tasmatic appearance of logics as an always present compliment of logic itself, in that it mobilizes means by which things occur in and for themselves in the mode of emergence, but also for a space for arranging the coming into being of ideas of the city that are beyond the habitual means of interrogating existing co-ordinates. Here, in the state of being promising, logics both pre-empt surprise and rely upon it to provide a gateway to emergence understood as the self-constitution of reality; a reality that is on the one hand seemingly unblemished by mess, and on the other forged in the full, ongoing complications of the cityscape in which it becomes manifest. This is a deeply ambivalent position. The physics of semantics in which such emergence is made is therefore worthy of attending to with all the precision and inventiveness that can be mustered, as it too becomes a space in which the city occurs.

1   Thomas Schelling, 'Models of Segregation', *American Economic Review*, 59:2 (1969), pp. 488–93.
2   Thomas Schelling, 'Dynamic Models of Segregation', *Journal of Mathematical Sociology* 1 (1971), pp. 143–86.
3   Jacob M. Epstein, 'Modeling Civil Violence: An Agent-Based Computational Approach', *Proceedings of the National Academy of Sciences*, 99:supplement 3 (14 May 2002), pp. 7243–50. Examples of work building on Epstein's model include Antonio A. Casilli and Paola Tubaro, 'Why Net Censorship in Times of Political Unrest Results in More Violent Uprisings: A Social Simulation Experiment on the UK Riots', *Social Science Research Network*, 14 August 2011, http://papers.ssrn.com/sol3/papers. cfm?abstract_id=1909467; Toby P. Davies, Hannah M. Fry, Alan G. Wilson and Steven R. Bishop, 'A Mathematical Model of the London Riots and their Policing', *Nature Scientific Reports* 3 (21 February 2013), article no. 1303.
4   Oscar Morgenstern and John von Neumann, *A Theory of Games and Economic Behaviour*, Princeton University Press, Princeton, 1947.
5   Thomas Schelling, *The Strategy of Conflict*, Harvard University Press, Cambridge, MA, 1960; 2nd edn, 1980. His paper 'Dynamic Models of Segregation' is revised in Thomas Schelling, *Micromotives and Macrobehaviour*, W. W. Norton, New York, 1978.
6   Schelling, 'Dynamic Models'. Schelling, *Micromotives*, ch. 4.
7   David Theo Goldberg, *The Threat of Race: Reflections on Neoliberal Racism*, Wiley-Blackwell, Oxford, 2009, p. 5.
8   Nina Simone, 'Mississippi Goddam', in *Nina Simone in Concert*, Philips, Eindhoven, 1964.
9   Richard Zeckhauser, 'Thomas Schelling, Ricochet Thinker', in Robert Dodge (ed.), *The Strategist: The Life and Times of Thomas Schelling*, Hollis Publishing, Hollis, 2006, p. x.
10 Martin Gardner, 'The Fantastic Combinations of John Conway's New Solitaire Game "Life" ', *Scientific American*, 223 (October 1970), pp. 120–3.
11 Edward F. Moore gives his name to systems of eight neighbours, expanded to use those at the corners in a rectilinear grid.
12 Ted Nelson, *Computer Lib/Dream Machines*, 2nd edn, Microsoft Press, Redmond, 1987, p. 108: 'All simulation is political. Every simulation program, and thus every simulation, has a point of

view. Just like a statement in words about the world, it is a model of how things are, with its own implicit emphases: it highlights some things, omits others and always simplifies.'

13 Joshua M. Epstein and Robert L. Axtell, *Growing Artificial Societies: Social Science from the Bottom Up*, Brookings Institution Press and MIT Press, Cambridge, MA, 1996.
14 See Axtell and Epstein's Sugarscape software.
15 Joshua M. Epstein, 'Why Model?', *Journal of Artificial Societies and Social Simulation*, 11:4, http://jasss.soc.surrey.ac.uk/11/4/12.html.
16 Stephen Graham, 'Software-Sorted Geographies', *Progress in Human Geography*, 29:5 (2005), pp. 562–80.
17 Claus Pias, 'On the Epistemology of Computer Simulation', *Zeitschrift für Medien- und Kulturforschung*, 1 (2011), pp. 29–54.
18 Bruno Latour and Vincent Lépinay, *The Science of Passionate Interests: An Introduction to Gabriel Tarde's Economic Anthropology*, Prickly Paradigm Press, Chicago, 2009, p. 19.
19 William Bunge, *Fitzgerald: Geography of a Revolution*, Schenkman Press, Cambridge, MA, 1971; reprint University of Georgia Press, Athens, GA, 2011.
20 Samir Chopra, 'Computer Programs are People Too', *Nation*, 29 May 2014.
21 Adam D. I. Kramer, Jamie E. Guillory and Jeffrey T. Hancock, 'Experimental Evidence of Massive-Scale Emotional Contagion through Social Networks', *Proceedings of the National Academy of Sciences of the United States of America*, 111:24 (17 June 2014), pp. 8788–90.
22 Epstein, 'Why Model?'.
23 Stuart Kauffman, *Investigations*, Oxford University Press, Oxford, 2000.
24 Robert Axtell, 'Economics as Distributed Computation', in Takao Terano, Hiroshi Deguchi and Keiki Takadama (eds.), *Meeting the Challenge of Social Problems via Agent-Based Simulation*, Springer, Heidelberg, 2003, p. 10.
25 Albert Müller and Karl H. Müller (eds.), *An Unfinished Revolution: Heinz von Foerster and the Biological Computer Laboratory, BCL 1958–1976*, edition echoraum, Vienna, 2007.

REFERENCES

Robert Axtell, 'Economics as Distributed Computation', in Takao Terano, Hiroshi Deguchi and Keiki Takadama (eds.), *Meeting the Challenge of Social Problems via Agent-Based Simulation*, Springer, Heidelberg, 2003.

William Bunge, *Fitzgerald: Geography of a Revolution*, Schenkman Press, Cambridge, MA, 1971; reprint University of Georgia Press, Athens, GA, 2011.

Antonio A. Casilli and Paola Tubaro, 'Why Net Censorship in Times of Political Unrest Results in More Violent Uprisings: A Social Simulation Experiment on the UK Riots', *Social Science Research Network*, 14 August 2011, http://papers.ssrn.com/sol3/papers.cfm?abstract_id=1909467

Samir Chopra, 'Computer Programs are People Too', *Nation*, 29 May 2014, http://www.thenation.com/article/computer-programs-are-people-too

Toby P. Davies, Hannah M. Fry, Alan G. Wilson and Steven R. Bishop, 'A Mathematical Model of the London Riots and their Policing', *Nature Scientific Reports* 3 (21 February 2013), article no. 1303.

Joshua M. Epstein, 'Modeling Civil Violence: An Agent-Based Computational Approach', *Proceedings of the National Academy of Sciences*, 99: Supplement 3 (14 May 2002), pp. 7243–50.

Joshua M. Epstein, 'Why Model?', *Journal of Artificial Societies and Social Simulation*, 11:4, http://jasss.soc.surrey.ac.uk/11/4/12.html

Joshua M. Epstein and Robert L. Axtell, *Growing Artificial Societies: Social Science from the Bottom Up*, Brookings Institution Press and MIT Press, Cambridge, MA, 1996.

Martin Gardner, 'The Fantastic Combinations of John Conway's New Solitaire Game "Life"', *Scientific American*, 223 (October 1970), pp. 120–3.

David Theo Goldberg, *The Threat of Race: Reflections on Neoliberal Racism*, Wiley-Blackwell, Oxford, 2009.

Stephen Graham, 'Software-Sorted Geographies', *Progress in Human Geography*, 29:5 (2005), pp. 562–80.

Stuart Kauffman, *Investigations*, Oxford University Press, Oxford, 2000.

Adam D. I. Kramer, Jamie E. Guillory and Jeffrey T. Hancock, 'Experimental Evidence of Massive-Scale Emotional Contagion through Social Networks', *Proceedings of the National Academy of Sciences of the United States of America*, 111:24 (17 June 2014), pp. 8788–90.

Bruno Latour and Vincent Lépinay, *The Science of Passionate Interests: An Introduction to Gabriel Tarde's Economic Anthropology*, Prickly Paradigm Press, Chicago, 2009.

Oscar Morgenstern and John von Neumann, *A Theory of Games and Economic Behaviour*, Princeton University Press, Princeton, 1947.

Albert Müller and Karl H. Müller (eds.), *An Unfinished Revolution: Heinz von Foerster and the Biological Computer Laboratory, BCL 1958–1976*, edition echoraum, Vienna, 2007.

Ted Nelson, *Computer Lib/Dream Machines*, 2nd edn, Microsoft Press, Redmond, 1987.

Claus Pias, 'On the Epistemology of Computer Simulation', *Zeitschrift für Medien- und Kulturforschung*, 1 (2011) pp. 29–54.

Thomas Schelling, *The Strategy of Conflict*, Harvard University Press, Cambridge, MA, 1960; 2nd edn 1980.

Thomas Schelling, 'Models of Segregation', *American Economic Review*, 59:2 (1969), pp. 488–93.

Thomas Schelling, 'Dynamic Models of Segregation', *Journal of Mathematical Sociology*, 1 (1971), pp. 143–86.

Thomas Schelling, *Micromotives and Macrobehaviour*, W. W. Norton, New York, 1978.

Nina Simone, 'Mississippi Goddam', in *Nina Simone in Concert*, Philips, Eindhoven, 1964.

Richard Zeckhauser, 'Thomas Schelling, Ricochet Thinker', in Robert Dodge (ed.), *The Strategist: The Life and Times of Thomas Schelling*, Hollis Publishing, Hollis, 2006.

ENTITIES

— 3 —

SOFTWARE STUDIES METHODS

What is the consistency of computational culture? What are the ways in which the objects of computer science and of its more informal offspring operate in and as the world? Looking into such questions, it can be readily seen that a cunningly diffuse and multi-layered aspect of the question of method is that of understanding what constitutes the problem. Luckily, for the development of such an inter- or anti-disciplinary field as software studies, computational media cultures are abundantly generative of such things. Problems flourish. From questions of the foundations of computing to the articulation of cultural tendencies and political systems across commodity platforms, via the questions of power, aesthetics and processes of subjectivity, problems abound, and that's only to mention a few that are properly named as such. Any short survey of methods in the field can therefore only be partial and indicative, picking out a few general trends. The kinds of problems addressed arose too at the emergence of software studies at the beginning of this century.[1] However, from such a starting point, software studies has become the grounds for a relishable diversity of methods, concerns, and conceptual and practical resources. This chapter will try to map a few of these and give some sense of their consistency and trajectories. In this, as a survey, it will necessarily be partial and limited due to the vitality and range of activity in the field. Read it then as an aperitif, before investigating further.

To frame the question of the problem, a little genealogy is in order. From a certain set of angles, software studies arose from a background of bemused frustration at the ways in which 'high-level' media theory would tend towards subsumptive generalization about the 'virtual', or about 'cyberspace', without attending to the howl and screech of a dial-up modem, or the particular dance of pixelated entities amongst the graphical user interfaces that constituted everyday activity in the 'knowledge economy'. A parallel here can be drawn with software art, which articulated itself in part against the media art and net art that often ignored the specific materials from which it was made, a condition that – as those materials became both increasingly interesting and increasingly over-coded – became untenable. Equally, as social theory drew upon the active constitution of society by objects, systems, media and tools, alongside those entities that had hitherto been understood to be social, the capacity to recognize what Scott Lash called 'technological forms of life' became pressing.[2] Amidst this too, the imperatives underlying the development of the field are driven by an emphasis on the complexly empirical and materialist, fortified by the empiricism of the abstract found both in the more generous reaches of the poststructuralist legacy and in those aspects of meta-mathematics and computer science that had always recognized the cultural dimensions of their activity.

More recently, software studies finds itself in the curious position of being a scholarly stick-in-the-mud as certain aspects of computational culture become sprinkled like glittery mica on trays of theoretical cupcakes: decorative, indigestible, and garnishing the semiotically retrospective and materially stale. Algorithms, for instance, are increasingly emphasized as an explanatory actor, although in a surprisingly large quantity of scholarship this explanatory power is asserted without their contextualization within the other systems in which they are embedded, and indeed, in a notable number of cases without even the requirement to ascertain what an algorithm might be. Indeed, a scan of the literature shows that it is entirely possible to have a social or literary theorist discourse on 'algorithms' without any references other than to others of their ilk. This kind of elective solipsism of disciplines is familiar to those navigating interdisciplinary terrains, and is also articulated through the kinds of citation politics that other such fields, such as feminist research, have become all too familiar with. We are in the amusing position where the emphasis on materiality in recent theory results in what is technical and important sounding being elevated to the same kind of generalizations that, say, the more banal pronouncements of postmodernity suffered from in their heyday. Social theory too often brings along its upstairs/downstairs split between high theory and empiricism.

There is an art to the interplay between the rigours imposed by attention to material qualities and conditions with all their constraints, limits and capacities, their specificities and individuations, and those entailed also by the particular material, epistemic and ontogenetic capacities of abstractions. In working on such a topic, software studies approaches might characteristically tend to identify specific algorithms, articulate their genealogy, recognize and work with their characteristics, and see them as part of a larger assemblage – one that is not in turn immune to the imperative of conceptual rigour.[3] All this requires something of an avidity for research. Such a condition also drives it towards non-canonical texts and sites as sources of interest. This in turn is a methodological choice that sets it at a tangent to theoretical work aiming to array itself solely amongst well-cited or paternalistically approved books. Showing that one is in dialogue only with those of the correct lineage is a rhetorical technique that has the democratic advantage that the canon is seemingly available to us all, whether we like it or not; but it also may be a technique effected as one of foreclosure. Part of this condition is due to the febrile pleasures of academic politics, in which it is seen that the study of new media has yet to establish itself fully as a legitimate field, and in order to do so must exaggeratedly exhibit the habits of conformism and deference special to the various overlapping pyramid schemes that are, amongst other things, operative in the university.

Another way of framing this question of methods is to arrive partially at it via two of the fields that contribute to software studies. Cultural studies and computing both emerged, in different ways, in the aftermath of the Second World War, both forged by the necessity of the interdisciplinary bringing together of multiple kinds of method, material and problematic. In different times, software studies emerges as a minor mutational fold within these discourses, at the cusp of the inventive enthusiasm of the world wide web and the internet, and the transition to the version of the same which we now inhabit. The various crises and possibilities in knowledge, technology, institutional forms and epistemic potential that each of these represents feed into the specific traits of software studies as a field.

With cultural studies, software studies shares a taste for vulgar objects that pass below the threshold of critical perception due to their mundane, technical or tedious nature. Ostensibly boring entities, manuals, slide presentations and technical specifications are all probed for interesting traces as admixtures of high technology and low theory. Just as crystals grow differently in variable electromagnetic fields, which can in turn be examined through the variations in growth pattern they contribute to, the relatively 'pure' formalisms that software articulates in such materials can also retain interesting patterns of resonance with wider formations.

Relatedly, one may sense into software by the ways it comes into composition with users. And here, ignorance of software's conventions has been thought to be highly revealing. It must be possible to read software in a way that is partially naive, stupid, heading in the wrong direction, mysterious, uninformed by a disciplinary history. To watch a person encounter a machine for the first time is exciting; one might learn, from their dissonant interpretation, what experienced preconceptions have become. Unfortunately, even with the micro-confusions of users moving between operating systems, today the state of inexperience with computational entities is a rare resource. But there are ways in which it is mobilized, bearing indeed some relation to Jacques Rancière's formulation of the 'ignorant', where people learn by moving along in a manner in which 'one shouldn't move along – the way children move, blindly, figuring out riddles'.[4] Indeed, given its value, the techniques of ethnography have been utilized to capture this moment, or to set up a pretext in which it can be removed from the story of a product.[5] There is a kind of sense in which this naivety, as a prerequisite component of the genesis of thought, may seek out new objects of encounter.

One of the ways such naivety may fruitfully manifest is by asking scrupulously simple questions. Indeed, the cunning and intelligence required for the deployment of a sufficiently simple question are of key methodological concern for programmers attempting to instruct machines, and for anyone working to elicit material from what is now commonly characterized as big data.[6] The artful projects of the working groups convened by Lev Manovich, such as *SelfieCity*, work in this mode,[7] and one can say that they operate at a number of levels. Ostensibly, they are navigations of certain sets of data. A question is asked of a flow of images that conform to a certain categorical norm: that of date, kind, genre, keyword, location and so on. These categorical terms are those that arise out of the specific nature of the system, which in part is that of a database whose genealogical roots are in set theory. Corralled as it often is within categorical architectures, and tucked, heavily filtered by a subset of such categories, behind application program interfaces (APIs), it is difficult to get significant traction on the material, except in reconfirming its preconditions.

To work around this, data is captured and *withdrawn* from such systems and then subject to other kinds of query; for instance, using colour saturation or hue to navigate the variation in colour of images tagged with the names of certain cities, or image-recognition software to analyse the tilt of the head characteristic of selfies given a certain location. The findings of such work are partly in this activation of the parodically positivist formalisms that undergird aspects of computational culture and subtend the ideas of big data. Genuinely trivial details in aggregate become something else; they constitute part of cultural form. To navigate these and to aggregate them in turn become part of the constitution of a dual capacity of critical exploration and seamless involvement that is both troubled and fascinating.

Working through and into the ways in which computational and networked forms change established modes of culture, politics and society and establish new ones has – like the traces of the forces acting on a crystal – been very palpable in certain cultural-economic forms such as publishing, music and film, where they have had massive systemic effects. In disciplines, such as philosophy, the articulation of these predispositions and capacities has been less immediately discernible but also intriguing, with not only the development of platforms and currents, and the mobilization of previously more marginal actants, but also cognitive speed-ups, trends and conceptual hazing becoming more visible. Computational forms here become one of the fields in which the crystal grows.

Related in certain ways to the question of operative stupidity and the principle of the pyramid scheme in academic citation patterns is something that may indeed be worth some study in itself: the entrenchment of Pareto-principle-type citation patterns due to the material specificity of contemporary publication.[8] When the search engine becomes the primary basis of scholarly research, the keyword becomes a crucial pivot for the articulation of fields. Thus, in speeded-up research cultures, ever-ready to announce what passes for a novelty, it is possible for communities of researchers working in related domains to bypass each other's work entirely due to over-dutiful following of links.

Earlier I noted that software studies methods include something of the fastidious, painstaking work of the archive following up a specific object. Here there is a useful correlation with work in the method of following the object, suggested by Kopytoff,[9] and in the figure of the boundary object formulated by Susan Leigh Star and James Griesemer.[10] One of the key factors to note is that many of the objects to be registered in software studies are multi-scalar. To fix only on the immediately empirical – say, on the position of a specific procedure within a wider assemblage – would also be to risk missing, via simply descriptive means, some of the more abstract dimensions of such an assemblage. The mathematical and logical conditions of such an entity are also inherently formed amongst non-uniform fields of metaphysical 'radiation' set in motion by mathematical conditions.[11] Equally, their articulation can be probed in relation to the epistemic conditions of certain kinds of data cultures and economies. To recognize the multidimensionality of the problem is by no means to deny the pleasures or necessity of micro-scalar analyses, but rather to emphasize, in relation to research methods, the ways in which positing an analysis of a part triggers in turn the positing of a vision of a putative whole.

To return, then, to the relation of the method to the problem, part of the work of software studies has been to burrow into and articulate the relations between different scales in which software becomes manifest without proposing any pre-existing, hierarchically ordered set of conditions to which such things must correspond, and without at the same time failing to notice that such orderings are multiple and highly operative. To this end, there is a discussion of software in terms of the data structures known as stacks in the work of Ben Bratton[12] and Rob Kitchin,[13] amongst others, examining the ways in which the mutual ordering and dependencies of separate scales of abstraction and operation produce functional wholes. When, via an overly normalized and normative empiricism, work in this domain risks an occasional simple recapitulation of systemic technical description, it is also challenged by a materialism operating 'below the stack' by, for instance, focusing on the social and even alchemical histories and qualities of the minerals that end up in dialogue with the logical operations of software in the work of artists such as Jonathan Kemp,[14] Martin Howse[15] and the group YoHa.[16] Both of these tendencies offer the potential of dialogue with the wider questions of infrastructure and the scholars, from Sergio Bologna[17] to Keller Easterling,[18] who have traced these interrelations via political economy and spatial approaches.

Questions of infrastructure appear too in much of the work assembling an understanding of the fundamental components of large-scale web platforms. There is a sense that a key movement in much contemporary work is an investigation of the operations, significance, underlying forces and consequences of social media and the apparatuses of production, storage, dissemination and analysis that they constitute. A number of articles have seen scholars address the functioning of, for instance, Google's PageRank or Adwords, Facebook's OpenGraph[19] and the shifting nature of database systems, from relational to NoSQL,[20] as well as other mechanisms that deftly bring together theoretical resources drawn from different strands of cultural and social theory, histories of organization and of mathematics, amongst others. Treating the entities of such 'abstract infrastructure' as inherently cultural, social and political, as well as interrogating the way in which computational media install and format the modes of coming into being and of becoming in the present, is fundamental to the questions that are formative to the genesis of methods.

One of the conditions here is the changing status of media. Fried-rich Kittler neatly boiled down the condition of media as being those mechanisms to do with the production, storage and dissemination of information.[21] The systems in the last paragraph added *analysis* to this triad. Analysis here is the breaking down of complex entities into what, at a certain scale, can be read as nominally fundamental units, and working out their immanent, potential or emergent relationships. Media have in many cases largely become a subset of computational systems. As a condition of their constitution as digital systems and, thanks to Alan Turing, as procedural systems that are inherently com-posed of discrete entities and steps, computers are constitutionally predicated upon analysis. Analysis and control combined are part of what make the move to computational generality such a significant, if not unprecedented, shift; and it is to the way in which this power of computational analyses is coupled with other forms that are native to the arts and humanities that we should now turn.

The collectively authored book *10 PRINT CHR$(205.5+RND(1));
: GOTO 10*[22] proposes that the single line of code set out in its title can be read, rewritten, divagated from, and used as the basis for memory and reverie in a compelling way. Here, close reading is the pivot on which a world can be spun out from a crystal of code. In related terms, a number of similarly minuscule objects have been examined for the way in which their minor variations can become highly revealing entry points into a wider set of phenomena. Anne Helmond's discussion of the historical changes to the hyperlink or URL – from something hard-coded into an HTML document, to an artefact generated on the fly by a database system on dynamic websites – exemplifies this approach.[23] By looking at such changes in technology, insights into the way in which websites are used and embody different modes of social and cultural activity can be readily elicited; for instance, in the trajectory from something hand-coded and available to all users, to being an ostensibly secure one-time-only transaction. Related articulations of such telling detail are evident in Ben Grosser's account of his plug-in, the 'Facebook Demetri-cator',[24] that removes numerical, quantitative and temporal data from the interface of the social media site. Another recent approach is to combine analytical methods from police data forensics with a historical survey of software manuals to draw up a history of

the various kinds of metadata that contain author information.[25] In these and many other projects there are numerous contributions to debates about what constitutes the object of study, entangled with the methodical means of staging such an encounter. Work by Wendy Chun, Alex Galloway, Annette Vee, Taina Bucher, Shintaro Miyazaki and numerous others specifically proposes methods integrated with particular lines of enquiry around certain scales at which software exists.[26]

An additional mode of analysis, drawn from technical practices, is that of reverse engineering. Here, Adrian Mackenzie suggests that 'One strategy is to begin by describing the most distinctive algorithmic processes present, and then ask to what constraints or problems these processes respond. From there we can start to explore how software transforms relations.'[27] Such a methodical frame corresponds to the process of observation and decomposition adopted in Robert W. Gehl's work on social media.[28] It also provides an impetus for research that works directly on software systems via means of programmatic comparison between input and output.[29] Such work involves setting up one system to interrogate another. Applied to a research target such as the predominant web-based services, this may involve establishing user accounts, scripts and servers that feed data into a system to generate results and then to make comparative analyses of them. Sometimes described as 'algorithm audit'[30] and strongly developed by researchers such as Latanya Sweeney,[31] such techniques are especially notable in formulating a progressive programme of research on the empirical operations of computational systems that form and constitute privatized forms of public resources.

One of the difficulties here is in negotiating the privileged position that quantification is allocated in different kinds of discourse, where the numerically describable stands in for the empirical. Such research is often that most taken up and, if not actually discussed, replicated in the press. Nevertheless, as a means of reflexively working into the way in which computational forms operate, it is an intensely valuable set of approaches. In a context too in which massive amounts of economic, social and cultural action are carried out in computational environments, it is a mode of action carried out on a tactical basis by multitudes of actors, not the least significant of these being algorithms employed by competing companies to understand the operations of others. We can say too, that as reverse engineering becomes a mode of sociability – one prods a person to see if they elicit, for instance, the signs taken for friendship – it is a mode that becomes increasingly omnipresent.

Methods result in many cases from the conjunction of an intensive question with a problem. A case that is interesting to the point of fascination demands subtle attention to crack it. Here, the mode of study adequate to a digital entity or process achieves the tender revelations of a hack. Exemplary in this regard are the edited volume and concurrently formed exhibitions of artworks put together by Olga Goriunova on the theme of Fun and Software.[32] One of the guiding concerns in this strand of Goriunova's work is to draw out the way in which software is formed in and as a question of obsessive pleasures of multiple kinds. The articulation of logics, processes, systems and other modes of computational artefact as they are manifest in, given grounds by and shaped by the nature of software, and provide in turn a condition of life that is both sensual and abstract, is richly drawn out in this series of projects. Crucial to note in the Fun and Software series is that scholarly modes of research are challenged by those that are anterior to the question of academic form. The condition of software is understood to be a fundamentally existential one. Aesthetics provides routes into such a question, but so also do the reflexive accounts of cultural and technical practitioners. There is a close involvement here too with the immanent mode of criticism established in software art and of the properly speculative dimension required when thinking about the various scales of conjunction of processes of abstraction and concretion to be found in software cultures.[33] Here, software studies develops close affinities with the philosophical approaches of writers such as Luciana Parisi that mobilize reflections on the ontological conditions of mathematical technologies.[34]

Following from this, the question of method is one coeval with multiple modes of being as much as with the problems they are crystallized into. Appropriate methods, then, involve grinding such crystals up, to see what they can do when ingested; describing what they mix with and the forms they take; or gazing deeply into them to divine the nature of the present.

NOTES

1   See for instance the 'Software Summer School' at the TechNiks series of events curated by Lisa Haskel in the Lux Gallery, London, in 2000; or the software section in Josephine Bosma et al. (eds.), *Readme! ASCII Culture and the Revenge of Knowledge*, Autonomedia, New York, 1999.

2 Scott Lash, 'Technological Forms of Life', in Lash, *Critique of Information*, Sage, London, 2002.
3 See for instance Adrian Mackenzie's tour de force on the Viterbi algorithm in *Wirelessness: Radical Empiricism in Network Cultures*, MIT Press, Cambridge, MA, 2010. The work of the Brussels-based Active Archives group (http://activearchives.org/wiki/Main_Page) is exemplary in working through the expressive capacities of the interplay of data structures and algorithms in relation to other media forms.
4 Jacques Rancière, *The Ignorant Schoolmaster: Five Lessons in Intellectual Emancipation*, trans. Kristin Ross, Stanford University Press, Stanford, 1991, p. 10.
5 Alex Wilkie, *User Assemblages in Design: An Ethnographic Study*, PhD thesis, Goldsmiths, University of London, 2010.
6 Rob Kitchin, *The Data Revolution*, Sage, London, 2014; Gannaelle Langlois, Joanna Redden and Greg Elmer, *Compromised Data: From Social Media to Big Data*, Bloomsbury, London, 2015.
7 Software Studies Initiative, *SelfieCity*, 2014, http://www.selfiecity.net.
8 Konrad Becker and Felix Stalder (eds.), *Deep Search: The Politics of Search beyond Google*. Studienverlag, Vienna, 2009.
9 Igor Kopytoff, 'The Cultural Biography of Things: Commoditization as Process', in Arjun Appadurai (ed.), *The Social Life of Things: Commodities in Cultural Perspective*, Cambridge University Press, Cambridge and New York, 1986.
10 Susan Leigh Star and James Griesemer, 'Institutional Ecology, "Translations" and Boundary Objects: Amateurs and Professionals in Berkeley's Museum of Vertebrate Zoology, 1907–39', *Social Studies of Science*, 19:3 (1989), pp. 387–420.
11 See, for an exploration of this set of conditions, M. Beatrice Fazi and Matthew Fuller, 'Computational Aesthetics', in this volume.
12 Benjamin Bratton, *The Stack: On Software and Sovereignty*, MIT Press, Cambridge, MA, 2016.
13 Rob Kitchin, 'Thinking Critically About and Researching Algorithms', *Programmable City Working Paper 5*, Maynooth University – NIRSA, Maynooth, 2014.
14 See, for the work of Jonathan Kemp, http://xxn.org.uk.
15 See, for the work of Martin Howse, http://1010.co.uk/org.
16 See, for the work of YoHa (Matsuko Yokokoji and Graham Harwood), http://www.yoha.co.uk.

17 Sergio Bologna, 'The Factory–Society Relationship as an Historical Category', trans. Ed Emery, Libcom.org, London, n.d.
18 Keller Easterling, *Extrastatecraft: The Power of Infrastructure Space*, London, Verso, 2014.
19 Irina Kaldrack and Theo Röhle, 'Divide and Share: Taxonomies, Orders and Masses in Facebook's Open Graph', *Computational Culture*, 4 (2014), http://www.computationalculture.net.
20 Paul Dourish, 'NoSQL: The Shifting Materialities of Database Technology', *Computational Culture*, 4 (2014), http://www.computationalculture.net.
21 Friedrich Kittler, *Literature, Media, Information Systems*, ed. and trans. John Johnston, G&B Arts, Amsterdam, 1997.
22 Nick Montfort, Patsy Baudoin, John Bell, Ian Bogost, Jeremy Douglass, Mark C. Marino, Michael Mateas, Casey Reas, Mark Sample and Noah Vawter, *10 PRINT CHR$(205.5+RND(1)); : GOTO 10*, MIT Press, Cambridge, MA, 2014.
23 Anne Helmond, 'The Algorithmization of the Hyperlink', *Computational Culture*, 3 (2013), http://www.computationalculture.net.
24 Ben Grosser, *Facebook Demetricator*, http://bengrosser.com/projects/facebook-demetricator.
25 See Matthew Fuller, Nikita Mazurov and Dan McQuillan, 'The Author Field', in this volume.
26 Wendy Chun, *Programmed Visions: Software and Memory*, MIT Press, Cambridge, MA, 2011. Alex Galloway, *The Interface Effect*, Polity, Cambridge, 2012; Annette Vee, 'Text, Speech, Machine: Metaphors for Computer Code in the Law', *Computational Culture*, 2 (2012), http://www.computationalculture.net; Noah Wardrip-Fruin, *Expressive Processing: Digital Fictions, Computer Games, and Software Studies*, MIT Press, Cambridge, MA, 2009; Taina Bucher, 'Objects of Intense Feeling: The Case of the Twitter API', *Computational Culture*, 3 (2013), http://www.computationalculture.net; Shintaro Miyazaki, 'Algorhythmics: Understanding Micro-Temporality in Computational Cultures', *Computational Culture*, 2 (2012), http://www.computationalculture.net.
27 Adrian Mackenzie, *Cutting Code: Software and Sociality*, Peter Lang, New York, 2006.
28 Robert W. Gehl, *Reverse Engineering Social Media: Software, Culture and Political Economy in New Media Capitalism*, Temple University Press, Philadelphia, 2014.
29 Martin Feuz, Matthew Fuller and Felix Stalder, 'Personal Web Searching in the Age of Semantic Capitalism: Diagnosing the

Mechanisms of Personalization', *First Monday*, 16:2 (7 February 2011), http://firstmonday.org/article/view/3344/2766; Bev Skeggs and Simon Yuill, *Values and Value*, https://values.doc. gold.ac.uk.

30 Christian Sandvig, Kevin Hamilton, Karrie Karahalios and Cedric Langbort, 'Auditing Algorithms: Research Methods for Detecting Discrimination on Internet Platforms', paper presented at Data and Discrimination: Converting Critical Concerns into Productive Inquiry, a pre-conference at the 64th Annual Meeting of the International Communication Association, 22 May 2014, Seattle.

31 Latanya Sweeney, 'Discrimination in Online Ad Delivery', *Communications of the ACM*, 56:5 (2013), pp. 44–54.

32 Olga Goriunova (ed.), *Fun and Software: Exploring Pleasure, Paradox and Pain in Computing*, Bloomsbury, London and New York, 2014. Exhibitions: Olga Goriunova (curator), *Funware*, Arnolfini, Bristol, September–November 2010; and *Fun with Software*, MU and Baltan, Eindhoven, November 2010–January 2011 (producers Annet Dekker and Annette Wolfsberger).

33 Related approaches such as design fictions and speculative design are important to map here.

34 Luciana Parisi, *Contagious Architecture: Computation, Aesthetics and Space*, MIT Press, Cambridge, MA, 2013.

REFERENCES

Active Archives, http://activearchives.org/wiki/Main_Page
Konrad Becker and Felix Stalder (eds.), *Deep Search: The Politics of Search beyond Google*. Studienverlag, Vienna, 2009.
Sergio Bologna, 'The Factory–Society Relationship as an Historical Category', trans. Ed Emery, Libcom.org, London, n.d.
Josephine Bosma et al. (eds.), *Readme! ASCII Culture and the Revenge of Knowledge*, Autonomedia, New York, 1999.
Benjamin Bratton, *The Stack: On Software and Sovereignty*, MIT Press, Cambridge, MA, 2016.
Taina Bucher, 'Objects of Intense Feeling: The Case of the Twitter API', *Computational Culture*, 3 (2013), http://www.computationalculture.net
Wendy Chun, *Programmed Visions: Software and Memory*, MIT Press, Cambridge, MA, 2011.
Paul Dourish, 'NoSQL: The Shifting Materialities of Database Technology', *Computational Culture*, 4 (2014), http://www.computationalculture.net

Keller Easterling, *Extrastatecraft: The Power of Infrastructure Space*, London, Verso, 2014.

M. Beatrice Fazi and Matthew Fuller, 'Computational Aesthetics', in this volume.

Martin Feuz, Matthew Fuller and Felix Stalder, 'Personal Web Searching in the Age of Semantic Capitalism: Diagnosing the Mechanisms of Personalization', *First Monday*, 16:2 (7 February 2011), http://firstmonday.org/article/view/3344/2766

Matthew Fuller, Nikita Mazurov and Dan McQuillan, 'The Author Field', in this volume.

Alex Galloway, *The Interface Effect*, Polity, Cambridge, 2012.

Robert W. Gehl, *Reverse Engineering Social Media: Software, Culture and Political Economy in New Media Capitalism*, Temple University Press, Philadelphia, 2014.

Olga Goriunova (curator), *Funware*, Arnolfini, Bristol, September–November 2010.

Olga Goriunova (curator), *Fun with Software*, MU and Baltan, Eindhoven, November 2010–January 2011.

Olga Goriunova (ed.), *Fun and Software: Exploring Pleasure, Paradox and Pain in Computing*, Bloomsbury, London and New York, 2014.

Ben Grosser, *Facebook Demetricator*, http://bengrosser.com/projects/facebook-demetricator

Anne Helmond, 'The Algorithmization of the Hyperlink', *Computational Culture*, 3 (2013), http://www.computationalculture.net

Martin Howse, http://1010.co.uk/org

Irina Kaldrack and Theo Röhle, 'Divide and Share: Taxonomies, Orders and Masses in Facebook's Open Graph', *Computational Culture*, 4 (2014), http://www.computationalculture.net

Jonathan Kemp, http://xxn.org.uk

Rob Kitchin, *The Data Revolution*, Sage, London, 2014.

Rob Kitchin, 'Thinking Critically About and Researching Algorithms', *Programmable City Working Paper 5*, Maynooth University – NIRSA, Maynooth, 2014.

Friedrich Kittler, *Literature, Media, Information Systems*, ed. and trans. John Johnston, G&B Arts, Amsterdam, 1997.

Igor Kopytoff, 'The Cultural Biography of Things: Commoditization as Process', in Arjun Appadurai (ed.), *The Social Life of Things: Commodities in Cultural Perspective*, Cambridge University Press, Cambridge and New York, 1986.

Gannaelle Langlois, Joanna Redden and Greg Elmer, *Compromised Data: From Social Media to Big Data*, Bloomsbury, London, 2015.

Scott Lash, 'Technological Forms of Life', in Lash, *Critique of Information*, Sage, London, 2002.

Adrian Mackenzie, *Cutting Code: Software and Sociality*, Peter Lang, New York, 2006.

Adrian Mackenzie, *Wirelessness: Radical Empiricism in Network Cultures*, MIT Press, Cambridge, MA, 2010.

Shintaro Miyazaki, 'Algorhythmics: Understanding Micro-Temporality in Computational Cultures', *Computational Culture*, 2 (2012), http://www.computationalculture.net

Nick Montfort, Patsy Baudoin, John Bell, Ian Bogost, Jeremy Douglass, Mark C. Marino, Michael Mateas, Casey Reas, Mark Sample and Noah Vawter, *10 PRINT CHR$(205.5+RND(1)); : GOTO 10*, MIT Press, Cambridge, MA, 2014.

Luciana Parisi, *Contagious Architecture: Computation, Aesthetics and Space*, MIT Press, Cambridge, MA, 2013.

Jacques Rancière, *The Ignorant Schoolmaster: Five Lessons in Intellectual Emancipation*, trans. Kristin Ross, Stanford University Press, Stanford, 1991.

Christian Sandvig, Kevin Hamilton, Karrie Karahalios and Cedric Langbort, 'Auditing Algorithms: Research Methods for Detecting Discrimination on Internet Platforms', paper presented at Data and Discrimination: Converting Critical Concerns into Productive Inquiry, a pre-conference at the 64th Annual Meeting of the International Communication Association, 22 May 2014, Seattle.

Bev Skeggs and Simon Yuill, *Values and Value*, https://values.doc.gold.ac.uk

Software Studies Initiative, *SelfieCity*, 2014, http://www.selfiecity.net

Susan Leigh Star and James Griesemer, 'Institutional Ecology, "Translations" and Boundary Objects: Amateurs and Professionals in Berkeley's Museum of Vertebrate Zoology, 1907–39', *Social Studies of Science*, 19:3 (1989), pp. 387–420.

Latanya Sweeney, 'Discrimination in Online Ad Delivery', *Communications of the ACM*, 56:5 (2013), pp. 44–54.

Annette Vee, 'Text, Speech, Machine: Metaphors for Computer Code in the Law', *Computational Culture*, 2 (2012), http://www.computationalculture.net

Noah Wardrip-Fruin, *Expressive Processing: Digital Fictions, Computer Games, and Software Studies*, MIT Press, Cambridge, MA, 2009.

Alex Wilkie, *User Assemblages in Design: An Ethnographic Study*, PhD thesis, Goldsmiths, University of London, 2010.

YoHa (Matsuko Yokokoji and Graham Harwood), http://www.yoha.co.uk

— 4 —

BIG DIFF, GRANULARITY, INCOHERENCE, AND PRODUCTION IN THE GITHUB SOFTWARE REPOSITORY

Matthew Fuller, Andrew Goffey,
Adrian Mackenzie, Richard Mills
and Stuart Sharples

This chapter will discuss the way in which Github, one of the largest dynamic repositories of software online, can be seen to operate as a mode of archive which in turn re-engineers the question of what an archive is. In very simple terms, Github is a place where software is stored online and from which it can often be downloaded. More expansively, it provides a sense of the archive as simultaneously a site of fine-grained analysis and of incoherence, of storage and of production.

To get to Github, we need to start with Git, a source code management (SCM) system designed by Linus Torvalds in 2005.[1] Git was initially based on the characteristics of a file storage system familiar to its author as the initiator of the Linux aspect of the GNU/Linux operating system.[2] Whilst it claims to be 'a stupid content tracker',[3] in practice Git is a highly sophisticated, decentralized and distributed way of writing code in groups on scales ranging from an individual to that of large organizations. Git encourages branching or multiple versions of the same project at the same time and provides many different ways of merging, tracking, duplicating and integrating code repositories distributed across many developers. It facilitates and encourages copies and variations as well as the tracking and auditing of changes in almost any kind of digital data.

Since 2007, Github.com – a separate organization – has served as a largely public host platform for Git repositories or 'repos'. It has encouraged software developers and programmers to store, work on and retrieve the source code and texts associated with software projects on many scales, again ranging from individuals to large organizations. It has augmented the many operations afforded by

Git with 'social coding' affordances such as 'starring', 'watching', the distinctive 'pull-request' mechanism, various more formal organizational arrangements (teams, organizations etc.) and visual descriptive devices (graphs in particular). Github has grown rapidly since 2007 to become perhaps the most important online code repository of the moment, hosting around 10 million projects in total with several million people contributing to them, albeit with widely varying levels of activity. We might understand Github as the formal enterprise that organizes – and somewhat ironically, centralizes – the informal, decentralized organization of Git.

Github itself publishes much data about the growth of repos. The public legibility of platform dynamics is typical of contemporary software-mediated culture: things are made to be readable by many. Github.com also produces and encourages the production of various forms of visualization and tabulation of what goes on there. To illustrate this legibility, we could choose important or famous repositories on Github – the Linux kernel, for instance, still led by Linus Torvalds, is a much-vaunted FLOSS (free, libre and open source software) project that has become economically and technically central to the development of the internet – and analyse the flows of meaning, texts and readers/writers connected to that repository.[4] Relatively quickly, individual contributions could be analysed, and we could begin to characterize the composition of the group of people who keep this important software object working and up to date. But this work is largely already done by Github.com itself.[5] Indeed, the site is characterized by a high degree of granularity of the data it holds. This is understood to mean the availability of multiple kinds of highly detailed, and to some degree tractable, information of the processes, material and actors it gathers. Since Github is notable for the 'socialization' of software production, in which the social media forms already mentioned are built into the archive, there is, in turn, a deep integration of quantification into the working processes of the archive.

Coding Processes and Architectures

The development of software has entailed a history of self-reflection of certain kinds. The discourse and practices of software engineering, for instance, were born of a need to intensify the quality and standardization of code, in turn stabilizing factors such as the culture of engineering and desirable qualities of personnel.[6] Here, we should also note the strong differentiation between the engineering and

70

software development approaches and the concomitant differences between hackers and engineers that run through them. Software engineering historically relies on the standardization and systematization of work in relation to large-scale projects. Hacking, by contrast, emphasizes informality and virtuosity.

Faced with the explosion of programming and the applications in which it is being deployed, computing has also developed numerous techniques of management or methodology, modularity and re-usability, to stabilize the nature of work and to make it more amenable to enjoyment or at least to management. Programming methodologies develop out of various formulations, such as the need to co-ordinate across often increasingly large-scale projects or, conversely, to develop project requirements as the system develops. Echoing such imperatives, examples such as Waterfall (a software development model predicated upon strict division of stages) involve an ordering and hierarchy of projects and products; conversely, Agile methodology is a mode of close collaboration between coders and clients, emphasizing the quality of working life, fast iteration of code, and the tight participation of the user. Alongside these organizational systematizations, programmers rework, add to and link pieces of code. This may seem an obvious statement, but the process also implies the development of languages, programming environments such as IDEs (integrated development environments) or the text editors (such as VIM or Atom) in which programmers work, as well as the use of systems of pre-written software at different scales such as frameworks, classes, libraries and objects. In parallel, and in the wider contexts of digital work, new conditions for the storage and management of files are generated. Music and architecture are related areas that generate thousands of memory-intensive files and variations on those files, implying archival necessities such as version control. In turn, the question of what constitutes a file is reconfigured: objects are now increasingly understood as a particular state space within a matrix of variable data, structured and inflected in turn by the specific qualities of the kind of media that is being worked, as in the difference between a text file and an architectural drawing, or a layer in an animation file. To a certain extent, these version-control systems can be seen as part of the general modularity of work in the gloriously undulating fields of the contemporary *Bürolandschaft*, echoing or reciprocating the modularity of paradigmatic computing systems such as Unix.[7] Part of the condition of such systems is a general move towards a relatively high degree of granularity of objects and, concomitantly, of the modes of analysis and use to which they may be put, something in turn affecting the nature of their condition as archive and as engines of production. We will explain this further later.

Within the specific domain of FLOSS code repositories, what is particularly interesting is that they fuse the distribution, production and consumption[8] or use of software into the same architecture. They constitute part of the establishment of a code commons that involves some of the means of negotiating over and managing disagreements, and they also provide the means of generating what we propose, following recent work in biology, to call *metacommunities*: sparsely or thickly connected populations of objects, users, producers. However, in distinction to the biological or ecological use of the term, calling these systems 'meta' means that they also partially draw up the matrix of possible operations that may constitute communities. Here, the software that encodes such operations is of crucial interest.

FLOSS code repositories include GoogleCode, Source-Forge, Savannah, Code Snippets and Tigris.[9] Some of these repositories support multiple version control systems. Savannah, for instance, supports CVS (Concurrent Versions System), Subversion, Git, Mercurial and Bazaar, though many if not most projects use CVS.[10] Some of these systems will be used in parallel, with code being developed on Git, and stable versions of a programme being made available by multiple sources. Equally, an organization may often make use of a public facing repository and have one or more private ones in which the daily work is done. Github, as a company, makes much of its money from providing the latter service on a commercial basis. There are also many smaller, project-specific repositories, such as Rastasoft, CPAN (Comprehensive Perl Archive Network) or Python.org, that provide the output of a specific group of programmers or, more expansively, the basic materials to work with a particular language. There are also sites that are not repositories but act as directories of projects.

What is crucial here is the question of version control. An example of simple version control for non-software use would be the wiki software that was originally developed for project documentation and collaboration around Agile software development and that now forms the basis for systems such as Wikipedia.[11] Version control allows users of a system to develop more than one version of a project, to have many people working on elements of a project simultaneously without overwriting each other's work, and to archive and make available completed or ongoing versions of a project as they develop.

Code repositories act as part of the mix of systems used in software development, such as the bug trackers, mailing lists, IRC (internet relay chat) channels and messaging applications that particular meta-communities or teams might work with in the development of a program. These operate by means of creating lists of work to do or by allowing fast means of communication that can be both synchronous and asynchronous. On another scale, code repos can be seen in relation to discussion forums such as Stack Overflow, privately owned operations that in turn sometimes shape and cull conversations according to commercial imperatives.

With many FLOSS projects, too, there is a merger between development and marketing, garnering new users and developers, that also constitutes the prospective shaping of a scene around the platform and the various constituencies that use it.[12] Equally, these projects often rely upon a legal and discursive framing via the use of free and open source software licences. These are generally defined and differentiated by the way in which they attempt to perpetuate the software either as a common good or as a resource free of the encumbrance of obligation to others. As we will see, this is also something subject to change.

Anatomies of Forks

One of the crucial aspects of Github's architecture is that it also upends what is called the 'taboo of the fork' in free or open source software. This is the taboo on splitting or duplicating a project, an act that often potentially breaks apart the community around the code. Git, the system that Github relies on, inverts this established software community ethic by making the fork its fundamental operation, something that in turn reframes the debate around the archive as the focus of storage, conservation, and communities of research.[13]

FLOSS has developed numerous terms for working with software and practices of copying and changing. *Cloning* a piece of software is copying it either at code level or at a higher level, for instance in terms of functionality and interface.[14] *Branching* is making a variant version of an existing body of code within a project, perhaps to create a prototype or for other purposes. *Derivations* are improvements or variations on an existing programme that differ whilst maintaining existing compatibilities. In this chapter, we are specifically interested in the way that Git, and by extension Github, has worked with the question of forking.

Forking is the practice of taking a body of code by making a copy of it and revising that code. Someone who forks some code may do so in order to improve it by making variations; to release a variant version of something modified for a more specific purpose. The term 'fork' has a variable genealogy within computing. In the POSIX operating system, a *fork* is a process making a copy of itself. A *fork bomb* is a work of hacker craftsmanship in which a process is launched to make a copy of itself.[15] As each subsequent process is launched, a further copy is made. One of the characteristics of a fork bomb is that it exponentially uses up the resources of memory of the computer. *Forking* software, as a technosocial operation, is often regarded as having a similar consequence: using up the attention and capacity of all the developers in a community. Unlike a fork bomb, however, such an operation cannot be ameliorated by a simple reboot. In this sense, the taboo on it has historically been a powerful one, since forking drains resources and creates a division in what is called the community. For Benjamin Mako Hill, author of a thoughtful text on forking in FLOSS development, prohibitions on forking operate as social taboo with large costs.[16] An alternative view, offered by artist and programmer Aymeric Mansoux, is that the inability to differentiate a project fully on Github, a situation that arises with the inversion of the forking taboo, leads to other kinds of problems: 'Forking has become so cheap, merging and collaborating became tedious and consensus is no longer such a loved value.'[17] The inversion of the taboo – indeed, automating it to the extent that there is a button on the Github interface reading 'Fork This Project' – may perhaps deserve a psychological reading which describes the trajectories of communities founded upon a crime (as if they arise any other way).

Forking is often studied as part of the field of software engineering, where it is generally analysed as part of the problem of efficiency, communication and duplication. Research into the quality assurance of software also typically relates an analysis of forks to the motivation and career-mapping of developers by marking their productivity and through various metrics. The economic analysis of software development projects may also be carried out in these terms. Quantitatively based empirical research on these systems is relatively intensive in terms of memory, computation and network, though involving analytical abstractions as a methodological imperative, and has historically tended to involve a close engagement with the problems of network outages and variability in processing power.[18]

Generations of Versions

Different version-control systems articulate the problems of forking, branching and cloning in different ways. Along with these variations, they generate variant ideas of the habitus of the programmer or developer, what forms the constitution or the pacing of a project, and what goes into the activity of software development. In order to trace this, before returning to the analysis of Github, we want to describe briefly the different generations of version-control systems and repositories.

The first generation of repositories is in many ways epitomized by CPAN, which is simply an index-based directory of software written in the Perl language, alongside software for working in Perl, that has been run since 1995. That it is a directory-based repository implies a high level of familiarity or willingness to attain expertise and mastery as the basic condition of programming. Software repositories of the first generation employ minimal interpretative filters, leading to a certain charm if not always a ready intelligibility to the uninitiated. There is a clear distinction between what they store and make available, the structure that indexes them, and the systems that are used to produce and work with the software.

The second generation of repos was set in motion by Sourceforge, a MySQL-based directory of software projects that became a central resource for FLOSS activity at the end of the twentieth century and after. This repo grew in the first wave of massification and visibility of FLOSS as a social and economic movement alongside the growth of discussion forums such as Slashdot, and is owned by the same company. Sourceforge ties project documentation and release notes into a download site but also brings in project rankings, user reviews of software projects, and user profiles, where users could be viewed according to the languages they used, the projects they are involved in and the stream of their activity. Alongside these, it brings in advertising for tech jobs and other related information. Users also have straightforward permissions as admin or developer, as well as team co-ordination tools for concurrency management (in wiki or source-code management environments). More recently, Sourceforge has incorporated Git, Mercurial, CVS and Bazaar as a range of systems that projects may use from its central site. Amongst these, it also includes cross-platform compatibility, allowing projects to migrate from one platform to another or to exist across platforms. As such, Sourceforge now epitomizes both the second generation and the third generation of repositories. This third generation consists of decentralized version-control systems such as Git, Mercurial or Bazaar. They are characterized by their speed of operation; the fine granularity of analysis of code, of use and of users that they allow; and their distributed infrastructure.

As software author and developer Joel Spolsky notes, Github tends to follow the requirements of freelancing FLOSS developers.[19] A more corporate, in-house version-control system would imply hierarchical levels of access governed by permissions structures, code reviews rather than promiscuous copying, and most likely a clear prohibition on the sharing of code. The data that is captured, stored and made addressable in certain ways implies a social, cognitive or processual order that can make use of it.

Amongst others, Philip Mirowski interprets neoliberal economics, particularly in the work of Friedrich Hayek, as the dream or ruse of a perfect information machine. There are certainly accounts of distributed version control systems that have such an inflection, or make the explicit correlation with idealized markets.[20] The wider question of open data in government may be a parallel here. What is counted as informative and what is not constitute some of the key functions of a social order. Bureaucracy arises, in James Beniger's terms, from the need to control the vast number of variables, information and contingencies in running an enterprise.[21] What we see in some sense in the present wave of social media is the adoption of bureaucratic forms in the management of friendship, dating, music acquisition and so on. These are all more ostensibly trivial aspects of life than the intercontinental import and export of goods, the movement of armies, and the mass markets of consumers implied by continuous production machines such as the conveyor belt. At the same time, their incorporation into control systems changes the nature of both in different, non-symmetrical ways.

Events in the API

As a typical social media platform, Github also publishes much data about what happens on Github.com through its APIs (application programming interfaces), an interface to provide information about the database and some of its contents to other software. The data provided by the API is indeed mainly intended for software applications and web services built around Github. But the combination of the Events API end point, the API that supplies a more or less 'live' feed of events on the Github.com platform, and the archived copies of events stored since 2011 at the GithubArchive[22] means that Github can in principle be analysed using what some currents in social science refer to as 'live methods' (research approaches based on the dynamics of experimental and collaborative events across a variety of media platforms).

The tools and devices for research craft are being extended by digital culture in a hyper-connected world, affording new possibilities to re-imagine observation and the generation of alternative forms of research data. Part of the promise of live methods is the potential for simultaneity in research and the possibility of re-ordering the relationship between data gathering, analysis and circulation.[23] The scale of the platform (only millions of participants, not hundreds of millions) and the existence of archives mean that social researchers can envisage analysing the whole of Github, not just one month of data or a selected group.

There are both great potentials and difficulties in doing so. The fact that we have ready access to the Github event timeline is testimony to this. But what is most available from that data is a set of eighteen pre-formed event types.[24] These event types subsume much of the traffic around Github but give us little way of deciding what is an important event and how to elicit – from the hundreds of millions of events in the event timeline – which ones matter and which ones do not. At the same time, we know from ethnographic and other studies of software that the very detailed and fine-grained tracking of work and activity that is inherent in Git means that, in principle, repos and software projects themselves can be analysed in great depth. Patterns of work, flows of meaning, borrowing and imitation of constructs and practices, and shifts in interest and importance should be publicly legible in the repos and, importantly, in the flow of code between repos. But the possibilities of perceiving these flows and patterns presuppose capacities to filter and select events in the stream that neither confirm the unsurprising importance of certain high-profile software projects (Linux, Mozilla, node.js etc.)[25] nor overwhelm us with the buzz of transient or ephemeral repositories, a discussion of which we will move to after also noting some of the other overall features of the system.

'Post-FLOSS' Archiving and the Archive as Engine

So, broadly speaking, what patterns of archiving are there? Users use Github in different ways: in a canonical open mode of use, making all code and forks visible; performing merges and the evaluation of code offline, invisible to others, but keeping what is published clean; and, in a related way, publishing changes in private Gits. There are also multiple hacks of the system, where a repo or a file might be named or entered on the fly by users that then rename a file locally to work on and subsequently reload it without reference to any broader project. Equally, the question of which pull, merge and commit has priority has to be resolved locally within the work group or organization around the repo. This means that large aspects of even the most well-organized repositories remain inscrutable.

Alongside the constraints on access to data via the API such as those already mentioned, Github works via the encouragement of contribution. Some of this encouragement is achieved through an efficient and useful system, via the extensive adoption of user experience design, contemporary 'flat design'-style graphic design and, of course, a cartoon mascot. Equally, the site operates by numerous types of granularity of access to analytics. There are numerous 'social' features such as letting you view the repos 'people you may know' have starred (starring being a mechanism to 'like' or draw attention to). Project sites include images, videos, comments and tags. Such features also extend to a greater metricization of programming culture, allowing users to view the rate at which something is updated, see the number of users following a project, peruse network diagrams of branches of code and so on. Here we have the archive also operating as a matrix of capture and semiotization devices, driven by the imperatives to rate, share, participate! As an economic factor, such hyper-auditing devices allow the site to become a means of finding and hiring programmers; Git and Github profiles become key to coders' CVs as a means of displaying the productivity, uptake and significance of the work produced. In this way, as in others, the archive is a site of production, an engine for the development of new software that involutes the sense of the archive as a repository of the unchanging past. Storage becomes the site of production when the form of production is variation.

This is not necessarily an entirely easy condition to navigate, and one that in turn ties back to the question of the fork. Github tends to encourage the possibility of multiple versions of the same code being developed, often in parallel, which sometimes fails to reap the full benefits of co-ordinated action. For instance, in a blog post, Ruby developer Seth B contends that in one version of some code he was wanting to work with, there were seventy versions of the same piece of code with incoherent information about which branch was in which state of development, including information as to where, if at all, a particular bug had been resolved.[26]

Github, one can thus say, is an environment for *making* a workflow rather than something that imposes a workflow of a certain kind. This implies that a project needs a certain kind of organization or at least a means of flagging or archiving defunct branches, those with 'dirty' code, experimental branches used for fixing and testing certain approaches, and so on. Discussions of Github online do tend to show the vexed question of how exactly to organize a repo well. Addressing this, quite a number of large-scale organizations with repositories maintain one that is public, where users are able to retrieve the latest versions of code, and that act more generally as public-facing websites. These organizations will also maintain a private repository where the actual development work is done.

Concomitantly, our findings from statistically analysing the Github archive show that the largest repos come accompanied by organizations; that is, organizations organize Git. Git and other such systems propose a set of abstractions of software development from and in which projects may compose themselves. The speed and granularity of changes are one of the 'innovations' of FLOSS. But within this is a variation in styles: the imperative to 'release early, release often', promulgated years ago by software polemicist Eric Raymond, can be compared to the Debian Linux distribution, which characteristically takes two years for the gestation of each stable release. Alongside the kinds of software development characteristic of the classical forms of FLOSS, we also see what can here be termed as 'post-FLOSS' forms of development. Post-FLOSS is characterized by a general indifference to the discussions of and loyalty to certain kinds of licences and the sense of ethics (GPL) or business models (Open Source) that these drew upon. Large amounts of the material placed online through Github tend to be without a licence assigned to it. This is not to say that some people don't use these licences or that the imaginary of software as culture that they map has no traction. Rather, they seem to exist alongside an expanded and incoherent universe of code objects, projects and practices that is somewhat different from the legendary world of the Unix greybeards, whose insistence on crafted, knowable code with powerful and rigorously applied abstractions and a matching ethos and legal apparatus has been so fundamental to the development of the internet and of free software. In the majority of cases on Github, code is uploaded to the repository, perhaps to be treated as public domain, or simply abandoned. What relationship this has to the wider ethos of the system and whether it signifies a change in the nature of programming work – showing it to be more or less precarious, perhaps, or marking the 'coming into public' view of another kind of coding practice – is unverifiable. Post-FLOSS inhabits conditions in which code objects, scripts, css files for the layout of a website, configuration files for customising the look and function of a program etc. form so much a part of everyday generic *stuff* that they are not worth protecting in the way that the adoption of a licence implies, even when that licence is available on a drop-down menu.

Diff as Infrastructure

Aside from the cluster of large-scale projects with their pattern of high levels of activity around complex software objects and systems, much of what is on Github tends to be of a much more diffuse kind, with high degrees of variation concerning project size, type and code, including the rapidity and scale of variations. We can say that in just about every parameter where variation is possible, it can be found. And here we note the source of *Big Diff* as this chapter's title. Diff is a Unix command that shows the differences between files. Git is similarly based on a file structure that works on the basis of marking the differences between objects stored in the repository. A diff is based simply on a character-by-character analysis of a file. Every change is logged and is retrievable by choosing the right commit.

Needless to say, this has interesting effects on the notion of the repository as archive. Archives tend to work with exemplars, not variations. With Git, as with all forms of computer memory that always involve making copies of files, objects no longer need to exist uniquely; indeed, they cannot do so if they are to be used within the system. The archive in this case comes into being as a process of structural differentiation rather than as a thing. Overall, Git is a massive graph structure and each code object, each archived file, is a set of trajectories across this graph. Based on a file structure that amasses hashes of symbols and diffs, the archive transitions into a systematization of the archive as an engine of minutely and massively assembled processes of addition and variation. Instead of the archive storing history as a set of exemplary if not necessarily unique entities, history is involuted in the archive rather than stored in it. With a system of versions at the core, versions generate histories and versions become generative. Different kinds of repos, such as public-facing repositories, working repos and empty repos, exist in memory and perhaps in use alongside those that are set up as websites, code deployment platforms, agile infrastructures, and mechanisms for publishing and working on apps and frameworks for making them.

This generativity is not simply one of a ceaseless, vitalist over-production. If we were to phrase it in terms of evolutionary modelling and to draw the archive as a form of fitness landscape, what we find is that there are millions of objects stuck in basins of activity. The phase space of the graph is a constellation of numerous entities, many of which are lonely asteroids drifting amongst thousands of archives of abandoned space junk, themselves giants against the millions of motes of dust that form their background.

Organizing Incoherence

One of the aspects of Github that echoes the problematic nature of much social media is that within the system it is impossible to have a 'delete' event, so once a file is on the system, there it stays. This is one factor that may lead to an understanding of Github as in many ways positively incoherent. To put this another way, any initial scan of the system as a whole will find a power-law distribution for the size of the projects. (Crudely put, most activity clusters around a small group of very large projects, with much of the remainder of the work being in tens of thousands of smaller projects of sizes decreasing in inverse proportion to their number.) Much of this is simply because there are low barriers to entry: a repo is easy to start but harder to maintain. Just as there are junk repos, uploaded only once, modified a few times or less, and left to drift, there are others that continue to gain occasional downloads years after posting. There is an enormously diverse range of patterns of use. Alongside lots of very small but somehow long-lived projects, there are people updating repos to check the differences between pieces of code, bots making various attempts to push changes, and multiple tools for managing and analysing Git data, potentially implying a form of recursive public or a certain kind of narcissistic fiddling that is not without its pleasures. Notably, many people use Github to circulate configuration files for text editors such as Vim and for operating systems such as OSX. Github is used as a platform for sharing machine configurations on a very large scale, and such files are rarely worked on as a project. The transverse movements of such files aren't really captured by the mechanisms of distributed version control, since they are so ephemeral. Equally, some users may also use Github as their mode of cloud back-up, with no contributions sought from others; they simply use additional features such as bug tracker and wiki as a means of interaction with users of their code. Here it's worth comparing this system to other code-sharing systems such as Pastebin, where files are just left alone on the off chance that they might be used or picked up by bots or onsite scripts scanning them for certain kinds of data: credit card information, serials, website layouts, URLs, usernames and passwords, scripts, My Little Pony porn and so on. With Pastebin, the 'drive-by commit' is all there is; the system is simply used as a generalized open notepad. Github is a far more variable and multidimensional field of entities with high degrees of differential use and relation to the idea of a project and, in turn, to the question of production and sharing.

As an archive, then, Github.com is exemplary in its crystallization of certain aspects of contemporary software cultures. It is a zone of massive, concerted activity and simultaneously a ground for the dumping and drifting of files characteristic of post-FLOSS; a space of atypical formations disparately linked across directory structures and smeared unevenly across timestamps and between users; a social factory of difference founded upon the violation of a communitarian norm that it in turn also constitutes; a site of perpetual audit and production; and an architecture for the free-form, the shapeless and the corporate that is in turn perpetually being built up for a hoped-for but deferred valuation on the stock market. As a site for unearthing the finely grained ambivalence of the contemporary archive, it is indeed something to keep tabs on.

NOTES

1 Git, online at http://Git-scm.com.
2 Git uses the MIT Licence, http://opensource.org/licenses/MIT.
3 Linus Torvalds, *Git Manual Page*, https://www.kernel.org/pub/software/scm/Git/docs.
4 The Linux Kernel is archived at https://GithubGithubGithub-Github.com/torvalds/linux.
5 One of the aspects of the discussion of archives in the era of open data and of big data is the way in which the archive as a site for the exercise and communication of expertise can sometimes be quite literally *dumped* – uploaded and then abandoned – following the idea that unspecified emergent forces will sort out the questions of legacy, interpretation and preservation that are characteristic of the archive as an institutional form. In rela-

tion to this aspect of the debate, this chapter, like others in this book, suggests that archival architectures find quite varied forms and that the archive as structured information, with attached practices of expertise, maintains the condition of being a mutable field in contemporary software development.

6   Nathan Ensmenger, *The Computer Boys Take Over: Computers, Programmers, and the Politics of Technical Expertise*, MIT Press, Cambridge, MA, 2010.

7   Tara Macpherson, 'US Operating Systems at Mid-Century: The Intertwining Of Race and Unix', in Lisa Nakamura and Peter Chow-White (eds.), *Race After the Internet*, Routledge, London, 2011.

8   For instance, in Github.io, which provides the conditions for software to run directly from Github servers.

9   Alongside the FLOSS-oriented systems, there are tens of proprietary source-control management systems, and many IDEs include version-control facilities.

10   Simon Yuill, 'CVS', in Matthew Fuller (ed.), *Software Studies: A Lexicon*, MIT Press, Cambridge, MA, 2008.

11   Bo Labouef and Ward Cunningham, *The Wiki Way: Quick Collaboration on the Web*, Addison-Wesley, Reading, 2001.

12   For instance, the Mozilla Foundation's currently regular Mozillafest.

13   In turn, there are a number of implementations of Git in several languages and that also run on various platforms: Gitorious, Gitlab, Gitprep (a direct clone of Github) etc.

14   The analysis of cloning here is often coded in relation to the question of intellectual property, predicated on the idea that one body of code may contain a direct copy of another.

15   See Geoff Cox, *Speaking Code: Coding as Aesthetic and Political Expression*, MIT Press, Cambridge, MA, 2012.

16   Benjamin Mako Hill, 'To Fork Or Not To Fork', lecture at Linuxtag 2005, Karlsruhe, http://mako.cc/writing/to_fork_or_not_to_fork.html.

17   Aymeric Mansoux, 'Fork Workers', presentation at Jonctions/Verbindingen festival, 2014, Brussels, http://vj14.stdin.fr/Fork_Workers.xhtml.

18   Audris Mockus, 'Amassing and Indexing a Large Sample of Version Control Systems: Towards the Census of Public Source Code History', in *MSR '09: Proceedings of the 6th IEEE International Working Conference on Mining Software Repositories*, IEEE Computer Society, Washington, DC, 2009.

19 Joel Spolsky, 'Town Car Version Control', *Joel on Software*, 11 March 2013, http://www.joelonsoftware.com/items/2013/03/11.html.

20 Philip Mirowski, *Cyborg Dreams: How Economics Became a Cyborg Science*, Cambridge University Press, Cambridge, 2002. See also Mirowski's acerbically perceptive, if partial, comments on Wikipedia in his postscript to Philip Mirowski and Deiter Plehwe's *The Road from Mont Pelerin: The Making of the Neoliberal Thought Collective*, Harvard University Press, Cambridge, MA, 2009.

21 James R. Beniger, *The Control Revolution: Technical and Economic Origins of the Information Society*, Harvard University Press, Cambridge, MA, 1986.

22 Githubarchive.org. The API is at https://api.github.com/events.

23 Les Back and Nirmal Puwar, 'A Manifesto for Live Methods: Provocations and Capacities', *Sociological Review*, 60(2012), pp. 6–17.

24 Constraints on access to data via the API also take other forms. Events support pagination; however, the per-page option is unsupported. The fixed page size is thirty items. Fetching up to ten pages is supported, for a total of 300 events.

25 Such projects dwarf most of the others in terms of the amount of code produced and by the quantity of lines written and the number of changes over time.

26 Seth B, 'Github, Your Network Graph Sucks!', *Sublog*, 30 August 2001, http://subimage.com/blog/2011/08/30/github-your-network-graph-sucks/#.VT5XiyHtmko.

REFERENCES

Seth B, 'Github, Your Network Graph Sucks!', *Sublog*, 30 August 2001, http://subimage.com/blog/2011/08/30/github-your-network-graph-sucks/#.VT5XiyHtmko

Les Back and Nirmal Puwar, 'A Manifesto for Live Methods: Provocations and Capacities', *Sociological Review*, 60 (2012), pp. 6–17.

James R. Beniger, *The Control Revolution: Technical and Economic Origins of the Information Society*, Harvard University Press, Cambridge, MA, 1986.

Geoff Cox, *Speaking Code: Coding as Aesthetic and Political Expression*, MIT Press, Cambridge, MA, 2012.

Nathan Ensmenger, *The Computer Boys Take Over: Computers, Programmers, and the Politics of Technical Expertise*, MIT Press, Cambridge, MA, 2010.

Bo Labouef and Ward Cunningham, *The Wiki Way: Quick Collaboration on the Web*, Addison-Wesley, Reading, 2001.

Tara Macpherson, 'US Operating Systems at Mid-Century: The Intertwining of Race and Unix', in Lisa Nakamura and Peter Chow-White (eds.), *Race After the Internet*, Routledge, London, 2011.

Benjamin Mako Hill, 'To Fork Or Not To Fork', lecture at Linuxtag 2005, Karlsruhe, http://mako.cc/writing/to_fork_or_not_to_fork.html

Aymeric Mansoux, 'Fork Workers', presentation at Jonctions/Verbindingen festival, 2014, Brussels, http://vj14.stdin.fr/Fork_Workers.xhtml

Philip Mirowski, *Cyborg Dreams: How Economics Became a Cyborg Science*, Cambridge University Press, Cambridge, 2002.

Philip Mirowski and Deiter Plehwe, *The Road from Mont Pelerin: The Making of the Neoliberal Thought Collective*, Harvard University Press, Cambridge, MA, 2009.

Audris Mockus, 'Amassing and Indexing a Large Sample of Version Control Systems: Towards the Census of Public Source Code History', in *MSR '09: Proceedings of the 6th IEEE International Working Conference on Mining Software Repositories*, IEEE Computer Society, Washington, DC, 2009.

Joel Spolsky, 'Town Car Version Control', *Joel on Software*, 11 March 2013, http://www.joelonsoftware.com/items/2013/03/11.html

Linus Torvalds, *Git Manual Page*, https://www.kernel.org/pub/software/scm/Git/docs

Simon Yuill, 'CVS', in Matthew Fuller (ed.), *Software Studies: A Lexicon*, MIT Press, Cambridge, MA, 2008.

— 5 —

THE AUTHOR FIELD

Matthew Fuller, Nikita Mazurov and Dan McQuillan

The Bind, Torture, Kill (BTK) case often crops up in the forensic literature as a shining exemplar of the fruitful police deployment of author field metadata intelligence.[1] The serial killer, alternatively called the BTK Strangler or the BTK Killer, was known for sending letters to the media expatiating upon his murders through the 1970s. Following a period of dormancy, the epistolary indulgence resumed again in 2004. In one of the later letters, the BTK Strangler asked the police if it would be possible to trace his letters if he started sending them on floppy disk. The police, responding via advertisement in a local newspaper, stated that it wouldn't be possible to trace him if he communicated in this way. Subsequently, in early 2005 the BTK Strangler did indeed send a letter to a news channel on a floppy disk. By imaging the floppy using the EnCase forensics suite, law enforcement agents were further able to apply EnCase's Deleted Files filter to scan the floppy image for any latent data still on the disc. Alongside the intended letter, they found another (thought to be) deleted Microsoft Word document. While the document, when opened in Word, did not seem to contain any potentially identifiable information itself, its surrounding metadata revealed that the document had been last modified by 'Dennis', with the affiliated organization being 'Christ Lutheran Church'. A subsequent sweep of the church's local website revealed that there was one Dennis Rader listed on the staff page. The metadata discovery led to identification of Rader, who was in turn linked to a variety of other physical evidence, and to his eventual arrest and confession.

The triumph of the state's metadata discovery and suspect identification is perhaps most jubilantly recounted by Shavers:

Rader would later learn that the metadata in the deleted file was recovered by law enforcement and traced directly to him by name. In mere minutes, 31 years of anonymity as a serial murderer unraveled as BTK was identified as the President of Christ Lutheran Church. Mere minutes. Mere metadata. A 31-year-old case broke wide open in minutes because of metadata.[2]

Naming Names

This chapter takes a small set of related data fields as its focus of interest: the author field and user ID, along with related material such as document instance IDs and other forms of metadata arrayed around author identification.

What is the author field? Users of word processing software such as Microsoft Word or its analogues such as Libre Office will know of it as the name that they enter in to a dialogue box when first installing and using the software. It is the name that is associated with the comments or track changes functions when modifying or sharing a document. The user ID may be acquired when starting up a computer for the first time, as with most mainstream operating systems. Equally, it can be assigned when setting up an account in large-scale multi-user systems, here it is the log-in name, the string of characters associated with everything carried out through a specific account.

The author field and user ID are curious entities in that despite their ostensive simplicity, their function is highly variable across different applications and software systems, and even within the lifespan of very widely used software the author field may come to the fore or recede, with different versions of an application introducing or phasing out the idea of the singular named user. In this chapter, we aim to track some of those variations and to draw out the way in which they not only establish an imagined ontology of use for software, but also establish and frame the user within a matrix of operations by which power is articulated in computational systems. Some of the features that are put into place by such systems are time, allocation of responsibility and records of action. Such things link the author field and the person or persons that answer to it into a wider framing of the possibilities of action and states of being, implicit and explicit variables in life set up as an array of possibles to be filled out.[3]

A Genealogy of the Author Field in Word Processor File Formats

A perusal of the manual for Electric Pencil,[4] the first personal computer word processor application, released in 1976, reveals no mention of any sort of identifying author field. Likewise, the comprehensive 450-page manual for Wordstar,[5] one of the most popular early word processors, released in 1979, noticeably contains no mention of an author function or user ID either. Notably, these earliest document formats were effectively plain text ASCII files, containing very few, if any, word processing codes – document mark-up syntax such as underlined text, superscript and subscript, footer/header-specified text and so on. The next decade saw the introduction of binary document formats which could contain data that was no longer readable as plain text and that could, significantly, be likewise erased should the binary document ever be converted to plain text. Indeed, an owner's manual for the Tandy WP-2 Portable Wordprocessor, whilst ultimately providing instructions for ASCII conversion for compatibility's sake, nonetheless prefaces the how-to by explicating the irreversibility of the act: 'If you convert a document to ASCII, the WP-2 removes these codes and all page setup parameters and does not restore them when you convert the file back into a non-ASCII format.'[6] This trend towards binary complexity went hand in hand with infusing word processor documents with metadata, albeit with the caveat that once the trend in file formats then shifted to open standards, the metadata was now there to stay, becoming entrenched in the discourse mechanics of word processing document formats.

Technical specifications for the Microsoft Word 5.0 binary file format reveal that by 1989 at the latest, Word DOC files were including author field metadata.[7] The field in question, labelled 'szAuthor', described curtly as simply the 'document's author', could contain a maximum of forty characters. Converting the binary Word DOC file into an ASCII TXT file, much like the conversion of the aforementioned Tandy WP-2 files, would result in an erasure of the underlying metadata, and thus a deletion of the author field and any information it may have contained.

However, what of the fate of the metadata when a binary format using proprietary syntax was converted to another binary format? O'Reilly's *Internet Forensics* guide contains the following suggestion under the heading 'The Right Way to Distribute Documents':

Most of these Word document problems could have been prevented if the authors had converted the files to PDF before distributing them. All of the Word-specific revision logs, comments, and edits would have been stripped out as part of that process. PDF files do have hidden information of their own but it is typically limited to identifying the software used to create the file, unless the author has explicitly added comments and the like using Adobe Acrobat.[8]

While it is technically true that the author field metadata contained in DOC files is not carried over upon conversion to PDF format, the claim that the metadata of PDF files is typically limited to exclude the author field is demonstrably false. When a DOC is printed to PDF, using Adobe's default PDF printer engine, the author field in the DOC does indeed get erased, but in its place Adobe's default behaviour is to insert the username into its own author field. That is to say that if one is logged into a particular computer on which one is doing the said file conversion with the username John Smith, the PDF properties will now contain John Smith in the author field metadata, in place of whatever information the original DOC possessed.[9] Thus the aforementioned advice is ineffectual for the removal of author field metadata, merely substituting one author field for another, and highlighting the resiliency of the author field function across various document formats and their accompanying metadata.

The 2000s saw the introduction of what we may term the third evolutionary stage of word processing document formats: binary file formats which nonetheless employed open file format specifications. In 2005, the Open Document Format (ODF) standard was introduced by the Organization for the Advancement of Structured Information Standards, itself having been based on Sun Microsystem's earlier OpenOffice.org XML format, used in, for instance, OpenDocument Text (ODT) files, which constitute the native output of OpenOffice's Writer application. A year later, Microsoft developed the Office Open XML format, used throughout its Office suite, effectively replacing DOC's binary format with the XML-based DOCX file format. Inverting the notion of the skeuomorph, a product element which is no longer functional but a stylistic or metaphorical reference to prior forms (for instance, grilles on electric cars, which have no technical need for them as there is no internal combustion engine to ventilate), Liu describes early forms of XML-like databases as a kind of prophetic relic or reverse skeuomorph. In their own time, they were proposed as instrumental to the progress of industrialism. But seen from our perspective, they are epistemological rather than instrumental stitches between past and present. They are an index or placeholder (rather than cause or antecedent) of the future.[10]

In other words, early forms of document author field metadata existing during the secondary stage of word processing format development were future-symptoms of the coming emphasis on metadata, as manifested today through increased mining efforts aided by format inter-operability and the aforementioned tenacious resiliency to deletion. As ODT and DOCX files now both use the Dublin Core Metadata Initiative (DCMI)[11] syntax set for encoding author field and other metadata, converting a Word DOCX file to an OpenOffice ODT file preserves the pervasive 'dc:creator' tag which carries with it the document author. Notable transmigrations nonetheless occur between the conversions. Consider author metadata represented thus in a DOCX file:

```
<dc:creator>Alice</dc:creator>
<cp:lastModifiedBy>Bob</cp:lastModifiedBy>
```

It now becomes modified to the following in the post-conversion ODT file:

```
<meta:initial-creator>Alice</meta:initial-creator>
<dc:creator>Bob</dc:creator>
```

The ultimate point is that the author field, whilst moving to alternate fields, nonetheless survives, *somewhere*, in the depths of the file. For instance, in order to locate the author field metadata in a DOCX document, one must first decompress the .DOCX file, then proceed to the /docProps/ subdirectory, and finally find the core.xml file. PDF files, in turn, whilst also supporting DCMI standards, include too their own XML-based Extensible Metadata Platform (XMP)[12] standard for encoding the author field, as will be discussed further later in the chapter.

We have thus seen how the development of word processing document formats and their accompanying metadata can be grouped into three stages: the first constituting plain text ASCII formats, which lacked author metadata altogether; the second constituting the introduction of binary formats, which also saw the accompanying introduction of word processor metadata, which could be excised by reverting to older ASCII formats; and finally the third stage being one of binary formats which employed inter-operable, open metadata standards that allowed for the easy porting of metadata from one document file format to the other. Throughout the said development we have observed the meticulousness with which metadata is preserved, rendering it resilient to erasure via conversion, at least between convoluted binary document formats. Despite ostensibly open schemas and standards, the author field could nonetheless thus be said to thrive on obfuscation introduced via a burgeoning, structured document file complexity.

Into Identity

In order to carry out an enquiry into the author field we work with material from the literature in criminal forensics.[13] In terms of documents this work is largely set out in manuals, how-to's and tutorials. Alongside the literature there is a related set of trade shows, conferences and conventions which function as means of consolidating the field. These operate across the commercial, state and academic sectors, with much of the literature exhibiting the functions of marketing as well as technical instruction. There is a sense of an emerging field broadcasting its importance to itself at the same time as it establishes professional norms and techniques. The particular difficulty of establishing criteria for specialist expertise is ramified by the numerous ways in which people acquire expertise in a field that is undergoing rapid development. Throughout its history, computing has often brought in 'outsiders' to fields that are yet to be fully stabilized with standard forms of knowledge and accreditation.[14] Computer security has often been a zone in which exploratory hackers and law enforcement agents at least come into some form of interface. Equally, however, such emerging fields are often filled with actors of a less easily registerable kind: chancers, start-ups, consultants, promulgators of new techniques with the heady but uncertain odour of snake-oil. Indeed, an early book on the then emerging field of computer crime goes so far as to suggest that those with known criminal pasts make ideal programmers and data entry operatives since they are, to a greater degree than ordinary citizens, already a known quantity.[15]

Coupled with this set of factors is the condition that identity in computational systems is regularly the subject of scandal and the mechanics of exposure. Doxing, revenge porn and identity theft are the more grassroots manifestations of such conflicts. The large-scale monitoring of populations by the USA's National Security Agency and the United Kingdom's General Communications Headquarters, under programmes such as PRISM and Tempora, are those which come from the state; and entrepreneurial operations on user identity are carried out by numerous companies, the most notable of which are Google and Facebook. For all of these operations, the identity of the user is an 'attack vector', a means of getting at a legally constituted human subject with a bank account, spending habits, associates, habitual and extraordinary locations and other associated quantities and predicates. Equally, techniques for using author information move across sectors: sexual shaming becomes a means both in intelligence operations, as in the attempted blackmailing of Islamist militants whose internet accounts were used to access pornography,[16] and in sexual bullying through the publication of intimate photographs and identification data online. The author field, the user ID, conflates the manifestations of a self previously zoned as public and private.

In other words, the author field is an exemplary contemporary entity operated upon by state actors, private sector operatives working across commercial and state sectors, and operatives working across the boundaries of legality and illegality, and articulating data across both communication and conflict. Characteristically, access to the user ID and password of voicemail accounts formed the basis for the 'phone-hacking' scandals that took place in the British media in recent years. Here, policing, the activities of 'bent coppers' and newspaper editors, proprietors and journalists, as well as a penumbra of 'private investigators' and other informants on the lives of celebrities and crime victims, formed a constellation that is highly diagnostic of contemporary formations of power.[17]

Given its multivalence, the user or the proper name given in the author field also operates as a means of operating on the reputation economy and for achieving recognition and gratification. In terms of the developmental curve of debates around digital culture, the author field can be temporalized as being characterized by invention, by multiple names, by assumed and invented identity in the theoretical and cultural extrapolations of the internet of the 1990s and early twenty-first century, and by an insistence on 'true names' in the present day as far as the operations of conglomerate platforms are able to determine things. It is the function of the name as a token with a vacillatory relation to identity that establishes it as of interest to so many parties.

The Author Field and Doubt in Criminal Forensics

Metadata is presented as a viable vector of intelligence gathering, ideally leading to successful target acquisition via positive identification and subsequent tracing. Metadata is hence here read as a proverbial silver bullet, intricately dug out, via the deployment of forensic software suites, from the entrails of a particular digital file, to be used in turn both to identify and to neutralize the purported originator. Within the realm of investigative data forensics, then, the author becomes quite literally coded as an entity of interest to law and order, with law enforcement thus meaning author identification and neutralization. The process of excavating the metadata author field is here presented as a means to apprehension. The forensic author function thus is not merely disciplinary, seeking to effectuate a feeling of ownership over any bit of produced data, but contains a latent punitive function.

The punitive function of the author field is seemingly predicated on an underlying certainty as to the veracity of the data next to the indicated field. Thus, forensic training manuals matter-of-factly state that metadata 'describes various characteristics of data, including when and by whom it was created, accessed, or modified'.[18] But what of the possibility that metadata itself may be created, accessed or modified, thus stripping away the legally comforting blanket of certainty so well worn in legal proceedings? Indeed, quite a number of forensic handbooks are generally quite sure to add a rejoinder to any of their exultations regarding the efficacy of any extracted metadata. Thus, alongside the boiler-plate legal meta-disclaimer typically found at the outset of forensic handbooks (for instance, 'Cengage Learning and EC-Council shall not be liable for any special, consequential, or exemplary damages resulting, in whole or part, from the readers' use of, or reliance upon, this material'[19]), there is also a general tempering admonition of any previous description of metadata extraction. 'A downside of metadata is that it is relatively easy to modify';[20] 'A word of caution: As with embedded strings, file metadata can be modified by an attacker';[21] 'Forensic examiners should be aware that metadata associated with Microsoft Office documents can be altered using freely available tools';[22] 'these headers could be easily removed or counterfeited by a forger using ubiquitous editing tools. And such header alterations are believed to be difficult to recognize and trace.'[23] The punitive function of the author field is thus here unbound by an uncertainty born of the potential of metadata malleability. The hapless author field persists, but is submerged and, since it can no longer be taken as absolute, undergoes the ignominy of being relativized.

The literature on criminal data forensics is concerned with a technics of certainty. In this regard we may be reminded of a quick exchange Pina Bausch places in the script for the dance theatre performance *1980*.

> Q: What frightens you?
> A: Certain people.[24]

Certain people are indeed frightening, but perhaps they are only side effects of the particular characteristics of the mechanisms for achieving certainty, and the means by which they are extrapolated. In the interplay of the duality set up in Bausch's phrase, the author is another mode of certain person: a dividual. The process for the identification of this kind of entity produces a token, a string of characters that stands in for certainty. And for criminal forensics, here is the problem: this token of certainty becomes a fulcrum on which doubt can be turned. Each aspect of the dividual can only ever be part of an infinitely extensible set; extensible, that is, until culpability or authorship is allocated. As such, the author field remains in the various metadata layers within the strata of the digital text, to be excavated and lavished with attention by forensic investigation. But alongside its part in rendering certainty possible, its fate may only be to be problematized and rendered inadmissible, subsiding once more into that familiar computational form, a tar-pit of inconclusion.[25] Metadata features may contribute to a decisive act of identification, of certainty about a certain person, equipment, payment, process or piece of data, but they may also hang around and stagnate rather than inexorably flow in the liquid way that information is supposed to. The author field may be just one more thing in a quagmire of document bloatware, of fragmentary patches of data, amidst a myriad of DOCs, PDFs, JPEGs and other metadata-laden debris. There is an art to extracting effective morsels of data from such a condition.

User ID

The user ID names a rendezvous for any number of attributes. A recent leak of Apple user IDs is instructive in this regard.[26] The leak, coming through an app development company, shows how the individual user always stands in the place of their universal figuration. However, this is not a cosmic universal, but one that only needs to be simply effective. In this case the range of all potential users is given numerically. Further variation can be elicited from a leak of data from the Snapchat app.[27] A, now defunct website, SnapchatDB.info, run by unknown parties, posted a data dump of 4.6 million Snapchat usernames, alongside corresponding phone numbers and approximate locations. Though the phone numbers in the leak were partially obfuscated, with the last two digits being redacted, the first three digits nonetheless reveal the North American area code (formally known as the Numbering Plan Area (NPA)), whilst the subsequent three reveal the Central Office Code (COC). This data could hence potentially be used to link the username to a city-specific geographic location beyond the general-area locations in the leak itself.[28] Thus here too we see the risks of numerical pairings of usernames with, in this case, (even partially obfuscated) phone numbers.

In order to give a sense of the operations available with such relatively trivial kinds of data, we give a couple of examples here. Attention to the specific qualities of the data as material is brought to the fore in this account, perhaps precisely because its relative dullness allows it to pass beneath the surface of ready perception. Such grey media are the characteristic forms of the present day. Case 1 looks at the author field in Adobe PDF. Case 2 examines JPEG metadata.

Case 1: Author

Portable Document Format (PDF) files use Adobe's own Extensible Metadata Platform (XMP) format to embed various bits of metadata in the file.[29] A variety of information encompasses the resultant metadata output, as delineated in the XMP Specifications, including the title, author, subject, keywords, creation date, modification date, application (used to create the PDF), document and instance IDs, and so on.[30] Of specific interest to the case study will be the author and document ID/instance ID fields.

PDF files generally have an author field, identifying the creator of the document. The author field can be inputted manually, or may be pulled automatically by the PDF print engine software used to generate the PDF.

To give a test case: if Alice is using a copy of Microsoft Word which, upon installation, she registered to 'Alice', and saves a Word Document (metadata.doc) to a PDF file (metadata.pdf$_0$), the PDF file will automatically have 'Alice' input to the relevant author fields of the resultant PDF's metadata. Specifically, the author field will be present twice in the resultant PDF's metadata (thus also highlighting metadata's potential for *resilience via redundancy*):

```
/Author(Alice)
<rdf:li>Alice</rdf:li>
```

Suppose that Alice then sends the resultant PDF (metadata.pdf$_0$) to Bob, and tells Bob that she does not want to be identified as the author of the PDF. Bob opens said PDF in Adobe Acrobat and accesses the Document Properties menu, from where he can redact the existent author field entry. From the Document Properties menu, Bob deletes Alice from the author field, thus leaving the field blank. Bob then saves the PDF (metadata.pdf$_1$), thinking that he successfully changed the author field.

To complicate and obfuscate matters further, Chuck learns of the PDF and thinks that instead of merely leaving the author field blank, Dave should be identified as the author so that he would bear any repercussions for the document, which would further protect Alice. Chuck thus opens metadata.pdf$_1$ and repeats the same author-changing process as Bob, albeit now changing the author field to 'Dave', and saves the PDF once again (metadata.pdf$_2$).

Bob then finally places the PDF (metadata.pdf$_2$) online for anonymous distribution. Eve downloads the file (metadata.pdf$_2$) and, incensed at its contents, seeks to find out who authored the document. Eve opens the Document Properties and sees that the author was Dave. She then sends Dave a sternly worded email.

Dave, understandably perplexed, downloads the same PDF (metadata.pdf$_2$) and similarly opens the Document Properties; albeit, being a bit more tech-savvy than Eve, Dave then opens the PDF not in Adobe Acrobat, but in a hex editor application. Dave then performs a search for the '/Author' and '<rdf:li>' fields.

Inside metadata.pdf$_2$ (which, one will recall, went through the following creation-chain of author-field manipulation: Alice [metadata.pdf$_0$] → (null) [metadata.pdf$_1$]) → Dave [metadata.pdf$_2$]), Dave finds the following:

```
/Author(Alice)
/Author(Dave)

<rdf:li>Alice</rdf:li>
<rdf:li>Dave</rdf:li>
```

Dave forwards his findings to Eve, who then directs her ire towards the original author of the PDF, Alice.

Thus, the apparently manipulated metada.pdf$_2$ had the original author field (which Alice, Bob and Chuck had presumed absent since metadata.pdf$_0$) clearly preserved in the latent metadata of the PDF.

Document ID/instance ID

To give another PDF-based example, suppose there is an eBook publisher, Terso, that generates individually serialized PDF eBooks upon each customer purchase. Thus, if Alice and Bob both bought the same eBook (alicesebook.pdf$_0$ and bobsebook.pdf$_0$, respectively), it would nonetheless be possible for Terso to identify whether it was Alice's or Bob's copy that was illegally distributed, on the basis of the unique serial number that could, say, be printed in the gutter of every page of the PDF.

Suppose that Bob is foiled by this initial mode of serialization, and thus does not share his PDF. Alice, however, being more tech-savvy than Bob, goes through her PDF and deletes the serial number found throughout the page gutters. Having thus removed the publisher-placed serial number watermark, Alice saves the file (making it alicesebook.pdf$_1$, though she may have renamed it to anonymousebook.pdf). Being weary of author-based identification, Alice further opens alicesebook.pdf$_1$ in a hex editor and manually deletes any author information, thus foiling any potential latent author metadata analysis.

Feeling confident that the document can now not be traced back to her, Alice then places her copy of the eBook online. In a week, Alice receives a terse email from Terso's lawyers, informing her of legal proceedings against her for copyright infringement. How was Terso able to identify that anonymousebook.pdf was linked to alicesebook.pdf$_0$, and thus was purchased by Alice?

The *XMP Specification* contains a specific subset entitled the XMP Media Management namespace, which 'contains properties that provide information regarding the identification, composition, and history of a resource'.[31] Of particular interest within this namespace are the document ID ('The common identifier for all versions and renditions of a resource') and instance ID ('An identifier for a specific incarnation of a resource, updated each time a file is saved'[32]) fields. Thus, the document ID value remains static for all modified versions of a document, while the instance ID changes with each iteration (or save) of the document.

aliceseebook.pdf$_0$ has the following metadata:

```
<xapMM:DocumentID>uuid:69bb8086-728d-4565-842e
-c84a3c754979</xapMM:DocumentID>

<xapMM:InstanceID>uuid:343902f9-808c-489f-af53-5cc921e774d8
</xapMM:InstanceID>
```

anonymousebook.pdf (which is in fact aliceseebook.pdf$_1$) has the following metadata:

```
<xapMM:DocumentID>uuid:69bb8086-728d-4565-842e
-c84a3c754979</xapMM:DocumentID>

<xapMM:InstanceID>uuid:343902f9-808c-489f-af53-5cc921e774d8
</xapMM:InstanceID>

<xapMM:InstanceID>uuid:11b3828a-bab0-4907-abdd-c8c3635900bd
</xapMM:InstanceID>
```

Thus despite the new instance ID of anonymousebook.pdf, the original, unifying document ID of aliceseebook.pdf$_0$ is retained as well (as is the initial instance ID, and indeed all subsequent ones).

One could at this point ask whether bobsebook.pdf wouldn't also match the document ID. The reason it wouldn't is that Terso's PDF generator engine generates a brand new PDF each time from the source files, as opposed to modifying an existent PDF on each purchase merely to append a new serial number. Thus bobsebook.pdf$_0$ and aliceseebook.pdf$_0$ would have two distinct document IDs.

An aside on the generation of the document/instance IDs

The document ID and instance ID values are known as universally unique identifiers (UUIDs), alternatively called globally unique identifiers (GUIDs). The *XMP Specification* does not stipulate a distinct method for their generation: 'This document does not require any particular methodology for creating a GUID, nor does it require any specific means of formatting the GUID as a simple XMP value.'[33] Instead, the specifications refer to IETF RFC 4122 ('A Universally Unique IDentifier (UUID) URN Namespace')[34] for recommended UUID generation guidelines. The *XMP Specification*, however, recommends against using the source machine's media access control address (MAC address) as a base for UUID generation because of 'privacy concerns'.[35] Though as there are no explicit guidelines within the specification, there is no underlying guarantee that various PDF generator engines will not in fact use, in part, the MAC address to generate the UUID, which will in turn become the document ID. Thus the document ID metadata may also be used by adversaries later to identify positively which source machine created a specific PDF by analysing the algorithm used by the specific PDF engine to generate document ID UUIDs, thus elucidating yet another potential surveillance vector afforded by the utilization of metadata.

Case 2: JPEG Metadata

PDFs are far from being the only file type to include metadata. JPEG (or JPG) photographs taken with digital cameras usually have extensive metadata embedded using the exchangeable image file format (Exif) standard.[36] Aside from a variety of camera specifications (such as shutter speed, exposure time, focal length and so on), Exif data can also include the make (brand), model and serial number of the source camera; the date, time and time zone in which the photo was taken; the name of the camera owner; and the Global Positioning System (GPS) co-ordinates at which the photo was taken. Exif data is not restricted to text-based data, and can include, for instance, an embedded thumbnail image of the original, unmodified photo. Mobile phones, such as some versions of the iPhone, automatically embed GPS co-ordinates unless the option is specifically disabled;[37] while popular photo editing software, such as some versions of Adobe Photoshop, automatically preserve the embedded original thumbnail of an image.

To take a test case, say a citizen journalist takes an accompanying photo of a source for an article whose location is confidential. The photo contains a street sign intersection and perhaps a house number in the background, which the journalist crops out to protect the source's location. Upon reading the article, those with an interest in identifying the source's location at the time of the article interview can extract the latent metadata from the published photo (using any number of freely available tools, such as ExifTool[38] or Exif Viewer[39]). They can thus identify the location from the embedded GPS co-ordinates as well as by identifying the street signs in the original, uncropped thumbnail image.

To take another test case, say a whistleblower anonymously publishes photos she took of a document classified as Top Secret.[40] Upon analysing the metadata, law enforcement officials, who have expressed an explicit interest in analysing Exif data,[41] do not find any GPS co-ordinates that would identify where the photo was taken, and thus the potential location of the whistleblower. However, they do find the following entries:

Model: Canon EOS 600D
BodySerialNumber: 309025041034

Upon contacting the identified manufacturer, they can at the bare minimum isolate the location from which the camera was originally purchased, possibly cross-referencing it to CCTV or bank card data, and if the owner ever registered the camera upon purchase, they may indeed be able to find the owner's identity as well.

Metadetail

We go into a relatively extended amount of detail here because, aside from showing the kinds of material, strings of symbols, and different kinds of editors and authoring systems that are involved in such cases, there is a nod towards the kind of fastidious, painstaking work that Foucault characterized as being required for work on the archive.[42] In these cases, though, the patient work of cross-referencing and detail checking is obligatory, because in the case of computational systems, any making of such an enquiry is to some extent *inside* the archive, a system of cross-referencing and interlocking agency of high degrees of granularity and multiple levels of redundancy, engineering processes of identification. Such metadata operates through an iterative mode of persistence, exploiting the resultant paradox of ephemeral, but numerically ordered variation (of instance IDs, of the imagined universality of a device ID) on the one hand and stable, steadfast identification (of what can in fact be the same sorts of data) on the other to foster tendencies towards an overarching, tenacious and unrelenting surveillance framework.

Equally, however, such cases evince the banality of metadata. To work on and within it requires a high degree of tacit knowledge, and the requirement always to attend to further developments, subsidiary forms of identification, requiring an expertise born only out of familiarity with procedures, kinds of data and the forms by which they are interrogated or called into being.[43] At the same time, the methods for ensuring identity are those that enable it to be erased, misattributed; that is to say, to be meticulously wrong. The variant forms of knowledge of those who work on and through identity may also not arrange themselves around the same enthusiasms, that for the state for instance; or for an inverse knowledge of the mechanisms of control. As a rough guide, it is better to avoid making oneself susceptible to the tender ministrations of a philologically inclined robot.

Lingering Certainty

User identification is often discussed in relation to the question of surveillance and the problematics associated with the construction of privacy. Identity, indeed, is a complex phenomenon in culture, one that in many ways undergoes a perpetual surfeit of technical specification. In the systems that we have discussed, identity is a function of the system that arranges it and whose signature is coeval with it. The author field is often complemented and qualified by numerous related fields. As we can see from the example of the PDF, the author field itself is somewhat recessive, almost superfluous compared to other forms of machine, document, location and user identification. We may suppose that in the kinds of document formats discussed, the author field may remain as a form of ritual acquiescence to being logged, or as a pleasurable interlude for the user who marks their imprimatur on an application's opening splash screen and whose word processing of learning, reticence and politesse may in turn be marked by discrete tags in comments and track changes.

In such a condition, as with other metadata, there is an increase of automation in writing. Not only does the computer have the agency of assigning the author, but alongside establishing the growth in the number of fields to be completed, a fully machine-generated condition of textuality, of data inscription, of the recording of the conditions registerable to the machine, becomes more palpable. If we are to calculate on the basis of sheer quantity, it is certain that machines now write more sequences of alphanumeric characters than have ever been directly authored by the human species. The author field is in a certain sense their valediction.

To put this another way, just as the signature is the guarantee of the document, part of the identification matrix, the author field can be read as a continuation of the historical series sign–seal–signature;[44] but it may also figure as an allocation of a certain computational role to a memory register that is nominally located outside of the machine – in the person of the author, where the person stands in for the author function. In this series, though, the author field rather lags behind other, later forms. The author field is not exactly superseded, but deprecated and supplemented, by other terms, such as log-in name, username and account name, as they are found in online systems and cloud 'services'. Here, the user ID complements the author field to the point of the latter receding as a rather vestigial form. One result of this is that whilst systems such as user ID develop to sustain and provide infrastructure for a univocal meaning, they are also populated with traces that ramify ambiguity. The author function is, if nowhere near dead, a bit foxed, vestigial, requiring of supplementary factors in the operations of certainty. The matrices of identification require the collaboration of other operators.

NOTES

1 E.g., Barry A. J. Fisher, William J. Tilstone and Catherine Woytowicz, *Introduction to Criminalistics: The Foundation of Forensic Science*, Elsevier, London, 2009, p. 295; John E. Douglas, Ann W. Burgess, Allen G. Burgess and Robert K. Ressler, *Crime Classification Manual: A Standard System for Investigating and Classifying Violent Crime*, 3rd edn, Wiley, Hoboken, 2013, p. 88; John E. Douglas and Mark Olshaker, 'Perpetrators', in Jonathan S. Olshaker, M. Christine Jackson and William S. Smock (eds.), *Forensic Emergency Medicine*, 2nd edn, Lippincott Williams & Wilkins, Philadelphia, 2007, p. 3; Bill Nelson, Amelia Phillips and Christopher Steuart, *Guide to Computer Forensics and Investigations*, 4th edn, Course Technology and Cengage Learning, Boston, 2010, p. 154; Brett Shavers, *Placing the Suspect Behind the Keyboard: Using Digital Forensics and Investigative Techniques to Identify Cybercrime Suspects*, Syngress and Elsevier, Waltham, 2013, p. 235; Lokendra Kumar Tiwari, Shefalika Ghosh Samaddar and Chandra Kant Dwivedi, 'E-Mail Forensics for Real Life Application in Evidence Building', *International Journal of Advanced Research in Computer Science*, 2:3, p. 288.
2 Shavers, *Placing the Suspect*, p. 235.
3 For a discussion of this problematic in relation to the 'human sciences' see François Laruelle, 'A Rigorous Science of Man', in Laruelle, *From Decision to Heresy: Experiments in Non-Standard Thought*, Urbanomic, Falmouth, 2012.
4 Michael Shrayer, *The Electric Pencil Word Processor: Operator's Manual*, 1977, https://www.sol20.org/manuals/pencil.pdf.

5 MicroPro International Corporation, *Wordstar CP/M Edition: Release 4*, MicroPro International Corporation, San Rafael, 1979, https://archive.org/details/Wordstar_Rel_4_for_CPM _1979_Micropro_International.

6 Tandy Corporation, *WP-2 Portable Wordprocessor Owner's Manual*, Tandy Corporation, 1989, https://archive.org/details/ WP-2_Portable_Word_Processor_Owners_Manual_1987 _Tandy, p. 66.

7 davidb, *Microsoft Word 5.0 (PC) Binary File Format* (Revision: 0.1), 1989, http://msxnet.org/word2rtf/formats/dosword5.

8 Robert Jones, *Internet Forensics: Using Digital Evidence to Solve Computer Crime*, O'Reilly Media, Sebastopol, CA, 2006, p. 148.

9 The propagation of the username into PDF author field metadata can be disabled by going into the Adobe Acrobat PDF printer properties, proceeding to the Adobe PDF Settings sub-menu and unchecking 'Add document information'; but the insertion of the username into the author field is nonetheless default behaviour for Adobe's PDF printer.

10 Alan Liu, 'Transcendental Data: Toward a Cultural History and Aesthetics of the New Encoded Discourse', *Critical Inquiry*, 31:1 (2004), pp. 49–84 at p. 72.

11 Dublin Core Metadata Initiative, 'DCMI Specifications', http:// dublincore.org/specifications.

12 Adobe, *Adobe XMP Developer Center*, https://www.adobe.com/ devnet/xmp.html.

13 In choosing to work with a forensic approach we are prompted by Matthew Kirschenbaum's work on the literary history of word processing. See his *Track Changes*, http://trackchangesbook .tumblr.com/mgk.html.

14 Nathan Ensmenger, *The Computer Boys Take Over: Computers, Programmers, and the Politics of Technical Expertise*, MIT Press, Cambridge, MA, 2010.

15 Donn B. Parker, *Crime by Computer: Startling New Kinds of Million-Dollar Fraud, Theft, Larceny and Embezzlement*, Charles Scribner's Sons, New York, 1976.

16 Ewen MacAskill, 'NSA "Collected Details of Online Sexual Activity" of Islamist Radicals', *Guardian*, 27 November 2013.

17 See Des Freedman, 'The Puzzle of Media Power: Notes Toward a Materialist Approach', *International Journal of Communication*, 8 (2014), pp. 319–34.

18 EC-Council, *Computer Forensics: Investigating Hard Disks, File and Operating Systems*, Course Technology and Cengage Learning, Clifton Park, 2010.

19 EC-Council, *Computer Forensics*, p. ii.

20 Matthias Kirchner, 'Notes on Digital Image Forensics and Counter-Forensics', in Kirchner, *Forensic Analysis of Resampled Digital Signals*, PhD thesis, Technische Universität Dresden, 2011, http://ws.binghamton.edu/kirchner/papers/ image_forensics_and_counter_forensics.pdf.

21 Cameron H. Malin, Eoghan Casey and James M. Aquilina, *Malware Forensics Field Guide for Windows Systems*, Syngress and Elsevier, Waltham, 2012, p. 378.

22 Ryan D. Pittman and Dave Shaver, 'Windows Forensic Analysis', in Eoghan Casey (ed.), *Handbook of Digital Forensics and Investigation*, Elsevier, London, 2010, p. 235.

23 Alex C. Kot and Hong Cao, 'Image and Video Source Class Identification' in Husrev Taha Sencar and Nasir Memon (eds.), *Digital Image Forensics: There is More to a Picture than Meets the Eye*, Springer, New York, 2013, p. 158.

24 Pina Bausch, *1980: A Piece by Pina Bausch*, performed at Sadler's Wells, London, 2014.

25 Frederick P. Brooks, Jr, *The Mythical Man-Month: Essays on Software Engineering*, Addison-Wesley, Reading, 1995.

26 The file obtained by the AntiSec hacker group contained '1,000,001 Apple Devices UDIDs linking to their users and their APNS tokens. the original file contained around 12,000,000 devices. we decided a million would be enough to release. we trimmed out other personal data as, full names, cell numbers, addresses, zipcodes, etc.' Antisec, SPECIAL #FFF EDITION – ANONYMOUS, http://pastebin.com/nfVT7b0Z. In original TXT format (130 MB): http://www.lasivian.com/files/permlinks/ iphonelist.txt; in size-optimized PDF (5.2 MB): http://ds4.ds .static.rtbf.be/article/pdf/iphonelist-1346775724.pdf. Of further interest: Aldo Cortesi, 'De-Anonymizing Apple UDIDs with OpenFeint', 2011, http://corte.si/posts/security/openfeint-udid -deanonymization/index.html;' Darrell Etherington, 'Apple UDID Leak Came from App Publisher, Not FBI', *Tech-Crunch*, 2012, https://techcrunch.com/2012/09/10/apple-udid-leak-came -from-app-publisher-not-fbi.

27 In CSV and SQL formats: https://thepiratebay.se/torrent/9419945/ Snapchat_Database_CSV__amp__SQL (see also Jon Skillings, 'Overexposed: Snapchat User Info from 4.6M Accounts', *CNET*,

2014, http://www.cnet.com/uk/news/overexposed-snapchat-user-info-from-4-6m-accounts).

28 The North American Numbering Plan Administration contains a Central Office Code Utilized Report tool which lists the approximate locales of COCs in any NPA: http://www.nanpa.com/reports/reports_cocodes.html.

29 Adobe, 'Adobe XMP: Adding Intelligence to Media', https://www.adobe.com/products/xmp.

30 Available at Adobe, *Adobe XMP Developer Center*.

31 Adobe, *XMP Specification Part 1: Data Model, Serialization, and Core Properties*, 2012, p. 28, https://wwwimages.adobe.com/www.adobe.com/content/dam/Adobe/en/devnet/xmp/pdfs/cc-201306/XMPSpecificationPart1.pdf.

32 Adobe, *XMP Specification*, p. 29.

33 Adobe, *XMP Specification*, p. 31.

34 P. Leach, M. Mealling and R. Salz, 'A Universally Unique IDentifier (UUID) URN Namespace', IETF RFC 4122, Internet Society, 2005, https://www.ietf.org/rfc/rfc4122.txt.

35 Leach et al., 'Universally Unique IDentifier'. For instance, the 'java.util.UUID mini-FAQ', 2005, http://www.asciiarmor.com/post/33736615/java-util-uuid-mini-faq, states that 'using a version 4 UUID could save you 20 months in a United States Federal Prison', alluding to the fact that the author of the Melissa worm was eventually identified from multiple Word DOC files having the same MAC-based GUID in their metadata as the original DOC which spread Melissa (see, e.g., Luke Reiter, 'Tracking Melissa's Alter Egos', *ZDNet*, 1999, https://www.zdnet.com/news/tracking-melissas-alter-egos/101974).

36 Camera & Imaging Products Association, 'Exchangeable Image File Format for Digital Still Cameras: Exif Version 2.3', CIPA DC-008-Translation-2012, http://www.cipa.jp/std/documents/e/DC-008-2012_E.pdf.

37 For instance, *Vice* journalists uploaded a photo of John McAfee when he was on the lam while being wanted for questioning by authorities in Belize; it was taken with the journalists' iPhone 4S, which included GPS co-ordinates (see Mat Honan, 'Oops! Did Vice Just Give Away John McAfee's Location with Photo Metadata?', *Wired*, 2012, http://www.wired.com/2012/12/oops-did-vice-just-give-away-john-mcafees-location-with-this-photo).

38 Phil Harvey, *ExifTool*, 2014, https://www.sno.phy.queensu.ca/~phil/exiftool.

39 Alan Raskin, *Exif Viewer*, 2012, https://addons.mozilla.org/firefox/addon/exif-viewer.

40 'Top Secret' being defined as a classifier 'applied to information, the unauthorized disclosure of which reasonably could be expected to *cause exceptionally grave damage* to the national security'; cf. 'Secret', 'the unauthorized disclosure of which reasonably could be expected to cause serious damage to the national security' (*Intelligence Community Classification and Control Markings Register and Manual: Version 5.1*, Controlled Access Program Coordination Office (CAPCO), Washington, DC, 2012, pp. 28–9, https://www.fas.org/sgp/othergov/intel/capco_reg_v5-1.pdf).

41 Anon., 'EXIF: A Format Is Worth a Thousand Words', *TechBeat*, Winter (2007), pp. 1–2, https://www.justnet.org/pdf/EXIF.pdf.

42 Michel Foucault, 'Nietzsche, Genealogy, History', in Foucault, *Language, Counter-Memory, Practice: Selected Essays and Interviews by Michel Foucault*, ed. Donald F. Bouchard, Cornell University Press, Ithaca, NY, 1977, p. 139.

43 See, for an account of related forms of expertise, Harry Collins, *Are We All Scientific Experts Now?*, Polity, Cambridge, 2014.

44 See Béatrice Fraenkel, *La signature: genèse d'un signe*, Gallimard, Paris, 1992.

REFERENCES

Adobe, *Adobe XMP Developer Center*, https://www.adobe.com/devnet/xmp.html

Adobe, 'Adobe XMP: Adding Intelligence to Media', https://www.adobe.com/products/xmp

Adobe, *XMP Specification Part 1:- Data Model, Serialization, and Core Properties*, 2012, https://wwwimages.adobe.com/www.adobe.com/content/dam/Adobe/en/devnet/xmp/pdfs/cc-201306/XMPSpecificationPart1.pdf

Anon., 'EXIF: A Format Is Worth a Thousand Words', *TechBeat*, Winter (2007), pp. 1–2, https://www.justnet.org/pdf/EXIF.pdf

Antisec, SPECIAL #FFF EDITION – ANONYMOUS, http://pastebin.com/nfVT7b0Z. In original TXT format (130 MB): http://www.lasivian.com/files/permlinks/iphonelist.txt; in size-optimized PDF (5.2 MB): http://ds4.ds.static.rtbf.be/article/pdf/iphonelist-1346775724.pdf

Pina Bausch, *1980: A Piece by Pina Bausch*, performed at Sadler's Wells, London, 2014.

Frederick P. Brooks, Jr, *The Mythical Man-Month: Essays on Software Engineering*, Addison-Wesley, Reading, 1995.

Camera & Imaging Products Association, 'Exchangeable Image File Format for Digital Still Cameras: Exif Version 2.3', CIPA DC-008-Translation-2012, 2012, http://www.cipa.jp/std/documents/e/DC-008-2012_E.pdf

Harry Collins, *Are We All Scientific Experts Now?*, Polity, Cambridge, 2014.

Aldo Cortesi, 'De-Anonymizing Apple UDIDs with OpenFeint', 2011, http://corte.si/posts/security/openfeint-udid-deanonymization/index.html

davidb, *Microsoft Word 5.0 (PC) Binary File Format* (Revision: 0.1), 1989, http://msxnet.org/word2rtf/formats/dosword5

John E. Douglas and Mark Olshaker, 'Perpetrators', in Jonathan S. Olshaker, M. Christine Jackson and William S. Smock (eds.), *Forensic Emergency Medicine*, 2nd edn, Lippincott Williams & Wilkins, Philadelphia, 2007.

John E. Douglas, Ann W. Burgess, Allen G. Burgess and Robert K. Ressler, *Crime Classification Manual: A Standard System for Investigating and Classifying Violent Crime*, 3rd edn, Wiley, Hoboken, 2013.

Dublin Core Metadata Initiative, 'DCMI Specifications', http://dublincore.org/specifications

EC-Council, *Computer Forensics: Investigating Hard Disks, File and Operating Systems*, Course Technology and Cengage Learning, Clifton Park, 2010.

Nathan Ensmenger, *The Computer Boys Take Over: Computers, Programmers, and the Politics of Technical Expertise*, MIT Press, Cambridge, MA, 2010.

Darrell Etherington, 'Apple UDID Leak Came from App Publisher, Not FBI', *TechCrunch*, 2012, https://techcrunch.com/2012/09/10/apple-udid-leak-came-from-app-publisher-not-fbi

Barry A. J. Fisher, William J. Tilstone and Catherine Woytowicz, *Introduction to Criminalistics: The Foundation of Forensic Science*, Elsevier, London, 2009.

Michel Foucault, 'Nietzsche, Genealogy, History', in Foucault, *Language, Counter-Memory, Practice: Selected Essays and Interviews by Michel Foucault*, ed. Donald F. Bouchard, Cornell University Press, Ithaca, NY, 1977.

Béatrice Fraenkel, *La signature: genèse d'un signe*, Gallimard, Paris, 1992.

Des Freedman, 'The Puzzle of Media Power: Notes Toward a Materialist Approach', *International Journal of Communication*, 8 (2014), pp. 319–34.

Phil Harvey, *ExifTool*, 2014, https://www.sno.phy.queensu.ca/~phil/exiftool

Mat Honan, 'Oops! Did Vice Just Give Away John McAfee's Location with Photo Metadata?', *Wired*, 2012, http://www.wired.com/2012/12/oops-did-vice-just-give-away-john-mcafees-location-with-this-photo

Intelligence Community Classification and Control Markings Register and Manual: Version 5.1, Controlled Access Program Coordination Office (CAPCO), Washington, DC, 2012, https://www.fas.org/sgp/othergov/intel/capco_reg_v5-1.pdf

java.util.UUID mini-FAQ, 2005, http://www.asciiarmor.com/post/33736615/java-util-uuid-mini-faq

Robert Jones, *Internet Forensics: Using Digital Evidence to Solve Computer Crime*, O'Reilly Media, Sebastopol, CA, 2006.

Matthias Kirchner, 'Notes on Digital Image Forensics and Counter-Forensics', in Kirchner, *Forensic Analysis of Resampled Digital Signals*, PhD thesis, Technische Universität Dresden, 2011, http://ws.binghamton.edu/kirchner/papers/image_forensics_and_counter_forensics.pdf

Matthew Kirschenbaum, *Track Changes*, http://trackchangesbook.tumblr.com/mgk.html

Alex C. Kot and Hong Cao, 'Image and Video Source Class Identification', in Husrev Taha Sencar and Nasir Memon (eds.), *Digital Image Forensics: There is More to a Picture than Meets the Eye*, Springer, New York, 2013.

François Laruelle, 'A Rigorous Science of Man', in Laruelle, *From Decision to Heresy: Experiments in Non-Standard Thought*, Urbanomic, Falmouth, 2012.

P. Leach, M. Mealling and R. Salz, 'A Universally Unique IDentifier (UUID) URN Namespace', IETF RFC 4122, Internet Society, 2005, https://www.ietf.org/rfc/rfc4122.txt

Alan Liu, 'Transcendental Data: Toward a Cultural History and Aesthetics of the New Encoded Discourse', *Critical Inquiry*, 31:1 (2004), pp. 49–84.

Ewen MacAskill, 'NSA "Collected Details of Online Sexual Activity" of Islamist Radicals', *Guardian*, 27 November 2013.

Cameron H. Malin, Eoghan Casey and James M. Aquilina, *Malware Forensics Field Guide for Windows Systems*, Syngress and Elsevier, Waltham, 2012.

MicroPro International Corporation, *Wordstar CP/M Edition: Release 4*, MicroPro International Corporation, San Rafael, 1979, https://archive.org/details/Wordstar_Rel_4_for_CPM_1979_Micropro_International

Bill Nelson, Amelia Phillips and Christopher Steuart, *Guide to Computer Forensics and Investigations*, 4th edn, Course Technology and Cengage Learning, Boston, 2010.

Donn B. Parker, *Crime by Computer: Startling New Kinds of Million-Dollar Fraud, Theft, Larceny and Embezzlement*, Charles Scribner's Sons, New York, 1976.

Ryan D. Pittman and Dave Shaver, 'Windows Forensic Analysis', in Eoghan Casey (ed.), *Handbook of Digital Forensics and Investigation*, Elsevier, London, 2010.

Alan Raskin, *Exif Viewer*, 2012, https://addons.mozilla.org/firefox/addon/exif-viewer

Luke Reiter, 'Tracking Melissa's Alter Egos', *ZDNet*, 1999, https://www.zdnet.com/news/tracking-melissas-alter-egos/101974

Brett Shavers, *Placing the Suspect Behind the Keyboard: Using Digital Forensics and Investigative Techniques to Identify Cybercrime Suspects*, Syngress and Elsevier, Waltham, 2013.

Michael Shrayer, *The Electric Pencil Word Processor: Operator's Manual*, 1977, https://www.sol20.org/manuals/pencil.pdf

Jon Skillings, 'Overexposed: Snapchat User Info from 4.6M Accounts', *CNET*, 2014, http://www.cnet.com/uk/news/overexposed-snapchat-user-info-from-4-6m-accounts

Tandy Corporation, *WP-2 Portable Wordprocessor Owner's Manual*, Tandy Corporation, 1989, https://archive.org/details/WP-2_Portable_Word_Processor_Owners_Manual_1987_Tandy

Lokendra Kumar Tiwari, Shefalika Ghosh Samaddar and Chandra Kant Dwivedi, 'E-Mail Forensics for Real Life Application in Evidence Building', *International Journal of Advanced Research in Computer Science*, 2:3 (2011).

AESTHETICS

— 6 —

ALWAYS ONE BIT MORE: COMPUTING AND THE EXPERIENCE OF AMBIGUITY

Fun is often understood to be non-conceptual and indeed without rigour, without relation to formal processes of thought, yielding an intense and joyous informality, a release from procedure. Yet, as Olga Goriunova's edited collection *Fun and Software* argues, fun may also be found, alongside other kinds of pleasure, in the generation, iteration and imagination of operations and procedures.[1] This chapter aims to develop a means of drawing out an understanding of fun in relation to concepts of experience in the culture of mathematics and in the machinic fun of certain computer games. Mathematical concepts of experience – as something to be effaced, in terms of the grind of churning out calculations; understood as the acme of human knowledge, bordering on the mystical; or at the same time prosaic, peculiar and thrillingly abstract – have been crucial to the motivation and genesis of computing. Experience may be figured as something innate to the computing person, or that is abstractable and thus mobile, shifting heterogeneously from one context to another, producing strange affinities between scales – residues and likeness amongst computational forms that can occasionally link the most austere and mundane or cacophonous of aesthetics. Amongst such, the fine and perplexing fun of paradox and ambiguity arises not simply in the interplay between formalisms and other kinds of life but as formalisms interweave, releasing and congealing further dynamics. There are many ways in which mathematics has been linked to culture as a means of ordering, describing, inspiring or explaining ways of being in the world, but it is less often that mathematics thinks about itself as producing figurations of existence, and such moments are useful to turn to in gaining a sense of some of the patternings of computational culture.

The Experience of Number

'There are no non-experienced truths.' This concise statement of the intuitionist position in mathematics comes from Luitzen Egbertus Jan Brouwer at the opening of his essay 'Consciousness, Philosophy and Mathematics'.[2] To put it the other way around, a truth, in mathematics, cannot be unknown even given a rigorous logical armature for its existence. A truth of such sort would be something like a statement of pi calculated to an accuracy of one digit more than that which is currently known to the calculator. Brouwer's argument would be that until that calculation is actually made, or a construction for it is given, pi is not *yet* that number but exists in a state of indetermination beyond that point. A positive way of putting this is that for Brouwer, mathematics is 'the free activity of the creating subject [*het scheppende subject*]',[3] a notion something rather akin to the slightly less purified notion of fun that we are working with here and having a familial relation to Oblonsky's assertion in *Anna Karenina* that 'Some mathematician has said pleasure lies not in discovering truth but in seeking it.'[4]

One of the key arguments of Brouwer's intuitionism was around the *principle of the excluded middle*. This principle states that for every mathematical statement, either it or its negation is true. As already mentioned with the example of pi, Brouwer believed that a number only came into existence when it was calculated, rather than existing in some state of ideal reality that is simply and imperfectly cited. This meant that for Brouwer, it would be possible to imagine correctly formulated mathematical statements that could be neither true nor false. Indeed, for him, no statement about a mathematical entity such as an infinite set could be known precisely in such terms; these entities had to be experienced, enumerated.[5]

The argument is against formalism in one way, and idealism in another, against the idea of universal pre-existing numbers. Brouwer's position is a kind of constructivism, building a form of inductive reason that is not determined in advance but composed of a rigorous relation to a world of abstraction. My intention is not to propound intuitionism here, but to use this work as a starting point to think through some of the context in mathematics and logic in which the computer was conceptualized, and then to draw this out in relation to the question of fun, in the broad, passionate, even obsessive, sense of the word that Olga Goriunova proposes. This will lead to asking whether fun needs to be experienced, and by whom or what, or if such experience can also move through, for instance, computers.

114

Further: how does fun circulate, what is its processuality when it also becomes computational and, to go in the opposite direction of tracing the ambit of fun to a wider assemblage, what forms of computing make such experience most palpable?

The way that intuitionism focuses mathematical thinking on experience, in the work of Brouwer (but to some extent also that of Henri Poincaré, a mathematician who always put the experiential and interpretative nature of his subject to the fore),[6] allows us to draw out some filiations to the experiential nature of software. Formalist mathematics, of the kind Brouwer was arguing against, presupposed that there were undiscovered truths that could be set out, in advance of their actually being known, by axiomatic reasoning which would implicitly have realized them. That is, the axiom comes before the number and before the calculation. For intuitionists, this makes the whole of classical mathematics a simply syllogistic exercise, and reduces its status as a science.

Brouwer proposes four forms of conscious experience: stillness, sensation, mathematics and wisdom, which are arrayed in a linear progression of state. Each of them builds an understanding of mathematics as primarily epistemological and mystical, in that 'research in the foundation of mathematics is inner enquiry with revealing and liberating consequences'.[7]

As is well known, one of the key controversies around the programme of formalist mathematics, and especially that of David Hilbert, was that generated by Alan Turing in work that led to the formulation of automatic computing in the famous paper 'On Computable Numbers, with an Application to the *Entscheidungsproblem*'.[8] If we read Turing's work with an eye to that of Brouwer, we can see some interesting correlations. Brouwer's definition of real numbers is propounded in the second part of Turing's short 'Correction', which was published in the following year and sets out a clarification of what is meant by a computable number.[9]

Whilst Brouwer opposed the idea of completed infinities as something that precludes experience, he tried to bring together the idea of the discrete and the continuous in a series of numbers; say, all those between zero and one. In the act of working these out, the sequence of numbers that you generate *is* that series, in its state of unfolding in your mind. Charles Petzold notes that 'In the intuitionist continuum, real numbers are always incomplete – unfinished and never to be finished.'[10] In this sense, numbers are like drives: eternal combustion engines, perpetual commotion machines; and as such intuitionism situates mathematics in time. (One experiences numbers in relation

115

to others, their 'two-ity', in that the number *one* already implies a movement towards *two*. Numbers imply a relation to the continuum as an ongoing.)

In §9 of 'Computable Numbers' Turing argues that a machine carrying out an algorithmically defined task is, at a certain level of abstraction, mathematically equivalent to a human carrying out the same task. If a machine finds the problem unsolvable given the algorithm, then so too would a human. There is a network of such problems that Turing works through at various times in the relationship between computing and intelligence,[11] but here Turing's machine provided a direct link to the work of Brouwer in that a calculation is always a process, occurring over time;[12] that a calculation is not (in terms of the problem staged in the paper) finely predictable – there is no machine that can decide in advance of the computation of an infinite set what the next number of that set must necessarily be; and that the work is limited to actually computable numbers, 'the subset of the real numbers that can actually be calculated'.[13] Needless to say, there is also an abrupt difference between Turing's and Brouwer's approaches, since Turing's work is here predicated upon the ability to disengage, or abstract, mathematical capacities.

Whether one takes an intuitionist or constructivist line, computation can be said to have a quality that is to certain degrees participative and processual. For Brouwer, this process was experience. Turing, however, liked to play with the ambiguity of things arising between the human and machine, the slippage of one into the other and their differentiation. Indeed, the radicality of the Turing Machine, as Alonso Church named it, was its invigoration of mathematical logic with things from outside of it.[14] Here, it is important to draw in one of the aspects of the discussion of Brouwer developed by Mark van Atten, whose phenomenological reading suggests that a key difficulty in the promulgation of intuitionism is its lack of reflexivity – that the position of the mathematician is fundamentally solipsistic.[15] Van Atten argues that Brouwer's figuration of mathematical consciousness (understood as four forms of thought) cannot be reflected on because to do so would require a further form of consciousness capable of such reflection and the production of figures of mutual understanding.

Because the Turing Machine alienates mathematics from the simply human creative subject, without succumbing to idealism, whilst still maintaining a relation to an understanding of computation as experience, its form of constructivism offers the possibility of articulating, if not necessarily achieving, such reflexivity. But equally in the movement of experience to computers, in circulation amongst machines, networks, codes, interpreters, interfaces and users, or various kinds, intents, states and arrangements, the simply phenomenological interpretation of the human individual requires supplement. And the way in which such a reflexive understanding of computational experience is constructed is emphasized, or becomes more explicit and tractable, in some kinds of procedures rather than others.

MMORPGs and the Demand for Experience

One way of understanding, via a difference, this experience of slippage crosses over into the cultural understanding of 'fair play' in games, and those that hack them. Here, there is an implicit requirement that computational processes are experienced, as something to be judged and interacted with on the basis of human skill. To experience them otherwise is to 'cheat'. An example of the persistence of such is in the rules governing many massively multi-player online role-playing games (MMORPGs) such as World of Warcraft or Runescape. Here, the use of macros, autotypers (to repeat messages), autoclickers (to repeat functions) and other kinds of bots is generally deemed to be an offence, a violation of the game.[16] But such things, bots especially, can, in turn, be means of having fun with the rather jaded rule sets of online gaming, through griefing or more interesting means. On the one hand, the prohibition on bots argues for an assumed level playing field: that *real* users are playing the game, not sets of competing scripts or mechanical devices tapping keyboards. In turn, the use of gold farmers, or professional players, in MMORPGs is seen as a betrayal of such experiential requirement, but also as part of the game, when players are increasingly plugged into wider sets of economic systems through games as backchannels.[17] The demand for a certain kind of subject as the experiential target of the operations of the manipulation of procedures, symbols and interactions that constitute such games suggests that computing is experiential, but experience is itself subject to what might politely be called 'variation'.

Machinic and Distributed Experience of Computing

In discussing computing as experience this chapter is concerned with arguing not that computers have, or experience, fun in the same way that humans do, or even that the latter classification of entity experi-

117

ence any particular kind of fun, but that computation itself can be fun, a form of passionate involvement that in some circumstances can also be said to be machinic and distributed. It is *machinic* in the sense that it implies multiple elements in states of relation, and *distributed* in the sense that it occurs across such relations, partly in the way in which different materials and their handling of processes conjugate and yield time.

As processing is distributed, a computing machine or piece of software might be said to take part, in its own terms, in Brouwer's sense, of the excluded middle. An example of such machinic and distributed interweaving can be found in the software art project Human Cellular Automata, which proposes that such a condition can be experienced.[18] But we can also suggest that, given the constructivist slant of Turing's work, there may be some other form of experience, or more strictly, open-ended undergoing, of mathematics that would not be human in the sense that Brouwer argues for, but would not strictly be simply axiomatic and deductive either.

In order to talk about circulating fun as being distributed and processual, it is useful to turn to some of the qualities of such relations, and to start to do so again through computing, maintaining a link to computing as experience. Brouwer talked about the experience of the creating mind, and proposed that mathematics was the ultimate exercise in free thought as such: this in the sense of mathematics as not only the purest form of thought, as the realization of the mind without any intrinsic relation to other aspects of the world, but also, because of that quality, as the most literally unencumbered, unfettered thought. This sense of the unencumbered quality of thought is useful to maintain, as a modality of the powers of abstraction. Here, though, such abstraction can also be seen to emphasize, and provide a precondition for, the combinatorial nature of thought in relation to and as part of other forms of experience, and, via Turing, for the constituent heterogeneity of computing. In order to get a sense of the nature of such experience it is useful to map some forms of relation that are not quite of the same order as this image of thought, but yet also significant in the experience of computation: ambiguity and paradox.

Ambiguity and Paradox

In his book *How Mathematicians Think*, William Byers differentiates the formalized, algorithmic means of doing maths from the moment of discovery. This is done in a somewhat different mode to Brouwer's, in that Byers aims to produce an alliance, or at least draw out affinities, between the constructivist and idealist or formalist schools through an emphasis on ambiguity; but this idea of ambiguity, one that Byers establishes through accounts and examples from many areas and ages of mathematics, is one that is also processual and experiential.

Ambiguity is a state which admits of more than one interpretation, or, more fully, of existence in a state in which, as Byers puts it, two (or more) 'self-consistent but mutually incompatible frames of reference'[19] have to be inhabited. In disciplinary terms we can think of the overlap of two not quite commensurable formalisms, such as that between logic and mathematics, or, in the example of geometry and arithmetic, fields which sometimes coincide but are not entirely mappable one to the other without causing interesting effects. As an example of such effects, one sees ambiguity in moments when the idea of a number as a quantity and as a process are linked, for instance in the number 'one third' being equal to 0.3 recurring in decimal notation. In the second version, knowing a number also involves calculation but requires as well a sense of the unreachable limit.[20] For Byers, understanding these two forms of the number requires a creative act, one with a certain affinity to Brouwer's intuition.

Interestingly here, we are also talking about different forms of notation. There is perhaps a case for a media theory of mathematical tools allied with ethnomathematics;[21] one that moves from pen and paper, to one-dimensional grids, through independent realms of abstract objects and the discourses that sustain them, to minds as putative entities, to other exciting forms of stationery.[22] But to move into more fully aesthetic terms, ambiguity emerges from the existence of two or more of these interpretative states. Ambiguity is not simply something requiring the gentle discernment of nuance or the capacity to take pleasure in the multifaceted, which it certainly can be. It can also present a being with a torn and bleeding reality in which one scale of a life is incommensurable with, yet bound up with, another scale that it cannot avoid. Its painfulness may also combine with another layer, that of the joy of being able to step outside of an overdetermination. Ambiguity manifests too as the double bind or the infernal alternative, experience squeezed into systemic imperatives, as much as it does as the subtle flickering of recognition of multiply nuanced being.[23] We can ask of different occurrences of ambiguity as a form of experience: how deeply can or must one inhabit ambiguity, what are its roles and latencies at different conjunctures of experience?

119

Given such an understanding of ambiguity, we can say that a paradox is a recursively nested ambiguity. That is, ambiguity is a statement or condition that contains the implication or fully stated condition of incompatibility with itself. Paradox is largely logical and semantic. Both paradox and ambiguity are essential to software. Both draw out the experiential and the temporal. Paradox breaks with the immediate time typical of statements made in first-order logic by forming a loop back to the condition of the formation of such thought, the decision to think, or the accident of thought. Both ambiguity and paradox are aesthetic modes that find particular forms in computation.

Fun Becomes Systemic

If computing is experiential, something that can be said to have roots in its mathematical underpinnings, how does such experience become fun? And then there is the question of aesthetics. Fun is often presented as wholesome enjoyment, a state of amusement in which the cares of the world are rinsed from us. In the entrepreneurial cast of the term, fun may also be an exhilarating intellectual and emotional overinvestment in a thing that leads to a technical and perhaps financial yield. But fun is itself ambiguous, being, in many cases, also perverse.

In an epigraph to his *Cent mille milliards de poèmes* Raymond Queneau cites Alan Turing as saying that 'Only a computer can appreciate a sonnet written by another computer.'[24] In order to enjoy such a poem, Queneau suggests, one would have to be something other than a straightforward literary reader. There is a funny set of unpackings here: the proposition of computer intelligence, one that would not correspond to that of humans, or things of other kinds, thus also implying a queer sympathy amongst a kind; but there is also a sense in which computing as cultural is somehow preposterous, and delightful as such, and indeed Turing in the article 'Computing Machinery and Intelligence' is intrigued by misidentification and guessing, a playfulness at the root of computing. There is a relay between computers set up by this proposal that is not one of strict computation in the sense of an immediate realization of first-order propositions manifest at the level of flows in circuits, but one of recognition and appreciation as yielding, revealing and hiding, enjoying something over time. Turing's understanding of experience in this article is vastly different to that established by Brouwer. Turing's is so concretely formulated in abstract terms that it can pass from one or more mode of realization to another, from the human computer to the abstract machine; Brouwer's is so interwoven in the experience of the abstract that it singularizes experience, is unutterable in words; but both are coupled with a relation to knowledge, to a subject and to a kind of existence.[25]

And, in the circulation of experience through time, we can say experience is something that, as Turing exemplifies in both his paper on the *Entscheidungsproblem* and the epigraph used by Queneau, also moves around, beyond people into devices, networks, arrays, processes. But in doing so, experience or undergoing itself undergoes changes in kind. Thus we can reframe the suggestion that, in the conditions of computational and networked digital media, in software cultures, ambiguity and paradox become machinic and distributed.

Such process may not be fluid and smooth, but perhaps halting, lame, encountering boredom. We can say that some of this is echoed in the repetitive language and constrained behaviours worked through by Beckett, in *Quad*[26] or other cases of his more procedural writings and scripts. As Deleuze asks, 'Must one be exhausted to give oneself over to the combinatorial, or is it the combinatorial that exhausts us, that leads us to exhaustion – or even the two together, the combinatorial and exhaustion?'[27] Complementary to this image, we can propose fun as a tendentially more joyous involvement in the combinatorial, one that does not necessarily run counter to the exhausted, but places finitude in undecided relation not only to the continuum, as for instance in phasing in music (exemplified in Steve Reich's *Drumming*[28] or the polyrhythmicality of breakbeats), but also to *escape* and to the powers of invention in relation to constraint; indeed, finds the two as mutually, ambiguously entangled.

Machinic Funs

For Guattari, 'The machine, every species of machine, is always at the junction of the finite and infinite, at this point of negotiation between complexity and chaos.'[29] Here, in machinic terms, are means by which the combinatorial may connect with exhaustion, but also, recursively, with other forms of combinatorial, generating paradoxes, ambivalence, multivalence. The machinic is part of a larger set which Guattari compares to Kleinian part objects, entities that rely for their actuation on kinds of coupling, tripling and connection, and which in such connection create being. The search for such coupling or tripling, their state of two-ity, results in sets of *projective–introspective* relations, generating subjectivities.[30] Such connectiveness in Klein is ambivalent, 'bad' as well as good and exploratory; generators of phantasy, nourishment and its denial; despisement, copious muddling and the ravages of yearning.

One paradoxical example of a machinic fun, which resonates with the concern for an ethnomathematical analysis of notation, arises from a use of numbers that is not mathematical but literary, yet still combinatorial. Claude Klosky's text 'The First Thousand Numbers in Alphabetical Order'[31] is a subtle and in a certain sense systematically hilarious work. Its simple procedure is to list the alphabetically written versions of the numbers from one to one thousand in alphabetic rather than numerical order. One could say that this is a kind of formalistic triumph, with an 'irrelevant' set of ordering principles that is axiomatically described by the work's title, yet here we are drawn to learn that not all formalisms are of the same order, and that in the shifting logic of this procedure there is the possibility of eliciting something new in the 'proper matter' of one by the application of another. The specific quality of the work is manifestly only recognizable through experience, that of actually working through at least some of the text. To read the whole one must be solemn, or raptured, a chatbot, or somehow else unlike a reader of text, to take on, in Craig Dworkins' terms, the role of a parser,[32] and to do so invites the mind to tingle with a kind of procedural pleasure that is somehow always syncopating the many itchy transitions between boredom and surprise. A formalism as such is itself always ambiguous, itself partial as it yields to, merges with or elides the suctions and trickiness of the different generative capacities of matter: alphabetism and number; the ego and the creative subject; computing and the ambiguities of fun.

Minecraft ALU and CPU by theinternetftw

A recent encounter that brought about such a pleasure was that with screen-capture documentation of the construction of two of the three basic components of a computer in the MMORPG Minecraft by a hacker named theinternetftw. Minecraft is a slightly clunky but very endearing-looking game, still in Beta at the time of theinternetftw's project, but one that has sophisticated sandbox gameplay untrammelled by set plots or points systems, and with a growing and avid user base. Minecraft is somewhat like an enormous constructor set,

122

in that everything is composed out of cubes, but one with monsters that attack you, wandering wildlife known as mobs or 'mobiles', a well-developed game physics of different natural materials (such as wood, iron, diamond, soil) that are to be sourced, worked and assembled and, in posing the highly manipulable components of the world, essentially form the core of the game. Minecraft is also cool because, as the name suggests, players go under the surface of the game, into the ground. Users make elaborate traps, laggily rendered rollercoasters, volcanoes spewing bitmapped lava, underwater glass tunnels with which to view pulsating rectilinear squid, meat factories (which mobs are lured into to be elaborately slaughtered and processed), and explore undocumented features and glitches. In turn, Minecraft takes the sandbox principle as a core recursive form. Users create enormous amounts of media around the game, and thousands of player-generated maps where games and scenarios developed within the game are circulated online as additional files allowing for different rule sets and genres to be adopted and played with on top of the Minecraft engine. Importantly, for this project and many others, one of the elements of the game, a type of material called Redstone, allows you to create basic logic circuits.[33]

The fundamental elements of a computer include an arithmetic logic unit (ALU), a central processing unit (CPU) and a program counter. The first of these was made in Minecraft by theinternetftw in autumn 2010, the second a few weeks later.[34] Invented by John von Neumann, an ALU performs addition and subtraction.[35] More sophisticated ALUs also do multiplication and division (as an extension of addition and subtraction) and include the Boolean logic of AND, OR and XOR (to return to Brouwer, the Exclusive Or being a way of framing numbers that generates the excluded middle). To make an ALU out of basic components such as transistor–transistor logic (TTL) chips is a familiar rite of passage for electronic engineering students, but it is the particular way in which this has been done which raises theinternetftw's work above the level of such an exercise.

Part of what is contradictorily fun about constructing a computer in this way is that working in Minecraft is pretty laborious. The scale of the circuit compared to that of the view of the player dramatically reverses the ratio that we are used to in viewing circuits, each byte of memory here corresponding to a block of space. The system is enormous and each block has to be put in place, one by one, mouse-click by mouse-click. It's also not an environment that is easily scripted, and this is a clunky process. It is therefore a relatively non-obvious situation in which to make such a machine – especially given that the Redstones need recharging every fifteen blocks, so that workarounds have to be made to cope with that. Examining this device moves us away from the idea of computation as something increasingly fast, increasingly small, into something that you can walk around, need to fiddle about with, fine tune, and observe happening. As, in many domains of application, computation moves out of the box into more and more aspects of space,[36] this is a project that generates a complementary dynamic, establishing computation in a way that is only legible as a spatial experience.

Such work also draws on the tradition of emulation hacks in which, say, to exaggerate slightly, a Cray supercomputer would be used to emulate a Sinclair Spectrum, running a Cray emulation. A computer becomes its own bug, but that bug is another machine, running itself. Formalisms mesh with, irritate, propitiate and explore each other, producing luminous declivities, skittering patterns, banqueting halls of mirrors, slag heaps of unprocessed symbols, states and efflorescences cross-pollinating at a myriad of uneven rates and via an entire zoology of third parties. In this regard, there's also something fascinating about using such a relatively graphically naff system to draw out what is now such a well-understood piece of engineering, rendering an iconic structure into something like a megalithic airport terminal, but one in 128-bit colour, with rectilinear sheep, pigs or chickens wandering around, and that at night runs the risk of being infested with zombies.[37]

Megalithic Chuckles

So how does the Minecraft Computer inflect the notion of machinic and distributed fun? There is a version of the excluded third in Philip Agre's description of technical knowledge in which a computer model 'either works or does not work',[38] but there is also a recognition of its insistence on empiricism in that 'Computer people believe only what they can build, and this policy imposes a strong intellectual conservatism on the field.'[39] The process and nature of computation are excluded in the first, but taken as a source of truth in the second, and here mathematics enters into its various kinds of relation to and distance from engineering, a discipline whose realism may often make it inventively as well as demonically otherworldly. Here though, a totemic piece of computer architecture, when translated into another domain of realization – that of Minecraft with all the curiosities and interest of its gameplay, logic, and visual and physical quirks – becomes something else, something fascinating, magnificently ridiculous, and done in a way which allows it to be explored.

Computing becomes about its experience as such; the machine is, in this instantiation, slower than many of the first electronic computers. Fun in software here lines up with a hackerly processual passion at a meeting point between complex orderings of many kinds, and also enrols the jointly incremental and transversal nature of invention which produces, through ambiguity, the capacity not only to see things in different lights, but also to draw hitherto unworked capacities out of them. Akin to Turing's symphony written for another computer, it is a computer made, paradoxically, within a computer. One can say, triumphantly, 'Look, I'm computing with the computer on my computer!' But it is an experience that also circulates via other means, drawing us into the monumental excitement of being able to add two to three via an enormous stone mechanism composed of pixels. In such paradox, and in a state of multiple ambiguities, computing finds itself reformulating the machinic compulsion to connect, refigure and experience of the part object. There is indeed a deep ambiguous fun in computing, in achieving such a microcosmic achievement on an epic scale.

NOTES

1   Olga Goriunova, *Fun and Software: On Pleasure, Paradox and Pain in Computing*, Bloomsbury, London, 2014.
2   Luitzen Egbertus Jan Brouwer, 'Consciousness, Philosophy and Mathematics', in *Proceedings of the Tenth International Congress of Philosophy*, North-Holland, Amsterdam, 1949, pp. 1235–49. See, for the context of this debate, Jeremy Gray, *Plato's Ghost: The Modernist Transformation of Mathematics*, Princeton University Press, Princeton, 2008.
3   Luitzen Egbertus Jan Brouwer, 'Volition, Knowledge, Language' (1933), in W. van Stigt, *Brouwer's Intuitionism*, North-Holland, Amsterdam, 1990, pp. 418–31. (The original title, *Willen, Weten, Spreken*, implies that, rather than abstract categories, these are things that are experienced, as willing, knowing and speaking.) See also, for a discussion, Mark van Atten, *On Brouwer*, Thomson Wadsworth, Singapore, 2004, p. 64.
4   Leo Tolstoy, *Anna Karenina*, trans. Louise and Aylmer Maude, Vintage, London, 2010, p. 192.

5 For an approach which translates between formalism and intuitionism, see Andrei Nikolaevich Kolmogorov, 'On the Principle of the Excluded Middle' (1925), in Jean van Heijenoort (ed.), *From Frege to Goedel: A Sourcebook in Mathematical Logic 1879–1931*, Harvard University Press, Cambridge, MA, 1967, pp. 414–37.

6 See, for example, the chapter 'On the Nature of Mathematical Reasoning', in Henri Poincaré, *Science and Hypothesis*, Dover, New York, 1952.

7 Brouwer, 'Consciousness'.

8 Alan Turing, 'On Computable Numbers, with an Application to the *Entscheidungsproblem*' (1936), in Turing, *The Essential Turing*, ed. B. Jack Copeland, Clarendon Press, Oxford, 2004, pp. 58–90. The problem consists in finding the limits to computability, problems that are too hard for an 'effective procedure' (a step-by-step method of working) to solve due to the nature of the number to be calculated.

9 Alan Turing, 'On Computable Numbers, with an Application to the *Entscheidungsproblem*: A Correction' (1937), in *The Essential Turing*, pp. 94–6. In this note, amongst other things Turing specifies an intuitive definition of the term 'computable number'. Without specific mention of Turing, an excellent exploration of the philosophical consequences of the intuitionist concept of number can be found in Aden Evans, 'The Surd', in Simon Duffy (ed.), *Virtual Mathematics: The Logic of Difference*, Clinamen Press, Bolton, 2006, pp. 209–34.

10 Charles Petzold, *The Annotated Turing*, Wiley, Indianapolis, 2008, p. 317.

11 See, e.g., Alan Turing, 'Computing Machinery and Intelligence' (1950), in *The Essential Turing*, pp. 433–64.

12 Petzold, *Annotated Turing*, p. 307.

13 Petzold, *Annotated Turing*, p. 307.

14 See Andrew Hodges, 'Alan Turing and the Turing Machine', in Rolf Herken (ed.), *The Universal Turing Machine: A Half-Century Survey*, Springer, Vienna, 1995, pp. 3–14.

15 M. S. P. R. van Atten, *Phenomenology of Choice Sequences*, Zeno Institute of Philosophy, Utrecht, 1999, p. 73.

16 There are other reasons for this prohibition as such programs are also occasionally Trojan horses.

17 See, e.g., Cory Doctorow, *For the Win*, Harper Voyager, London, 2010; Edward Castronova, *Synthetic Worlds*, University of Chicago Press, Chicago, 2005.

18 This project, first performed at the Software Summer School in London in 2000, and subsequently elsewhere, consists of a crowd of people arranging themselves into a grid formation and carrying out a set of instructions inspired by James Conway's 'Game of Life'. See Matthew Fuller, *Human Cellular Automata*, http://www.spc.org/fuller/projects/the-human-cellular-automata.

19 William Byers, *How Mathematicians Think: Using Ambiguity, Contradiction and Paradox To Create Mathematics*, Princeton University Press, Princeton, 2007, p. 28.

20 Byers, *How Mathematicians Think*, pp. 40–1.

21 Brouwer, who thought of language simply as a shed residue of, or impediment to, mathematics on the one hand, or an inexact technique for memorizing mathematical constructions on the other (see his, *Cambridge Lectures on Intuitionism* (1951), Cambridge University Press, Cambridge, 1981), would rather probably be appalled at the idea. Edsger Dijkstra, on the other hand, always alert to the medial conditions of thought, suggests of the photocopier that 'No future history of science can ignore the change the advent of the copying machine has made' ('Twenty-Eight Years', EWD 1000, *Edsger W. Dijkstra Archive*, University of Texas, https://www.cs.utexas.edu/users/EWD/index10xx.html).

22 Of signal relevance here is the approach exemplified by Bernhard Siegert in 'Cacophony or Communication? Cultural Techniques in German Media Studies', trans. Geoffrey Winthrop-Young, *Grey Room*, 29 (2008), pp. 26–47.

23 For the double bind, see Gregory Bateson, Don D. Jackson, Jay Haley and John H. Weakland (1956), 'Toward a Theory of Schizophrenia', in Gregory Bateson, *Steps to an Ecology of Mind*, University of Chicago Press, Chicago, 2000, pp. 201–27. The 'infernal alternative' is posed by Isabelle Stengers and Phillipe Pignarre in *Capitalist Sorcery: Breaking the Spell*, trans. Andrew Goffey, Palgrave Macmillan, London, 2011.

24 Turing in Raymond Queneau, *Cent mille milliards de poèmes*, Gallimard, Paris, 1961.

25 Here we can develop a relation to Foucault's understanding of experience. Looking back, he reformulates to some extent a thematic running from his earlier work to his later: *experience*. That is to say that 'forms of knowledge, matrixes of forms of behaviour, and the constitution of subjects and modes of being' are experiential, rather than static (Foucault, *The Government of Self and Others: Lectures at the Collège de*

France 1982–1983, ed. Arnold I. Davidson, Palgrave, London, 2010, p. 5).

26 Samuel Beckett, 'Quad', in Beckett, *Collected Shorter Plays*, Faber and Faber, London, pp. 289–94.

27 Gilles Deleuze, *Essays Critical and Clinical*, trans. Daniel W. Smith and Michael A. Greco, Verso, London, 1998, p. 154. See also Samuel Beckett, *Quad et autre pieces pour la television, suivi de L'Épuisé par Gilles Deleuze*, Éditions de Minuit, Paris, 1999.

28 Steve Reich, *Drumming* (1970–1).

29 Félix Guattari, *Chaosmosis: An Ethico-Aesthetic Paradigm*, trans. Paul Bains and Julian Pefanis, Power Institute, Sydney, 1995, p. 111. See, for further, previous discussion of such an approach, Félix Guattari, *The Anti-Oedipus Papers*, Semiotext(e), Los Angeles, 2006, and the riddling of reality with such machines in Gilles Deleuze and Félix Guattari, *Anti-Oedipus: Capitalism and Schizophrenia*, trans. Robert Hurley, Mark Seem and Helen R. Lane, Athlone, London, 1984.

30 The term 'part objects', used in general discussion in object relations theory, runs through much of Klein's work. See, e.g., Melanie Klein, 'Some Theoretical Conclusions Regarding the Emotional Life of the Infant,' in Klein, *Envy and Gratitude and Other Works 1946–1963*, Hogarth Press and the Institute of Psycho-Analysis, London, 1975.

31 Claude Klosky, 'The First Thousand Numbers in Alphabetical Order', in Craig Dworkin and Kenneth Goldsmith (eds.), *Against Expression: An Anthology of Conceptual Writing*, Northwestern University Press, Chicago, 2011, pp. 148–57. It is notable that this piece of work would change each time it is translated into another language as the alphabetical ordering of the letters would differ, rendering the formalism that generates the work, as given in its title, fundamentally playful.

32 Craig Dworkin, *Parse*, Atelos, Berkeley, CA, 2008.

33 For a description of the use of Redstone to create circuits, see http://www.minecraftwiki.net/wiki.

34 For video of the first ALU see http://www.youtube.com/watch?v=LGkkyKZVzug. For initial documentation of the CPU see http://www.youtube.com/watch?v=sybOqi_dgX0&feature =related. The program counter and a revised ALU (of 11 October 2010) are shown at http://www.youtube.com/watch?v=sybOqi_dgX0&feature=related. The cheerful and laconically enthusiastic tone of the commentary by theinternetftw makes these a

pleasure to watch. The full computer seems not to have been built; however, a number of others have since developed Minecraft computers of various sorts, including, in June 2011, a dual core CPU by anomalouscobra and jomeister15 (see http://www.youtube.com/watch?v=EaWo68CWWGM&feature=related) and, in September 2011, a full gaming computer 'Redgame' by laurensweyn, video of which is at http://www.youtube.com/watch?v=lB684ym3QY4&feature=related.

35 John von Neumann, *First Draft of a Report on the EDVAC*, Contract No.W-670-ORD-4926, between the United States Army Ordnance Department and the University of Pennsylvania. Moore School of Electrical Engineering, University of Pennsylvania, 30 June 1945.

36 See Rob Kitchin and Martin Dodge, *Code/Space: Software and Everyday Life*, MIT Press, Cambridge, MA, 2011.

37 The slight naffness of Minecraft, its clunky aesthetics, the laboriousness of the construction work within it, alongside the exuberance of imagination involved and expended in it by millions of players, are a subtext of the hugely popular Yogcast series of comedic, lackadaisical commentaries on Minecraft, posted on YouTube. In the last few years, since Minecraft has come out of Beta, a highly active scene of 'Let's Play' video makers has emerged with their own channels.

38 Philip Agre, *Computing and Human Experience*, Cambridge University Press, Cambridge, 1997, p. xi.

39 Agre, *Computing*, p. 13.

REFERENCES

Philip Agre, *Computing and Human Experience*, Cambridge University Press, Cambridge, 1997.
M. S. P. R. van Atten, *Phenomenology of Choice Sequences*, Zeno Institute of Philosophy, Utrecht, 1999.
Mark van Atten, *On Brouwer*, Thomson Wadsworth, Singapore, 2004.
Gregory Bateson, Don D. Jackson, Jay Haley and John H. Weakland (1956), 'Toward a Theory of Schizophrenia', in Gregory Bateson, *Steps to an Ecology of Mind*, University of Chicago Press, Chicago, 2000.
Samuel Beckett, 'Quad', in Beckett, *Collected Shorter Plays*, Faber and Faber, London, 1984.
Samuel Beckett, *Quad et autre pieces pour la television, suivi de L'Épuisé par Gilles Deleuze*, Éditions de Minuit, Paris, 1999.

Luitzen Egbertus Jan Brouwer, 'Volition, Knowledge, Language' (1933), in W. van Stigt, *Brouwer's Intuitionism*, North-Holland, Amsterdam, 1990.

Luitzen Egbertus Jan Brouwer, 'Consciousness, Philosophy and Mathematics', in *Proceedings of the Tenth International Congress of Philosophy*, North-Holland, Amsterdam, 1949.

Luitzen Egbertus Jan Brouwer, *Cambridge Lectures on Intuitionism* (1951), Cambridge University Press, Cambridge, 1981.

William Byers, *How Mathematicians Think: Using Ambiguity, Contradiction and Paradox To Create Mathematics*, Princeton University Press, Princeton, 2007.

Edward Castronova, *Synthetic Worlds*, University of Chicago Press, Chicago, 2005.

Gilles Deleuze, *Essays Critical and Clinical*, trans. Daniel W. Smith and Michael A. Greco, Verso, London, 1998.

Gilles Deleuze and Félix Guattari, *Anti-Oedipus: Capitalism and Schizophrenia*, trans. Robert Hurley, Mark Seem and Helen R. Lane, Athlone, London, 1984.

Edsger Dijkstra, 'Twenty-Eight Years', EWD 1000, *Edsger W. Dijkstra Archive*, University of Texas, https://www.cs.utexas.edu/users/EWD/index10xx.html

Cory Doctorow, *For the Win*, Harper Voyager, London, 2010.

Craig Dworkin, *Parse*, Atelos, Berkeley, CA, 2008.

Aden Evans, 'The Surd', in Simon Duffy (ed.), *Virtual Mathematics: The Logic of Difference*, Clinamen Press, Bolton, 2006.

Michel Foucault, *The Government of Self and Others: Lectures at the Collège de France 1982–1983*, ed. Arnold I. Davidson, Palgrave, London, 2010.

Matthew Fuller, *Human Cellular Automata*, http://www.spc.org/fuller/projects/the-human-cellular-automata

Olga Goriunova, *Fun and Software: On Pleasure, Paradox and Pain in Computing*, Bloomsbury, London, 2014.

Jeremy Gray, *Plato's Ghost: The Modernist Transformation of Mathematics*, Princeton University Press, Princeton, 2008.

Félix Guattari, *Chaosmosis: An Ethico-Aesthetic Paradigm*, trans. Paul Bains and Julian Pefanis, Power Institute, Sydney, 1995.

Félix Guattari, *The Anti-Oedipus Papers*, Semiotext(e), Los Angeles, 2006.

Andrew Hodges, 'Alan Turing and the Turing Machine', in Rolf Herken (ed.), *The Universal Turing Machine: A Half-Century Survey*, Springer, Vienna, 1995.

Rob Kitchin and Martin Dodge, *Code/Space: Software and Everyday Life*, MIT Press, Cambridge, MA, 2011.

Melanie Klein, 'Some Theoretical Conclusions Regarding the Emotional Life of the Infant', in Klein, *Envy and Gratitude and Other Works 1946–1963*, Hogarth Press and the Institute of Psycho-Analysis, London, 1975.

Claude Klosky, 'The First Thousand Numbers in Alphabetical Order', in Craig Dworkin and Kenneth Goldsmith (eds.), *Against Expression: An*

Anthology of Conceptual Writing, Northwestern University Press, Chicago, 2011.

Andrei Nikolaevich Kolmogorov, 'On the Principle of the Excluded Middle' (1925), in Jean van Heijenoort (ed.), *From Frege to Goedel: A Sourcebook in Mathematical Logic 1879–1931*, Harvard University Press, Cambridge, MA, 1967.

Minecraft Wiki, *Redstone*, http://www.minecraftwiki.net/wiki

John von Neumann, *First Draft of a Report on the EDVAC*, Contract No.W-670-ORD-4926, between the United States Army Ordnance Department and the University of Pennsylvania. Moore School of Electrical Engineering, University of Pennsylvania, 30 June 1945.

Charles Petzold, *The Annotated Turing*, Wiley, Indianapolis, 2008.

Henri Poincaré, *Science and Hypothesis*, Dover, New York, 1952.

Raymond Queneau, *Cent mille milliards de poèmes*, Gallimard, Paris, 1961.

Steve Reich, *Drumming* (1970–1).

Bernhard Siegert, 'Cacophony or Communication? Cultural Techniques in German Media Studies', trans. Geoffrey Winthrop-Young, *Grey Room*, 29 (2008), pp. 26–47.

Isabelle Stengers and Phillipe Pignarre, *Capitalist Sorcery: Breaking the Spell*, trans. Andrew Goffey, Palgrave Macmillan, London, 2011.

Leo Tolstoy, *Anna Karenina*, trans. Louise and Aylmer Maude, Vintage, London, 2010.

Alan Turing, 'On Computable Numbers, with an Application to the *Entscheidungsproblem*' (1936), in Turing, *The Essential Turing*, ed. B. Jack Copeland, Clarendon Press, Oxford, 2004.

Alan Turing, 'On Computable Numbers, with an Application to the *Entscheidungsproblem*: A Correction' (1937), in Turing, *The Essential Turing*, ed. B. Jack Copeland, Clarendon Press, Oxford, 2004.

Alan Turing, 'Computing Machinery and Intelligence' (1950), in Turing, *The Essential Turing*, ed. B. Jack Copeland, Clarendon Press, Oxford, 2004.

— 7 —

COMPUTATIONAL AESTHETICS

M. Beatrice Fazi and Matthew Fuller

It is the contention of this chapter that computation has a profound effect on the composition of digital art. We understand computation as a method and a force of organization, quantification and rationalization of reality by logico-mathematical means. The computational precedes and yet grounds the digital in its technical, social and cultural manifestations: it finds in digital technologies a fast, efficient and reliable technique of automation and distribution, yet remains a notion wider and more powerful than the digital tools that it subtends. Art, operating with the digital prefix and taking on many of the characteristics of the contemporary world, is inherently interwoven with the specific features of computational structures. At the same time, though, it can be said that aspects of digital art have yet to be sufficiently considered from that perspective. To some extent this is understandable, given the immense flexibility – and, often, resultant opacity – of computational systems. Digital art, however, builds upon and works through the computational, sharing its limits and potentials while also inheriting conceptual histories and contexts of practice. For this reason, we contend that an aesthetics of digital art is, at a fundamental level, a computational aesthetics.

Medium Specificity

The crux of our argument can be summarized in the particular kind of medium specificity of the aesthetics of digital art, a specificity that we see pertaining to this art's primary computational character. When making a claim for the computational specificity of digital art, however, we abstain from flattening this proposition onto openly 'modernist' arguments, or following on with the sets of uneasy quali-fications and rejoinders that come after such positions. We are wary of the essentialism that such an argument would imply, mourn or efface. It is our contention, however, that the risk of 'computational essentialism' is diminished by the nature of computation itself. It is somewhat perverse to look to Greenberg as a point of orienta-tion, but it will serve to make the point: traditionally, a modernist medium-specific aesthetics would call for the individuation of a 'raw' materiality, which – in operation and in effect – amasses and defines the potential for artistic expressivity of a certain medium, a modern-ism of attenuation.[1] In the case of computational aesthetics, however, such a prescription is more difficult to sustain. How is one to match the material promises of a medium if this medium does not have an idiotypic substantial form (such as canvas, paint, marble or mud), but rather has to be understood as a method and a force that, through rules, constraints and capacities for expression, continually renego-tiates its own structures of existence? In other words, what makes computation special in terms of its mediality – and thus perhaps dif-ferent from any other media coming into composition with art – is the impossibility of describing it simply as an intermediary 'substance'.

Art, thankfully enough, is not simply communications. The rela-tion of art with its media has been complex – a relation that is dis-avowed as much as it is explored, and through which one can trace the histories of many modalities or kinds of art that may themselves not cohere into a stable lineage. Art always propagates, rather than necessarily progresses, by disrupting and reinventing its terms of growth and domains of operation. Computation, however, has, in a certain sense, been a more historically delimited domain. To some extent this is due to the relative youth of the field as an organized discipline. At the same time, we argue, computation's development through mathematics, logic, philosophy and physical engineering gives it an equally rich genealogy. With its folding out into culture and the social, and indeed in its entanglement with art, it is undergoing further mutation, and its complex lines of invention and imagination find new forms of growth.

Recognizing this, critical discourse in recent years has developed cultural and artistic understandings of some of the mechanisms and components (algorithms, values, parameters, functions, codes and so on) through which computation operates, for instance via the emer-gence of fields such as software studies.[2] We would like to supplement this discussion with a consideration of computation's mediality as a mechanism of ontological and epistemological production. In terms of our medium specificity argument, this implies that computation is a medium in so far as it actualizes modes of being, levels and kinds of agency, and procedures of thought and configuration.

The ontological and epistemological expressions of computation are concretized and become operative at various scales: in the cultural, the societal and the political, as well as in art and elsewhere. Through a double articulation, computation changes these fields, yet maintains its own specificity; a specificity that is in turn affected, in variable ways, by the mutational forces of these fields' characteristics. Calling for a recognition of the medium specificity of computation in digital art thus means taking up the challenge of considering a mediality that surpasses the bounds of its grossly material instantiations and circumstances. In fact, acknowledging medium specificity involves reconsidering the notion of matter altogether, via the mobilization of all categories of the computational (whether sensuous, or logical, or both), and in the light of the ontologies and epistemologies that computational systems initiate or participate in.

A problem that immediately follows from this argument about medium specificity is how computation can be understood and spoken of, and by which means its consequences in the area of digital art can be mapped out. In attempting to address these questions, we advocate not a 'programmatic aesthetics', but a way of understanding the things that are explicitly or implicitly taken into account when working with computational systems. Computational aesthetics is certainly partially entwined with the computing machine, and in many particular works founded on very specific articulations of that interlacing. Yet the existence of computational aesthetics is not exclusively tied to a particular past, present or future technology.

Computation, we contend, is a systematization of reality via discrete means such as numbers, digits, models, procedures, measures, representations and highly condensed formalizations of relations between such things. To compute involves abstractive operations of quantification and of simulation, as well as the organization of abstract objects and procedures into expressions that can (but also may not) be thought of, perceived and carried out. Attending to computational aesthetics, then, puts in question the forces of all degrees and kinds that participate in these abstractions, and enquires what level of autonomy one should assign to such forces and abstractions. Similarly, a medium-specific computational aesthetics addresses the ways in which other techniques and genealogies (e.g., language, science, mathematics and art itself) conjoin, contribute to or contrast with computation, and thus result in often irreconcilable, convulsive or, conversely, reductive interrelations of other aesthetic approaches, ontological commitments, knowledge structures and arenas of practice. The impact of computation on other hitherto distinct fields constitutes, to a large extent, the status of the problematic of contemporary forms of life. We can therefore conclude that computation is as much a condition as it is a medium.

Computational Construction

It is in the light of these and related issues that the condition of computational aesthetics has to be understood not as given but as constructed. This claim, however, comes with two important qualifications.

To construct is to build up, to compose, to compile. A construction requires, in varying measures, a dose of planning and an amount of improvisation, the laying of foundations and the addition of decoration, the work of an engineer and the effort of a craftsperson. In this sense, a construction is less the straightforward manufacture of a result or an output than a heterogeneous process of creation. Constructing a computational aesthetics is a similarly inventive and procedural endeavour. It is, we claim – alongside the recognition of ecology and the invention of economies – a requisite for contemporary thought, imposing key issues proper to twenty-first-century culture. For example, questions such as how to define numerically determined rules for the analysis, codification and prediction of the world; how to account for digitally interfaced modes of sensing; and how to theorize new spatio-temporally distributed and networked prospects for cognition.

If it is a truism that computational technologies have brought about a fundamental epistemological break,[3] constructing a computational aesthetics means coming to terms with both the disruptions and the opportunities that this break initiates in modes of perceiving, acting and cognizing. In fact, it involves coming to terms with these conditions while looking for and articulating computational aesthetics' internal epistemological validations – those that are inherent to the theories and practices of computation itself. The construction of computational aesthetics, therefore, calls for a reworking of many of the conceptual categories, classes, types and criteria involved in aesthetics, noting that aesthetics is in turn understood here as a theory of construction – again! – of what constitutes experience. In other words, we are arguing, on the one hand, that to understand digital art in terms of an aesthetics of computation is key to the status of contemporary culture, which indeed is a computational culture. On the other hand, however, the very notion of computational aesthetics for us goes well beyond a theory of 'art made with computers', and becomes an investigation of the more foundational and formative aspects of the reality of the computational itself. In this respect, the reworkings of the aesthetic that we are here advocating are acts of both discovering and inventing the unfamiliar, the nameless, that which has been forgotten and is yet to be known: computational aesthetics must construct its own concepts.

Our first qualification of computational aesthetics' mode of construction should be read in the light of what we consider the restrictions or limitations of a traditional 'constructivist epistemology' for addressing the potential for conceptual discovery and invention. To claim that computational aesthetics is not given but has to be constructed would seem to echo the slogans of social constructivism, according to which situations are constructed by the interpretations that humans give of them. While there are some conditions and circumstances in which such an approach may also gain significant traction in digital art, we are keen to stress that the sociocultural constructivist position is not what we argue for, and that the construction of computational aesthetics advocated here is irreducible to the social constructivist epistemological paradigm. We would like to take a distance from the sociocultural constructivist agenda to extend the significance of 'construction' from an epistemological level to an ontological one. Which is to say: when constructing computational aesthetics one creates not only ways of knowing reality, but reality itself. To be more explicit, we understand the construction of computational aesthetics as a process that is 'internal' to the notion of computation, and should therefore not be approached from any particular disciplinary ground. Computer science alone cannot fully account for the modes of existence of the aesthetics of computation, but neither can cultural theory, philosophy or art. To say that computational aesthetics is not inferred from some particular disciplinary area, however, also means that its actuality cannot be subsumed under individual categories such as the societal, the cultural and the economic, or of course the aesthetic, although this actuality can surely be more or less successfully interrogated from such perspectives.

Computational aesthetics does not arise from a void; it is of course part of society, culture and economy – if we can, for a moment, accept the ruse that these things are adequately nameable. At the core of this issue lies, for us, the following point: to understand construction as the methodology proper for an immanent investigation of computation. We believe that social and cultural constructivism, in wanting to accommodate and assimilate difference, reiterates instead a 'transcendent' take on computational practices and technologies. From this transcendent perspective, human social histories or human cognitive processes are equally relative amongst each other, yet still causally superior to the events that they are said to construct. We argue for another view: that the construction of computational aesthetics is not solely based upon the determinism of a particular identity-forging co-ordinate, such as a time in history or a group of people, but that this construction is in fact incidental to computation's capacity of being an immanent operation of production of its own as well as other entities' modes of existence. Computational aesthetics is not produced by the social but is social. Similarly, it is not the result of a certain culture; it is culture. The diversities of the planes into which computational aesthetics cuts are not the transcendent cause of the aesthetics; these planes and multiplicities of contexts, intentions, norms, actions, perceptions etc. must themselves – to appropriate Deleuze and Guattari's claim – be made.[4] With this assertion we do not mean to say that in the aesthetic investigation of computational media anything is equal to anything else. On the contrary, we affirm that the realities of computational aesthetics are produced in the expressions that the aesthetics of computation finds for itself. The construction of such aesthetics is always in the computational event.

Having clarified this, we should note that, while we are wary of a simply sociocultural constructivist approach, our position also differs from what one could call an 'autopoietic' constructivism that would frame construction as a self-producing and self-organizing operation of subjective experiencing. This, then, is our second qualification of computational aesthetics' construction, a qualification that perhaps can help us to clarify our proposal for an immanent investigation of computational aesthetics. According to the autopoietic dialectics between observing and observed systems, everything relates to the environment in so far as it establishes and stabilizes itself in relation to it. The observer thus constructs her own world self-reflexively; that is, by positioning herself in relation to an environmental situation.[5] Without disavowing the importance of autopoietic constructivism for some fields (such as theories of cognition, which see it as variously involved with the world), we believe that this type of constructivism becomes particularly problematic when applied to computational aesthetics. In our opinion, autopoietic approaches to digital art seem to overlook the fact that computation is full of encounters between levels of expressivity and actuality that cannot interact in terms of subjects and objects, or within the confines of an environmental 'outside' or an 'inside' of the system.[6]

Many of these encounters or determinations in fact concern the (human) users of computation, not computation itself. We believe instead that the construction of computational aesthetics also involves incongruences and incompatibilities: in computation there are many particular cases but there is also an at least implied pretence to universality; the different speeds of eternity and fracture are often disjointed, and the diverse scales of what is too big to count or too small to see are frequently beyond subjective perception. In this sense, the construction of computational aesthetics needs to be radicalized from within the limits and potentialities of the computational itself, and not imposed upon the experiential positioning of an observer (whoever or whatever this latter is supposed to be). In other words, what we are advocating here is the capacity of computational aesthetics not simply to represent reality, but to contribute to the immanent constitution of reality itself.

Ten Aspects of Computational Aesthetics

In order to cut into the condition of computational aesthetics, we would like to offer a short overview of some of the features and characteristics that, to a greater or lesser extent, and to varying degrees of combination, articulate the reality of computation. It should be stressed that we are not looking for the ultimate qualities and values of either computation or aesthetics. Rather, we take these characteristics and features as modes of existence of the computational that infiltrate (and, in some cases, pervade and direct) its ontological and epistemological productions. In other words, these features and characteristics inform computation's modalities of being, levels of agency, and procedures of thought that mark the medium specificity of digital art, on the one hand, and its constructive nature, on the other. There is therefore no claim either that the list that follows is an exhaustive itemization of the conditions of computational aesthetics, or that aspects or combinations of it are exclusive to computational aesthetics and do not surface in other contexts and kinds of art, or aesthetics more broadly. What we suggest, instead, is that computational aesthetics brings the modes listed into a sharper focus and degree of compositional strength. If aesthetics can be understood as a theory of how experience is constructed, then this list attempts to account for some of the modalities of the computational that partake in such constructions. In some cases the items on this list help to sustain those constructions and to bring them into the empirical realm; in others they clash with the very category of experience altogether. The examples we offer are equally meant to provide an illustration of how computational aesthetics not only produces and regulates, but also points beyond, its own ontological and epistemological validations, and thus always has to be found and investigated in the computational event.

1 Abstraction and concreteness

Computation sets in motion some fundamental reorientations of culture, and of the circumstances in which art occurs, in that it endures as a conjoint condition of the abstract and the concrete.[7]

On the one hand, computation is a technique of abstraction. Layers of abstractions are piled up, from the hardware and the machine language right up to the graphic user interface; they manage the in-betweens of electronic circuits and symbolic procedures, and thus safeguard the operability of computing machines. In this respect abstraction is a self-contained dimension of existence of the computational. Historically and conceptually, computation draws upon the formal abstractions of logic and mathematics. Abstract mechanisms of inference drive it, while formal languages and symbol manipulation are among the abstract means that ground the very possibility of algorithmic 'effective procedures'. On the other hand, however, computation is as concrete as the world in which it participates. Computation not only abstracts from the world in order to model and represent it; through such abstractions, it also partakes in the world. In this sense, computation is a technology of material agency: there are the actions of algorithms organizing commercial warehouses, air traffic and administrative records; there are the social associations of networked practices, which aggregate and shape both the technological and the cultural; and there are the solid effects of software applications, which intervene in and bring about modes of knowing, trading, writing, playing, perceiving, interacting, governing and communicating.

The qualities of abstraction and concreteness have innumerable effects in terms of the constructivism and medium specificity of computational aesthetics. One effect is that the abstract structures of computation can move fast from one instantiation or occurrence to another (an algorithm can be used for sorting rice grains, faces or patterns of pixelation, for instance). The movement across multiple sites and occasions of a work is one way of tracing the variable characteristics of computational aesthetics across social forms, and of highlighting some of the ways in which the computational is often built into the latter. Tracing aspects of such a genealogy, the work of YoHa (Matsuko Yokokoji and Graham Harwood) and Graham Harwood – epitomized in *Lungs (Slave Labour)* (with Mongrel),[8] *London.pl*[9] and *Coal Fired Computers* (with Jean Demars)[10] – amongst others, works with the abstractions of relational database systems both to concretize their schema and to establish relational calculus as a grammar of composition that links labour, primary accumulation, mechanisms of power and the materialities of organic and non-organic forms of life.

2 Universality

Universality in computation is established at the conceptual level of the machine. In the 1930s the computer science pioneer Alan Turing famously developed a thought experiment that put the mental activity of computing in mechanical and finite terms in order to imagine a universal device (subsequently known as the Universal Turing Machine or UTM) that would be able to replicate the behaviour of any other Turing Machine. Anything mechanically computable could and would be computed by such a universal device, as it would be capable of processing any algorithm fed into it.[11] The UTM is the basis of the 'von Neumann architecture' for stored-program computers,[12] and thus the foundation of present-day computing devices, which are in fact general-purpose and can be programmed to emulate each other. Such functional generality is perhaps the most basic, yet crucial conceptual premise of modern computational endeavours. Moreover, the amplification of functional operations also underpins the possibility of understanding computation as a technique of abstraction that is already geared towards universality. Computation generates and disseminates abstractions that are general and inclusive. In its renegotiation of structures of existence, computation aims to encompass and produce the universality of formal methods of systematization and of all-purpose models of reasoning.

Artists may respond to this universality by attending to the specificity of particular instantiations of computational forms, as in the wave of attention that has been paid to retro-computing platforms and to Game Boy hacks. The artist group Beige (Cory Arcangel, Joe Beuckman, Joe Bonn and Paul B. Davis), for example, looked for constraints in order to address the question of universality and thereby reveal universality's nature by noting its particular, historical concrescence in styles of design, the development of genres of game and so on.[13] In their work, computing was always filtered through the quirks and constraints of a particular system with all its clunkiness and idiosyncracy. *Super Abstract Brothers*, for instance, replaced the sprites and landscape of a Nintendo Entertainment System cartridge game with blocks of colour.[14] Alternatively, the nature of claiming universality itself may be a foundational point of exploration for certain artists, such as David Rokeby,[15] whose multifarious and rigorous works probe and ally with the various ways in which algorithms and other procedural and interpretative acts of computers shape and condense as spaces and behaviours. One example amongst many is *N-Cha(n)t*,[16] where a circle of computers run generic speech-recognition and speech-to-text programs. The machines hear and interpret each other, responding with further speech. The resulting cycling mixture of interpretation and response also implicitly offers the capacity for people to loop themselves into the feedback cycles of chuntering vocalizations and tangential interpretations in which machine intuition, logic and chance are intriguingly interwoven.

3   Discreteness

Something is defined as discrete if it is disjointed, separated, distinct, detached or discontinuous. Discreteness is arguably the hallmark of the digital. Digital systems by definition are discrete systems: they represent, store and transfer information in terms of discontinuous elements or values (binary digits, for example). The computational, as we have explained, is not synonymous with the digital: the digital should be understood as an automation of the computational. Computation itself, however, is also marked by discreteness. As a rule-governed activity, computation arranges calculation procedures through the sequential succession of countable and separable states. The 'valid reasoning' that computational mechanisms are meant to encapsulate and model is explicated via the manipulation of quantifiable entities into a finite sequence of well-defined steps. The time and memory that such a sequence employs in order to perform the computation are also finite; so too are the input that set it in motion and the outcome that it generates.

The discreteness of computation is often at odds with the continuity of interactions proposed by affective philosophies, system theories and cognitive phenomenologies, which – in art, culture and science – focus on the dynamic becoming of relations and connections. Discreteness also prompts questions about the recognition one is willing to give to computational entities, on the one side, and computational processes, on the other, and invites further investigation as to

141

whether a theoretical and technical reconciliation between the two is possible.

The discreteness of a computational object may also be used for comedic effect, as in the game Surgeon Simulator,[17] where a patient, body parts, surgical tools, transplant organs and the paraphernalia of an operating theatre are all to be worked on by interacting with a first-person shooter (FPS)-style interface. The game is a device-based Grand Guignol that reaches the level of slapstick in the clashing, clumsy interactions of the handled objects' levels of discreteness.

Discreteness also allows for the re-composition of things and their fixture in new positions, thereby generating both new kinds of commodity forms and new commonalities. This potential is illustrated in its violation by Yuri Pattison's 'e ink pearl memory',[18] in which discreteness is employed as a means of disrupting the transcendental role of the commodity. Here, amongst other forms and arrangements of informational matter, such as a small spill of photocopier toner, treated Kindle eBook readers are modified to display fixed abstract images; that is to say, they are 'broken', becoming finite, discrete. Conversely, the discreteness of digital material such as software or music also allows for an establishment of its sharing or commonality in certain ways. This aim is a prominent aspect of numerous computational initiatives, but becomes most obvious in free software, and in file-sharing ventures such as the Pirate Bay, a project itself sometimes manifesting explicitly as art through the Piratbyrån (Bureau of Piracy).[19] As different levels of discreteness, alongside the ability to copy wholes or parts, combine with computing resources such as memory or bandwidth, discreteness also plays a part in the development of expressive styles and modes of computing at multiple scales, including the determination of degrees of granularity in the resolution of images.

The ability to keep things separate is by necessity a key factor of the ethico-aesthetic dimensions of computational technologies' political nature,[20] determining what they reveal or make tractable, as well as what they hide. The regimes of what links, what can be analysed, what pools together and what remains apart are core to the nature of such systems.

4 Axiomatics

Computation is axiomatic. The modes of abstraction, universality and discreteness already discussed are key features of the axiomatic character of computational systems, and of the many parallels between computation and logico-mathematical reasoning. Via this axiomatic character, these parallels distinguish past and present conceptions of digital computing machines.

As is well known, Alan Turing established the notion of computability after discovering a particular class of numbers that cannot be computed.[21] Turing demonstrated, however, that what is computable can be determined algorithmically; that is, through a mechanized principle of deductive inference, 'with every tiny step of reasoning in place'.[22] What had been an informal notion of computation was hence formalized into the axiomatic parameters of the logico-mathematical comprehension of correct inference. In this sense, to compute became to manage discrete quantities, and to do so by following abstract and finite inferential rules with universal applicability.

Today the axiomatic nature of computing subsists in and thrives on its many formalisms. The axiomatic method is central to symbolic notation and procedural execution: for every calculating process, whether a basic operation or a more convoluted function, the computational system engages, and then reiteratively re-engages, with the general problem of determining consequences from a handful of validly symbolized premises. It is because of the unavoidability of axiomatics in computation that digital art and theory alike cannot leave the formalizations of computation to the computer scientist's classroom. Instead, digital art and theory need to take up the challenge of thinking and creating an aesthetics of computation that takes into account, if it does not limit itself to, the inferential and rule-based character of computational systems, while remaining aware of the ways in which computation borrows methods from mathematics and logics.

5 Numbers

Computation holds a multifaceted and profound relationship to numbers. Of course, contemporary computers are 'metamedia'[23] capable of accomplishing much more than merely 'crunching' numbers. However, the computing machine's relation to the numerical remains intimate. This is due partly to computation's discrete and quantitative nature, and partly to the fact that a computing machine has to operate within the parameters of a calculation.

The very idea of number has continuously changed over time, stretching and convoluting to encompass new categories and attributes, and has become something different again in its encounter with the medium specificity of computation: a means of establishing relations among abstractive methods, formal systems and concrete tasks that are governed in turn by the operation of numbers. Although this recursion to some degree existed before in techniques such as calculus, it is fundamentally different in computation in terms of the quantity and density of operations. Numbers in computation show various qualities and behaviours. As a unit of measurement, numbers are used, for instance, to portion pixels, megahertz and registers in memory. As a mathematical entity, numbers are the objects of the many types of counting that computers carry out: counting of amounts, of sequential steps, of variables, of inputs, of time and so on. As an incommensurable quantity, numbers approximate the risk of infinite loops within recursive functions. As a digital representation, numbers mirror electronic binary states in binary digits. As a symbol, numbers are elements of codes and scripts, and cement the possibility of encryption, while also being means of organizing, prioritizing and enacting such qualities and behaviours.

6   Limits

Computation is limited, in a quite fundamental way. Its limitations are inherent in the axiomatic nature of computational systems. In mathematical logic there are undecidable propositions; in computability theory there exist problems that cannot be solved via purely mechanical procedures. The formal notion of computation itself is founded upon the discovery that some programs will not halt and some functions will not be calculated. Some things just cannot be computed.

The existence of limits in computation is unsettling but also empowering. Amongst the most troubling consequences of these limitations is the comprehension that while computing machines do indeed process many tasks, they do not process just anything. Techno-cultural agendas proposing an all-embracing and all-solving computational rationality are thus faulty at their very outset. Errors, bugs and glitches might be more or less probable, depending on the specific case. Yet they are always logically possible, as is a formalist misapprehension of a situation or a condition.[24] One of the most interestingly enabling outcomes of the limits of computation, however, results from turning this internal failure into the very method through which computation operates. Limitations, just as with the previously discussed principle of universality, are established at the conceptual level of the computing machine: they are intrinsic to the axiomatic character of computational formalization. Given the necessary provisions, the formal deductions of computational systems nevertheless have been turned into systems of unprecedented instrumental power. To the cultural theorist, the philosopher and the artist, such mismatches and ambiguities surrounding promises of delivery and potentials for machine breakdown or misrecognition offer an equally finely textured occasion for speculation, and are also one of the qualities of computation gamed in the exercise of power.

7 Speeds

Art stages different relations to time: for instance, in the way a dance slows, speeds, accentuates, draws attention to the minuscule or raises it to the level of the cosmic. A relation to, modulation and creation of time and timings characterize a work and articulate its mode of being in the world. Computational aesthetics enters into relation with such articulation by intervening in time in certain ways.

The intensity of computational speed is characteristically emphasized as being core to its novelty and to its world-making capacities. When the audience is supposed to pay attention to a rapidly unfolding complex process in the film *The Matrix* (1999), for instance, the scene is rendered to film in great slowness, as if to suggest that, in order to yield something comprehensible to the human sensorium, what passes in less than a moment in computational terms must necessarily be drawn out over minutes. Computational speed is thus about experiential intensity as much as it is about strict measure; yet it is also about the mobile threshold of the capacities of computing itself to structure its own modes of existence. The speed of calculation of a computer was, from the very outset, in monstrous disproportion to the capacities of humans, just as machine weaving had been to the movements of earlier generations of hand-weavers. This scale of disproportion is fluid, and forms a complex set of texturing of expression that manifests in anything from interaction times in musical instrumentation to media-archaeological concerns regarding speed of execution or bandwidth in the conservation of aesthetic objects.

This issue connects to a subsequent characteristic of speed within computational aesthetics: its constructivist nature. As a consequence of the UTM, the timing of many kinds of processes can be brought about within the machine. Computing has no inherent 'native' speed but provides means of staking out and arranging relations to speeds. While intensification of speed is one mode in which computational expression is staged, extension of a work over time is also a significant tendency, especially in works such as Jem Finer's *Longplayer* (2000–)[25] and Gustav Metzger's proposed *Five Screens with Computer* (1965),[26] where the unfolding of a work is arrayed in relation to monumental time. Finer's project, sited in London's Trinity Buoy

Wharf at the time of writing, assembles a system for making a non-repeating piece of music play for a period of exactly one thousand years. Metzger's plan was to erect a run of five 30-by-40-foot panels of stainless steel 25 feet apart. Each panel would be 2 feet deep and constructed from 10,000 picture elements of plastic, glass or steel, each of which would be ejected over a period of ten years, eventually resulting in the annulment of the work.

8 Scale

Scale effects are core to the development of computing in the present era. By scale effects we mean the ways in which a specific kind of structure or process can be instantiated both across a relatively small number of instances and for a tendentially infinite quantity of them. Systems designed to navigate and conjoin multiple scales, such as the golden mean or Corbusier's Modulor,[27] exist within numerous aesthetic forms as a means of arranging elements or of making and assisting a judgement about these forms' efficacy or beauty. Computing, however, allows for these systems of judgement and composition to be integrated into the technology in which these systems themselves are realized.

In systems such as the world wide web, limitations of scale due to material considerations tend towards the negligible, resulting in the use of the term 'scale-free' to describe the web's patterns of network growth. The specific qualities of the scale-free nature of such a system contrast with other aspects of computational aesthetics. This is due to the quality of universality of systems such as finite state machines, which have a very small scale that can exist alongside systems of larger scales. Most notably, however, there may be transitions across the scales. A multitude of small-scale finite state machines, for instance, can be conjoined in order to generate a system of great complexity that can be described as scale-free. Computational aesthetics, then, includes, as a core constituent, the movement in and out of scalar reference. Concomitantly, the tendency towards a scale-free aesthetics in certain works operating on the basis of these networks can be observed and is to be expected in the future.

The scale-free nature of certain computing forms is coupled in dynamic ways with currents such as globalization, which was explored in early internet art by Shu Lea Cheang in Net Nomad projects such as *Buy One Get One*.[28] Artists such as Ai Weiwei have used this condition in creating a global constituency for their work, in a period in which the artist – perhaps due to the demise of the reputation of figures such as the politician and banker – also becomes a potential candidate for the role of 'moral hero'. Other artists, such as The Yes Men, Übermorgen or Paolo Cirio have used the unstable conditions implied by these scale-free networks and globalization as a departure point for exploring sociotechnical expressions of networked forms as they mesh with various political and institutional configurations. [29] Paolo Cirio's loophole4all.com,[30] for instance, is a website and service that allows users to select the names of tax avoidance entities nominally framed as companies or trusts legally located in the Cayman Isles. Once these entities are selected, since they need to keep their status shady, the project suggests that their names and tax-free status can be used for invoicing by citizens, thus ensuring the same fiscal opportunities to a wider range of users.

The question of scale is also linked to the development of platforms for cultural expression, since the potentially scale-free nature of a project in technical respects aligns with the capacities of expression of specific social and cultural forces and the individual histories embedded in them. The development of platforms such as the video analysis and combination site Pad.ma (2008–)by a coalition of groups based in Mumbai, the early picture-sharing platform Nine(9) (2003) or the text discussion site aaaaarg.org,[31] in their combinations of invention and specificity and their amalgamation with other groups, histories and resources, exemplifies such a condition.

9 Logical equivalence

In earlier discussions of digital media much attention was paid to the question of whether a particular experience or thing qualified as 'real' or as 'virtual'. Recognizing the medium specificity and the constructivism inherent in computational aesthetics suggests that it might be more fruitful to pay attention to the discussion of forms of logical equivalence.

A system can be said to be logically equivalent to another if it yields the same behaviours and functions, independent of each system's underlying material structure. Logical equivalence is a quality that is foundational to computing as a thought experiment, arising out of the need to equate computing activity with the mental processes of a person. Alan Turing describes the procedure of making a calculation as a series of mental processes and note-making, abstracting the procedure to a formally describable set of steps that can then be instantiated in a machine.[32] The result is an axiomatic procedure that can be universally applied to any computable problem (the a priori limits of the axiomatic procedure itself, however, remain intractable). Simulation is one effect of establishing logical equivalence between systems. An entity or process may be ordered in such a way that it is rendered more or less behaviourally identical to that which it models. At the same time, there may be play within the kinds of equivalence that are operative. At a certain scale, for example, a system may display logical equivalence to another, yet be composed of substantially different materials. There may also be interplay with the subjective experience of each different instantiation of a logically equivalent event or performance. The musicological concept of interpretation may be pertinent here. The translation of behaviours and entities from other contexts into computational ones implies an evaluation of what constitutes meaningful forms of equivalence and thereby the intensification of aesthetic, along with ethical, judgements. The interplay of these conditions has proven to be very fertile ground for exploration for many artists.

In his ongoing *Status Project*,[33] for instance, Heath Bunting sets out to establish a logically equivalent description for the process of attaining membership of various kinds of social formations (such as nation states or video libraries). Being a certain age, having an address, having a name, being able to produce and refer to other specific documents: by following certain set and delimited procedures, one may acquire a position that can be computed as verifiable within a logically describable system of veridiction, a statement that is true according to the worldview of a particular system.

The condition of logical equivalence has also driven much work in the field of bio art, where the reduction of the characteristics of DNA to its base pairs TCAG (T = thymine; C = cytosine; A = adenine; G = guanine) allows for the re-articulation and the handling of the amino acids that they signify and partially render tractable. In the project *The Xenotext*, the poet Christian Bök exploited this context to encode a short poem in a bacterium that would in turn produce readable protein, via the use of Bök's interpretative system, the Chemical Alphabet, as further fragments of poetry.[34]

10 Memory
Within computing, the fact that both data and the instructions that act upon that data are stored as data has significant consequences. Not the least of these is that, since a computational machine can be completely copied with great ease under the conditions of logical equivalence, the conditions for an effective digital commons can be produced. The fact that both a computer and the data that runs on it

(including the operative and executable data software) can be copied creates interesting situations in politics and economics, situations that also have consequences for art and contribute to the social and economic force of computing at large.

Memory also introduces other conditions and forms of computational aesthetics: possibilities both for all actions and interactions to be logged in order to be restaged or analysed, and, within different configurations, for the (partial or full) reversibility or irreversibility of an action. Moreover, memory presents conditions of delay and storage, so that an event may unfold in computational time at a different moment. Related to the question of speed, time – as it manifests in the interrelation between processing and storage and in the interaction between the computational system and a subject, such as a musician, dancer or gameplayer – becomes a crucial factor in the developments of the aesthetic modality of both specific systems and computational systems as a whole.

Memory, understood as the extent of the capacity to process data, also has significant effects for digital art. These effects are readily observable in 8-bit aesthetics,[35] where constrained data architectures are adopted or simulated for the pleasures of their nostalgic and simplified forms. However, they can also be seen in the use of any constrained computing system – that is to say, any at all. We can also argue that memory is exemplified in an interplay between learning and the relentless lack of it in computing. Kryštof Kintera's human-scaled robot *Revolution* (2005)[36] beats its hooded head endlessly, over and over, against a wall. This is not a generative error, as a glitch would be, but a machinic ability to repeat without recourse to reflection.

If – Then

At this point any reader will probably have added some other aspects of computational aesthetics to this list. Our aim is not to be complete here. Indeed, part of the question of the aesthetics of contemporary digital media, particularly as they are developed by artists, is to advance and proliferate frameworks for recognizing further modes of existence for the computational. The task of doing so is a collective one, and cannot be reduced to a schematic list of qualities, or to a set of conditions imported into art directly from an understanding of different forms of computer science. Once again, we would like to stress that computational aesthetics, and the immanent investigation

149

of it, reside in the computational event. Computing and its aesthetics are no longer 'owned' by the disciplines and fields that grew up closely in and around it. The computational mundanity of everyday objects and processes, as well as the more explicitly critical and speculative modes of computational forms, may be interrogated by means of the characteristics that we have discussed here. At the same time, the nature of the computational may be changed altogether by bringing more conditions and forms of existence into its purview. All of this together, along with the very flexibility of computational reality, means that these considerations can only ever be a provisional and partial mapping. There is much to invent and to be dazzled by, much texture to be found. One might also discover a strange, dull, as yet unnameable familiarity in certain repetitions and compulsions that may indeed travel unremarked from art installations to office work and social forms. To go beyond such a list means to engage in a preliminary process of recognizing and operating the aesthetic dimensions of computation. As critical experimental work moves more substantially in this direction, the force and method of computation may become more open to understanding, discovery and invention.

NOTES

1   Clement Greenberg, *Art and Culture*, Beacon Press, New York, 1961.
2   Matthew Fuller (ed.), *Software Studies: A Lexicon*, MIT Press, Cambridge, MA, 2008.
3   For instance, Bernard Stiegler argues that the irreducible ambivalence of technological rationality is altering all forms of knowledge, and thus 'we must learn to think and to live differently' ('*Die Aufklärung* in the Age of Philosophical Engineering', *Computational Culture*, 2 (2012), http://computationalculture. net/comment/die-aufklarungin-the-age-of-philosophical -engineering).
4   Gilles Deleuze and Félix Guattari, *A Thousand Plateaus: Capitalism and Schizophrenia*, trans. Brian Massumi, Continuum, London, 2004, p. 7.
5   Humberto Maturana and Francisco Varela, *The Tree of Knowledge: The Biological Roots of Human Understanding*, Shambhala, Boston, 1992.

6 Although such conditions of internality and externality may also be part of, or indeed be imperative in, aspects of the computational method (as with the specific forms of modular architectures, object-oriented environments, the limited modes of abstraction layers such as interfaces, and so on).

7 The history of art is, in some respects, that of an interplay between the abstract and the concrete, as they are understood and made manifest by different means over time. In a sense, we live at a moment in which the abstract itself, as a force and a method, is understood to be of highly diverse character. The modes of abstraction in art, having generated a history of significant range, now also manifest this proliferation, the consciousness of which in turn has its own effects.

8 Graham Harwood with Mongrel, *Lungs (Slave Labour)*, 2005, http://www.mongrel.org.uk/lungszkm.

9 Graham Harwood, *London.pl*, 2004, http://www.mongrel.org.uk/londonpl.

10 YoHa, with Jean Demars, *Coal Fired Computers*, 2006, http://yoha.co.uk/cfc.

11 Alan Turing, 'On Computable Numbers, with an Application to the *Entscheidungsproblem*' (1936), in Turing, *The Essential Turing*, ed. B. Jack Copeland, Clarendon Press, Oxford, 2004.

12 Martin Davis, *Engines of Logic: Mathematicians and the Origin of the Computer*. W. W. Norton, New York, 2000.

13 Beige, http://www.post-data.org/beige.

14 Beige, *Super Abstract Brothers*, 2000, http://post-data.org/beige/abstract.html.

15 David Rokeby, http://www.davidrokeby.com.

16 David Rokeby, *N-Cha(n)t*, 2001, http://www.davidrokeby.com/nchant.html.

17 Bossa Studios, *Surgeon Simulator*, 2013, http://www.surgeon-simulator2013.com.

18 Yuri Pattinson, 'e ink pearl memory', in Tom Clark, Rozsa Farkas and Harry Burke (eds.), *Arcadia Missa Open Office Anthology*, Mute, London, 2013, pp. 58–61.

19 Piratebyrån, http://piratbyran.org.

20 Here we are referring to the 'ethico-aesthetic paradigm' of Guattari, who draws the expression from Mikhail Bakhtin, and uses it to denote the way in which collective subjectivity can, through the techniques and practices epitomized in (but not limited to) art, constitute and project itself towards alterity and

heterogeneity. For Guattari, aesthetics has ethical and political implications, in so far as 'to speak of creation is to speak of the responsibility of the creative instance with regard to the thing created, inflection of the state of things, bifurcation beyond pre-established schemas, once again taking into account the fate of alterity in its extreme modalities' (Félix Guattari, *Chaosmosis: An Ethico-Aesthetic Paradigm*, trans. Paul Bains and Julian Pefanis, Power Institute, Sydney, 1995, p. 107).

21 Turing, 'On Computable Numbers'.
22 Gregory Chaitin, *Metamath: The Search for Omega*, Peter N. Nevraumont Books, New York, 2005, p. 30.
23 Lev Manovich, *Software Takes Command*, Bloomsbury, London, 2013.
24 This narrow or voluminous gap is, for instance, that occupied by the discussions of so-called ethicists in their prevarications on the operation of automated warfare, such as that carried out by drones.
25 Jem Finer, *Longplayer*, 2000–, http://longplayer.org.
26 See Simon Ford, 'Technological Kindergarten', *Mute*, 1:26, 4 July 2003.
27 Le Corbusier's 1954 Modulor is a scale of proportions that was based on the golden ratio and developed on the model of the human body. Le Corbusier, *The Modulor: A Harmonious Measure to the Human Scale Universally Applicable to Architecture and Mechanics*, Birkhauser, Basle and Boston, 2004.
28 Shu Lea Cheang, *Buy One Get One*, 1997, http://www.ntticc.or.jp/en/archive/works/buy-one-get-one.
29 Yes Men, http://www.yesmen.org; Übermorgen, http://www.ubermorgen.com; Paolo Cirio, http://www.paolocirio.net.
30 Paolo Cirio, *Loophole for All*, 2013, http://loophole4all.com.
31 Pad.ma, 2008–, http://pad.ma; Mongrel, *Nine(9)*, 2003, http://www.mongrel.org.uk/nine; aaaarg.org, http://aaaaarg.fail.
32 Turing, 'On Computable Numbers'.
33 Heath Bunting, *The Status Project*, 2005–, http://status.irational.org.
34 Bök, *Xenotext*.
35 Olga Goriunova, *Art Platforms and Cultural Production on the Internet*, Routledge, London, 2012.
36 Jana Horáková, 'The Robot as Mitate: The Media Specific Aesthetic Analysis', in *Device_Art*, Kontejner, Zagreb, 2012.

REFERENCES

aaaarg.org, http://aaaaarg.fail
Beige, http://www.post-data.org/beige
Beige, *Super Abstract Brothers*, 2000, http://post-data.org/beige/abstract.html
Christian Bök, *The Xenotext*, 2011, http://www.poetryfoundation.org/harriet/2011/04
Bossa Studios, *Surgeon Simulator*, 2013, http://www.surgeonsimulator2013.com
Heath Bunting, *The Status Project*, 2005–, http://status.irational.org
Gregory Chaitin, *Metamath: The Search for Omega*, Peter N. Nevraumont Books, New York, 2005.
Shu Lea Cheang, *Buy One Get One*, 1997, http://www.ntticc.or.jp/en/archive/works/buy-one-get-one
Paolo Cirio, http://www.paolocirio.net
Paolo Cirio, *Loophole for All*, 2013, http://loophole4all.com
Martin Davis, *Engines of Logic: Mathematicians and the Origin of the Computer*, W. W. Norton, New York, 2000.
Gilles Deleuze and Félix Guattari, *A Thousand Plateaus: Capitalism and Schizophrenia*, trans. Brian Massumi, Continuum, London, 2004.
Jem Finer, *Longplayer*, 2000–, http://longplayer.org
Simon Ford, 'Technological Kindergarten', *Mute*, 1:26 (4 July 2003).
Matthew Fuller (ed.), *Software Studies: A Lexicon*, MIT Press, Cambridge, MA, 2008.
Olga Goriunova, *Art Platforms and Cultural Production on the Internet*, Routledge, London, 2012.
Clement Greenberg, *Art and Culture*, Beacon Press, New York, 1961.
Félix Guattari, *Chaosmosis: An Ethico-Aesthetic Paradigm*, trans. Paul Bains and Julian Pefanis, Power Institute, Sydney, 1995.
Graham Harwood, *London.pl*, 2004, http://www.mongrel.org.uk/londonpl
Graham Harwood with Mongrel, *Lungs (Slave Labour)*, 2005, http://www.mongrel.org.uk/lungszkm
Jana Horáková, 'The Robot as Mitate: The Media Specific Aesthetic Analysis', in *Device_Art*, Kontejner, Zagreb, 2012.
Le Corbusier, *The Modulor: A Harmonious Measure to the Human Scale Universally Applicable to Architecture and Mechanics*, Birkhauser, Basle and Boston, 2004.
Lev Manovich, *Software Takes Command*, Bloomsbury, London, 2013.
Humberto Maturana and Francisco Varela, *The Tree of Knowledge: The Biological Roots of Human Understanding*, Shambhala, Boston, 1992.
Mongrel, *Nine(9)*, 2003, http://www.mongrel.org.uk/nine
Pad.ma, 2008–, http://www.pad.ma
Yuri Pattinson, 'e ink pearl memory', in Tom Clark, Rozsa Farkas and Harry Burke (eds.), *Arcadia Missa Open Office Anthology*, Mute, London, 2013.

153

Piratebyrån, http://piratbyran.org
David Rokeby, http://www.davidrokeby.com
David Rokeby, *N-Cha(n)t*, 2001, http://www.davidrokeby.com/nchant.html
Bernard Stiegler, 'Die Aufklärung in the Age of Philosophical Engineering', *Computational Culture*, 2 (2012), http://computationalculture.net/comment/die-aufklarungin-the-age-of-philosophical-engineering
Alan M. Turing, 'On Computable Numbers, with an Application to the *Entscheidungsproblem*' (1936), in Turing, *The Essential Turing*, ed. B. Jack Copeland, Clarendon Press, Oxford, 2004.
Übermorgen, http://www.ubermorgen.com
Yes Men, http://www.yesmen.org
YoHa, with Jean Demars, *Coal Fired Computers*, 2006, http://yoha.co.uk/cfc

— 8 —

PHRASE

Matthew Fuller and Olga Goriunova

1

Different elements of the world make themselves available to different perspectival operations. In the context of computational and networked digital media, one of these has been the device established in hypertext as the link. As realized in the world wide web, the link mixes the orders of the semantic or linguistic and the logical. A link asserts a relation between things and also makes one happen. Because of its dual position, the link became a crucial means of understanding and ranking websites and their relative importance. Epitomized in algorithms such as PageRank[1] or HITS[2] or in software that mapped the topology of the web by such links,[3] this understanding of the link allowed a further formalization of this entity of dual character, a formalization that in turn created new volatilities, opportunities and problems.

Our concern in this chapter is with a related entity of multiple character that can be called a phrase. Phrases exist as conceptual, technical and experiential entities in domains that are codified in mark-up languages, choreography and linguistics, but which they cannot be boiled down to. They operate as one of a series of micro-to-macro objects, entities in their own terms at a certain scale, but also as mediations of part–whole relations. We see them as articulating a crucial relation between the formal and the subjective, between the logical and the experiential, between the numerical and the gestural. That is, phrases are means of both understanding and experiencing technosocial relations.

In this text we aim to focus on a particular kind of phrase: those that exist in relation to computational systems and their users. Here, phrases are entities that either individually or together participate in technosocial processes. Just as certain software will view a website as a collection of links, certain perspectival operations may see phrases simply as formally defined objects and couplings between them, but they also provide the means for making connections with objects of other kinds, to more elusively formalizable things and behaviours such as conversational ruses or rhetorical manoeuvres, or as with dance they may involve gestures.

Phrases can be largely technical (an algorithm, a comments facility on a website, a filter in a sorting system, a means of gathering votes, an interface element); can be bodily or performative (a gesture, the provision of a mechanism); or can be both (the offering of a microphone at a public meeting, the movement of a player-object-logic-sound in the use of an electronic instrument such as Michel Waisvisz's 'The Hands'[4]); or they can be largely rhetorical or experienced in language. In terms of scale, although we say that networks are composed of phrases (phrases in software), phrases themselves can be rather large-scale or micro-scaled, but they also act momentarily to suture scales together or make them distinct. The development of phrases allows for the possibility of opening up intersubjective processes and the spaces for the articulation and development of new ones. In such a context phrases can also act as tools or vehicles for reflexive, performative, enactive, demonstrative and experimental social research.

2

In dance, a phrase is often understood as a particular discrete sequence of small movements that flows or stutters together to make a whole, nested into or arrayed along with others between pauses: the flowing arch of an arm in relation to the twist of the head; the oscillations of the waist, buttocks, legs, back wineing to a beat coming through a wall of speakers. In sound- and sign-related sciences, a phrase is neither a sentence nor simply composed of words. A sentence or collection of words does not necessarily make up a phrase. A phrase can be a single word, consisting of a single phoneme. Strictly speaking, within linguistics, a phrase is the largest phonetic unity; it is a space in between pauses, a basic component of speech.[5] The defining characteristic of a phrase is intonation, which is itself melody, rhythm and logic, among other qualities. Phrases are performative and mixed with breathing too much to exist in literature.

All that language-specific music and pulmonary excitation cannot get away from sense. Such sense, though, is related directly to the nonsensical, to beauty. A phrase can be a sticking together of words that do not make the same meaning on their own; that is, it is undecomposable; in such a case it can be called an idiom. Everyone, and especially everyone different from everyone else, can make idioms and produce a personal phraseology, so that a phrase is not necessarily a basic universal component. At the same time, a phrase communicates expressively, tastily, individually and illogically in the context of a specific language and requires a device of distance in approaching it in translation. Here, phrases are not bricks to build larger constructions with, and they do not surround us in their nicely ordered, gridded and ranked sextillions. A phrase is a lucky device; it can occur, become fashionable or firm, or can dilapidate. It may last only a moment.

In order to expand on this, it is worth noting a related development. In recent theorizations of new media, particularly those coupled with an interest in the articulations of the literary, attention is often paid to the development of an appropriate unit of analysis that mixes the cultural and technical in discussing the operations of computational fictions, games, playable narratives and other such mechanisms. Noah Wardrip-Fruin describes a series of these as 'Terms for Thinking about Processes' and provides a useful overview of the discursive current in proposing his own useful addition to the series, 'operational logics'.[6] Operational logics happen inside the black box of computers, but are also manifest at the interface and in the behaviours of objects. They form a rich processual vocabulary of behaviours that game designers and writers work with. Examples of operational logics from outside of games are edge detection in picture editors, find and replace in word processors, or the movement or generation of onscreen objects or interface sounds via a relation between physical controllers and what is handled by them. Operational logics are means by which we learn how a program works, often by analogy with others, without necessarily reading the manual, but they also contribute a lot to the feel of a computational entity or operation. One of the gains to be made by the development of such terms is in being able to abstract a computational logic without always having to drill down to the level of its specific implementation. Thus, one can speak about software without necessarily analysing code (although this may be essential in some cases) and find a critical vocabulary more adequate to emerging computational cultural forms.

Related to but distinct from this current of work there is also a tendency in new media studies that aims to identify or invent distinct units which can be strapped safely within a taxonomic framework of meaningful units ordered into ranks and sets. Whilst it is not our intention to suggest that such systems are not operative, particularly in computing, such a normative aspiration is one that extends beyond its capacity to describe or work with the ranges of material aimed at, producing a skin, rather than the snake which shed it.

3

Mikhail Bakhtin's *Toward a Philosophy of the Act* is a useful point of triangulation for what we are trying to devise here.[7] This essay establishes a means of understanding the interrelation between the concrete real, or universal, as it is manifest in a particular moment and the individual experience of that moment in historical, subjectival terms. The first of these terms is understood as an abstract scale, that of theory and ideas which move without the necessity of modification from one instantiation to another. The abstract scale of theory, however, is impossible without the other term of experience, the historically actual deed of its actualization. Each of these scales drives and shapes the other. Theory works by its own autonomous laws, forcing consequences by the momentum of its own inner logic, generating theoretical 'subiectum' or consciousness that must be inhabited. Such a logic might perhaps be found in numbers such as those generated as the Fibonacci series or in reckoning Champernowne's number.[8] At the same time, it is impossible to inhabit theory without the contamination and propulsion engendered by the other side of the dualism of cognition and life. Life, which is always too complex for theory, is also what occupies it, drives it.

Bakhtin proposes a quality, answerability, with which to understand the interrelationship of these terms: 'the answerability of the actually performed act is the taking-into-account in it of all the factors – a taking into account of the sense validity as well as of its factual performance in all its concrete historicity and individuality'.[9] At once ethical and aesthetic, answerability is one of the means by which Bakhtin's work connects to that of those, such as Félix Guattari, who later took it up, and related it to the machinic volition of functional assemblages of partially incommensurable materials.[10] Early on in the text Bakhtin relates the scale of the concept, that of the theoretical machine, to that of the 'world of technology' which is driven by its own 'immanent laws' and has 'long evaded the cultural task of understanding the cultural purpose of that development'.[11] The world of technology is kin to the abstract scale of the concept, uninhabitable, and here it exhibits a tendency to evil. However, it does not permanently lose an ability to live, be lived in and riven with the lived experiences which in turn drive it. The scale of abstraction, of scientific reason, has its own distinct modality, its own patterns of accession, diminution or growth, but can also open itself to the unity of life.

The world of cognition in this sense is distinct from Plato's idea of the essences; it does not need to be discovered, but to be invented. This theoretical world is composed of archipelagos of more or less pure abstraction and reasoning, all of which are alien, provocative, thrilling and incompatible with the historically situated, lively beings who can think through, make real and therefore complexify this unin-habitable, arid world and make it meet the unity of the real, making it juicy, turning it into something else. Phrases are points at which Bakhtin's world of technology commingles without merging with that of emotional and subjective volition, with historical and fleshy experience, to produce identifiable moments of transition between the two, producing new elements which themselves cohere to produce the technosocial and at the same time break up the idea of the 'concept without brains', to capture it in their folds.

4

Whilst mathematically based network analysis has shown that complex, large-scale networks, if that is what one is looking for, can be elucidated across many material and social domains, most researchers working in this area agree that a pressing challenge is to find ways of tracing the articulations of such 'line and dot' net-works with more culturally, materially and socially complex forms of understanding.[12] Phrases make useful objects and methods of study in relation to the larger scale of networks because they often provide a point of indistinction between the technical and the social (and the human). Equally, as phrases, they are in themselves distinct entities. This means that they are, partially, alienable from their context, but not too readily.

Phrases test the degree to which social dynamics in the context of applications and social networking platforms undergo formalizations of relation between people, ideas, objects and processes. They are also a means of entering triggering and sensing into the grammars and diagrams through which such technosocial dynamics can be built, felt, understood and changed.

Michel Serres asks whether we can 'conceive of an intersubjective origin for simple machines'.[13] We wonder how they emerge when one or more of those entities has already gone over such a threshold. Do phrases, as simple machines that cross from the human to non-human and back, emerge as a result of interactions between people, or do they also function as attractors for certain kinds of processes of subjectivation? How do they frame and induce certain kinds of action, imaginary and agency, and how do such things also overflow them?[14] In an era when relatively crude social networking technologies aim to diagrammatize and interpellate the social, and in turn ask to be gamed and manipulated, this is a crucial question to ask of software development.[15]

Phrases emerge from sociotechnical devices, in the contexts of computer-mediated communications and in offline but partly computational events. Phrases participate in building media ecologies, connecting the gestural to the logical, the procedural to the bodily, the formal to the informal, skills to structures. Phrases are what work well in the performance of the world, but they can also be used to understand it. A couple of examples may serve to clarify what we mean to indicate.

The IBM Votomatic voting machines, which became notorious during the Floridian phase of the 2000 election of President George W. Bush, exhibited what might be called a certain expressivity in operation. The punchcard-based voting machines gave considerable variation to the way in which a hole was punched in the voting card to indicate the choice of candidate. The so-called 'hanging chads' were scraps of card that should have been punched out by the machines, but which were left attached, rendering the card nominally unreadable. This machinic gesture was carried out each time as a phrase, sloppily, deftly, drawing on the kind of humanization of error supposedly removed by the use of machines. In this case, the phrase is certainly largely technical, but carries a concatenation of relations to other kinds of judgement, action and behaviour.[16] Rather than being a singular unit of action corresponding to an affirmation, the act produced a generalized, perhaps targeted, doubt.

The People Speak is a company of artists, programmers, designers and other people that develop events for 'social decision making'.[17] They mix formats adapted from TV chat and quiz shows with other kinds of structures in order to produce readily understandable and

160

hopefully thus inclusive kinds of public forums. We have mentioned that moving a microphone might constitute a certain kind of phrase. One of their projects, Talkaoke, is 'a mobile talkshow' where 'what we're going to talk about is up to you'.[18] The people who come and sit round the portable, neon-lit circular table with a charismatic, motormouth host in the middle are those who direct the conversation. The host simply and skilfully picks up the pace, provides a bit of tempo to its fast, multiform improvisation. One of the key acts in this is the movement of the mic. The phrase that starts someone's time to speak may include bending the arm at the elbow, proffering the mic, making eye contact, uttering some words. It is a phrase that says start, say something, seduce, shock, open your mouth; it impels one to think, or to show that one is not thinking, to take part in the game or get out. Its phrasing can be aggressive, quizzical, eager, but it connects the user and interlocutor into a circuit of speech, into video (shown on nearby screens), into the circulation of statements, jokes, questions, thoughts and phrases made by others, and offers amplification.

5

A phrase is both steady and not-already-there, but the genesis and usage of phrases are core to the operation of computational networks as they increasingly entangle the social. Phrases make meaning but escape full description; they are something that happens that makes something happen; just as cards may be shuffled violently, elegantly, with flair or clumsiness, data is sorted with greater or lesser concern for time and resources. Depending on the algorithm chosen, such a sorting process moves one entity about in different ways in relation to others that are not simply equivalent to the fixed execution of instructions, but imply something akin to a dance, where the parts move according to a pattern, but one which is modified according to the characteristics of those elements being sorted as they in turn change the speed and order in which they are sorted. The phrasing of Bubblesort, a slow sorting algorithm,[19] is tellingly idiosyncratic. The sorting process starts at the beginning of a dataset, swapping neighbouring entities backwards and forwards according to whether they are attributed a smaller or greater value (commonly numeric or alphabetic), returning to the beginning of the dataset once each pass has been made, until no swaps are necessary. The permutational movement of such algorithms, the data they come into composition with, the multiple systems they are embedded in are themselves expressive; that is, they exude phrases.

A phrase, then, is not simply a cyborg event, mixing the technical and bodily, formal and fleshy, into one entity of priorly parcelled human and non-human which even when fused implies a dualism. In its technosocial manifestation a phrase may encompass such parts, or more, but is also special in its unity, in its force and performance at multiple and tangential scales, and irreducible to any of them. Experimental art practices, such as live-coding or the durational ensemble performances of Shu Lea Cheang and Martin Howse, establish themselves in part as effective collision sites for the generation of unprecedented phrases experienced and endured by all sorts of entity.[20]

Phrases can be mundane, functional or brilliant, but they are not all units of the same order; in our proposition for the phrase as a device, we think only in as much as we ask questions. How does a phrase assemble itself to become a real unity of an order and ensemble that are not predetermined? What does it yield to say that the participative drive of its elements mingles together with the technological and conceptual to be experiential? Taking part in the world of mixed matters, a phrase appears as an aesthetic as much as an ethical consideration. Aesthetics implies life and the generation of experiences, the fundamental scale at which phrases are registered and a crucial way to understand what makes a phrase a phrase – a scale that also, like those of the architectonics of relations established in rationally ordered conditions and of the experiential or participatory, induces the need for an ethics.

The phrase acts, to come back to Bakhtin, in the space where we do not know how to exist, where we are not, and where, nevertheless, we are. Can we study such phrases, technical, computational, emotional, formal, social, at the point of our existence, and not in the abstract aftermath? What capacities would be required to think, interact and act in terms of phrases where we are, and is such a domain somewhere theory can go?

A phrase emerges at a moment of encounter as a force and a formulation that makes a work, an object, real. As a phrase traverses scales, every time along a new vector, making an ensemble come into existence, it becomes key to experiencing and understanding the genesis of the reality in question. The fabric of a phrase, however, cannot be limited simply to its multiplicity. Drawing together combinations of codes, forces, statements and energies without the experiential and participative scales that a phrase takes can assist in rather rich interpretative acts, orderings and games but does not necessarily engender an insight.

Equally, it is not necessary that such an approach only has 'intuition' to rely on, leaving the material to speak to us in articulating its own phrases. Such a constitutive suppleness, however, itself implies that, in the search for ways to make sense of digital material and in allowing for the technical and networked to appear, we do not invent a kind of re-calcified structuralism where all elements are readily searched for and synthesized along the lines of something akin to laws or look-up tables.

Tuning in to the scale, texture and experiential nature of a phrase therefore implies an approach allowing a tenderly close reading, a way of working with things that are materially rich but not cumbersomely materialized, a proximity that requires the taking of a distance sufficient to allow for the phrase to form and give itself over without turning itself in.

NOTES

1 Sergei Brin and Larry Page, 'The Anatomy of a Large-Scale Hypertextual Web Search Engine', *Computer Networks and ISDN Systems*, 30:1–7 (April 1998), pp. 107–17. See also Amy N. Langville and Carl D. Meyer, *Google's PageRank and Beyond: The Science of Search Engine Rankings*, Princeton University Press, Princeton, 2006.

2 The HITS (Hyperlink Induced Topic Search) algorithm is a forerunner of Google's well-known PageRank that sorts pages according to their relative status as 'hubs' (links from) and 'authorities' (linked to). See John M. Kleinberg, 'Authoritative Sources in a Hyperlinked Environment', *Journal of the ACM*, 46:5 (1999), pp. 604–32.

3 See I/O/D, *I/O/D 4: The Web Stalker*, http://bak.spc.org/iod, and Martin Dodge's *Cybergeography* research page, http://personal-pages.manchester.ac.uk/staff/m.dodge/cybergeography.

4 Michel Waisvis, *The Hands*, http://www.crackle.org/TheHands.htm.

5 Roman Jakobson famously worked on speech sounds and sound systems of languages; see Roman Jakobson, *Selected Writing. Vol. 1: Phonological Studies*, ed. S. Rudy, Mouton, The Hague and Paris, 1971. See also L. Zinder, *Obschaja Fonetika* [*General Phonetics*], Vysshaja shkola, Moscow, 1979; A. Reformatskii,

Vvedenie v Jazykovedenie [*Introduction to Linguistics*], Aspect Press, Moscow, 2000.

6   Noah Wardrip-Fruin, *Expressive Processing: Digital Fictions, Computer Games and Software Studies*, MIT Press, Cambridge, MA, 2009.

7   Mikhail M. Bakhtin, *Toward a Philosophy of the Act*, trans. Vadim Lupianov, ed. Vadim Lupianov and Michael Holquist, University of Texas Press, Austin, 1993.

8   Champernowne's number was established in 1933 by David G. Champernowne and consists of a decimal fraction in which the decimal integers are concatenated as one number, in increasing order, one term after another: 0.12345678910111213. See David G. Champernowne, 'The Construction of Decimals Normal in the Scale of Ten', *Journal of the London Mathematical Society*, 8 (1933), pp. 254–60.

9   Mikhail Bakhtin, *Art and Answerability: Early Philosophical Essays*, trans. Vadim Liapunov, ed. Michael Holquist and Vadim Liapunov, University of Texas Press, Austin, 1990, p. 28.

10 Félix Guattari, *Chaosmosis: An Ethicoaesthetic Paradigm*, trans Paul Bains and Julian Pefanis, Power Institute, Sydney, 1995; Maurizio Lazzarato, 'Bakhtin's Theory of the Utterance', trans. Arianne Bove, *Generation Online*, http://www.generation-online.org/p/fp_lazzarato6.htm.

11 Bakhtin, *Philosophy of the Act*, p. 7.

12 See, e.g., the 'Outlooks' chapter in, M. Newman, A. Barabasi and D. J. Watts, *The Structure and Dynamics of Networks*, Princeton University Press, Princeton, 2006.

13 Michel Serres, *The Parasite*, trans. Lawrence R. Scher, University of Minnesota Press, Minneapolis, 2007.

14 Florian Cramer, 'Buffer Overflows', in W. Sützl and G. Cox (eds.), *DATA Browser 4. Creating Insecurity: Art and Culture in the Age of Security*, Autonomedia, New York, 2009, pp. 45–51.

15 The critical analysis of software systems, in software studies and elsewhere, is one place to turn for the development of such work. Social networking sites are designed to probe, extract, invent and analyse modes of interaction, a situation in which such sites also develop both pre-emptive designs, anticipating use, and post-facto designs, arising out of the non-standard usage of their resources and mechanisms by users. Since we are no longer in the phase of invention of such software but in that of its infrastructural and strategic normalization, an understanding of the

networks of phrases meshing the interpersonal and the formalized needs also to recognize the profound degree of serialization and repetition involved, despite, and occasionally because of, the ways in which it may still be lively.

16 The electronic voting machines which largely replaced the card-based ones in some cases were hardly less open to doubt; see Ariel J. Feldman, J. Alex Halderman and Edward W. Felten, *Security Analysis of the Diebold AccuVote-TS Voting Machine*, Center for Information Technology Policy, Princeton University, 13 September 2006.

17 The People Speak, http://www.theps.net.

18 Talkaoke, http://talkaoke.com.

19 Owen Astrachan, 'Bubble Sort: An Archaeological Algorithmic Analysis', in *Proceedings of ACM SIGCSE '03*, ACM, New York, 2003. For a clear visualization of the working of common generic sorting algorithms, see D. R. Martin, http://www.sorting-algorithms.com.

20 For live-coding, see the site maintained by a loose alliance of live-coders, TOPLAP, http://www.toplap.org. For the documentation of an event by Cheang and Howse, see Shu Lea Cheang, Martin Howse et al., *Moving Forest*, Berlin 2008 and London 2011, http://www.movingforest.net.

REFERENCES

Owen Astrachan, 'Bubble Sort: An Archaeological Algorithmic Analysis', in *Proceedings of ACM SIGCSE '03*, ACM, New York, 2003.

Mikhail Bakhtin, *Art and Answerability: Early Philosophical Essays*, trans. Vadim Liapunov, ed. Michael Holquist and Vadim Liapunov, University of Texas Press, Austin, 1990.

Mikhail M. Bakhtin, *Toward a Philosophy of the Act*, trans. Vadim Lupianov, ed. Vadim Lupianov and Michael Holquist, University of Texas Press, Austin, 1993.

Sergei Brin and Larry Page, 'The Anatomy of a Large-Scale Hypertextual Web Search Engine', *Computer Networks and ISDN Systems*, 30: 1–7 (April 1998), pp. 107–17.

David G. Champernowne, 'The Construction of Decimals Normal in the Scale of Ten.' *Journal of the London Mathematical Society*, 8 (1933), pp. 254–60.

Shu Lea Cheang, Martin Howse et al., *Moving Forest*, Berlin 2008 and London 2011, http://www.movingforest.net

Florian Cramer, 'Buffer Overflows', in W. Sützl and G. Cox (eds,), *DATA Browser 4. Creating Insecurity: Art and Culture in the Age of Security*, Autonomedia, New York, 2009.

Martin Dodge, *Cybergeography*, http://personalpages.manchester.ac.uk/staff/m.dodge/cybergeography

Ariel J. Feldman, J. Alex Halderman and Edward W. Felten, *Security Analysis of the Diebold AccuVote-TS Voting Machine*, Center for Information Technology Policy, Princeton University, 13 September 2006.

Félix Guattari, *Chaosmosis: An Ethicoaesthetic Paradigm*, trans. Paul Bains and Julian Pefanis, Power Institute, Sydney, 1995.

I/O/D, *I/O/D 4: The Web Stalker*, http://bak.spc.org/iod

Roman Jakobson, *Selected Writing. Vol. 1: Phonological Studies*, ed. S. Rudy, Mouton, The Hague and Paris, 1971.

Jon M. Kleinberg, 'Authoritative Sources in a Hyperlinked Environment', *Journal of the ACM*, 46:5 (1999), pp. 604–32.

Amy N. Langville and Carl D. Meyer, *Google's PageRank and Beyond: The Science of Search Engine Rankings*, Princeton University Press, Princeton, 2006.

Maurizio Lazzarato, 'Bakhtin's Theory of the Utterance', trans. Arianne Bove, *Generation Online*, http://www.generation-online.org/p/fp_lazzarato6.htm

D. R. Martin, *Sorting Algorithms*, http://www.sorting-algorithms.com

M. Newman, A. Barabasi and D. J. Watts, *The Structure and Dynamics of Networks*, Princeton University Press, Princeton, 2006.

A. Reformatskii, *Vvedenie v Jazykovedenie [Introduction to Linguistics]*, Aspect Press, Moscow, 2000.

Michel Serres, *The Parasite*, trans. Lawrence R. Scher, University of Minnesota Press, Minneapolis, 2007.

Talkaoke, http://talkaoke.com

The People Speak, http://www.theps.net

TOPLAP, http://www.toplap.org

Michel Waisvis, *The Hands*, http://www.crackle.org/TheHands.htm

Noah Wardrip-Fruin, *Expressive Processing: Digital Fictions, Computer Games and Software Studies*, MIT Press, Cambridge, MA, 2009.

L. Zinder, *Obschaja Fonetika [General Phonetics]*, Vysshaja shkola, Moscow, 1979.

— 9 —

FERAL COMPUTING: FROM UBIQUITOUS CALCULATION TO WILD INTERACTIONS

Matthew Fuller and Sónia Matos

In 'The Coming Age of Calm Technology', Mark Weiser and John Seely Brown are clear in their assertions that what really 'matters' about technology is not technology in itself, but rather its capacity to continuously recreate our relationship with the world at large.[1] Even though they promote such an idea under the banner of 'calm technology', what is central to their thesis is the mutational capacities brought into the world by the spillage of computation out from its customary boxes. What Weiser and Brown's work tends to occlude is that in setting the sinking of technology almost imperceptibly, but deeply, into the 'everyday' as a target for ubiquitous computing, other possibilities are masked; for instance, those of greater hackability or interrogability of such technologies. Our contention is that making ubicomp (ubiquitous computing) 'seamless'[2] tends to obfuscate the potential of computation in its reworking of computational subjects, including societies, modes of life, and interrelations with the dynamics of thought and the composition of experience and understanding.

Even though we recognize the bifurcation of 'calm' technology into new feral logics, ubicomp's development – through techniques of identification, naming, tracking, sorting, monitoring and responding – has been precipitated, if not always inspired, by a research agenda inherited from military programmes inaugurated during the Second World War and after.[3] This same 'military' heritage continues to define much of the research agendas of significant academic and industrial institutions, directly influencing their epistemological orientations. Doing 'calm' requires, then, an overemphasis on the machine, keeping the deployed human component stable and unexcited and focusing essentially on the development of frameworks that in turn calmly interpret and act on the calmed user. Such an approach

167

can be seen to operate in opposition to a deeper understanding of human–computer symbiosis, one that may even step out of this dyad to engage with a wider understanding of systems and ecologies. What is crucial to recognize here is that this agenda, infatuated with an ontological positivism simple enough to teach a machine, establishes distinct conceptions of ubiquity that ramify into computational technology, human action and cognition and the environments in which these occur. As it stands, many of the problems experienced by ubiquitous computing as a progressive research programme can be found in the reliance on such an ontology and its apparently stable concatenations of misidentification and mismatched response, delimiting the potential of new logics into simplified models of calculation.

Despite its partial 'military' heritage, ubiquity is effectively bifurcating from this calculative approach, challenging much of the practice of computer programming and other layers of the ordering of computers, now diversified by networks, embedded systems, new graphical user interfaces, the world wide web and wireless devices, networks of sensor-actuators, and the multiform variations introduced to computing by its deep embedding in the social, technical, biological, aesthetic and political dimensions of life. This renewed context has, particularly within the field of computer science, shifted from a view of 'computation as calculation' to one of 'computation as interaction',[4] deviating from the core of its first-order programming philosophy, from computation as 'number crunching' to an object-based and distributed approach.[5] The growth of computation into a new, feral state has also affected the ways in which user relations within artefactual ecologies can be understood, extending previous research frames. Here, the emphasis on the ideal of 'computation as calculation' has not only affected the field of computer science, but also influenced the field of cognitive science[6] and those concerned with computation as metaphor, instrument, field or infrastructure.

Once again, ubiquitous computing and its propensity for distribution as part of environments, opening new space for variable kinds of users and contexts, has shifted the idea of cognition as analogous to the workings of computational devices to an idea of cognition as situated, embedded and distributed. This idea has much in common with what Heinz von Foerster and others named 'second-order cybernetics'.[7] Indeed, amongst other contexts, this field has a lasting influence, or even undergoes a revival in contemporary computational design laboratories, as for instance in the development of robotics.[8] One of the main goals of second-order cybernetics was the attempt to study complex systems, including humans and machines, under a new light, attending in particular to the way in which they formed patterns of reflexivity, gained a recursive sense of self and of the wider processes which that self co-composed. Crucially, they also emphasized the study of systems that are analytically indecomposable, such as memory, or which grow as part of a 'conversation' or other form of structural coupling,[9] making the distinction between subject and object, observer and the observed, simply a neat, but disabling, perceptual gimmick.

One of the founders of the cybernetics movement, Norbert Wiener, posed the need to interlink the new worlds of 'automata' with distinct social interests and concerns, where the decentralization of authority should accompany the decentralization of computation.[10] This project would soon be obfuscated by scientists such as John von Neumann, whose vision of their use tended to relegate computational power exclusively to the interests of the military and industrial establishments. This limitation was inaugurated at the same time cybernetics disengaged from domains – unfortunately – characterized as 'humanist', finally closing the computer into itself.[11] As a consequence, the inherited 'military' agenda has contributed to the divide between cultural approaches to technology and the means for a technical imaginary on the one hand and those that characterize themselves as 'scientific' on the other. Today, an expansion of the scope of interdisciplinary approaches within the distinct domains that study human–computer interaction and computing cultures more widely are moving towards a potential reversal of this 'trend'. Here, ubiquitous computing has played a decisive role. Its propensity for distribution throughout the environment has opened space for a new range of contexts, users and artefacts, raising new, complex questions that extend beyond the premise of perfecting artificial intelligence. What once was the concern of an engineering-driven discipline is now delivered to a wider field of intelligences and skills beyond any discipline.

Interaction: The Extension of Computation beyond Calculation

Both the fact and ideation of ubiquitous computing and its characteristic embeddedness have driven the need for an exploration of new human–computer relations, shifting the research motto from, in one description, 'proactive computing' to 'proactive people'.[12] The shift arises not only from a new conception of human–machine symbiosis – of the sort originally theorized and supported by Lick-lider,[13] towards mutual proactivity – but also from a challenge from within the field of computer science itself. Essentially, this shift has been accompanied by a transformation of the understanding of what computation is and how it might be done, dislodging from a model where computation is seen as a series of fixed functions that are out-lined to achieve a certain specified goal. Computation as something 'centralized, sequential and result-oriented', and primarily focused on the execution of calculation, moves tentatively or eagerly, but perhaps inexorably, towards an understanding of 'computation as interaction'.[14] Here, dynamic relations become key. A computation does not simply equal the achievement of a result, measured by an ever-increasing metric of acceleration towards that result, but tends towards a collaboration with the user or other elements in a wider ecology, understood through a connective multiplication of the capac-ities of each entity in the computational composition.

Where the 'calculative' approach has persisted in the disavowal of computational artefacts beyond their formal description as varia-tions upon calculus, it has also tended to make difficult or to prevent the recognition of any external influence or of the multi-layeredness of computational situations. Concerning the embeddedness of com-putational gadgets throughout the environment, it has particularly influenced the ways in which certain dogmatic computational frames have pushed forward 'result-oriented' rather than 'process-oriented' programming styles.[15] Such imperatives have often dissuaded engaged professionals from elaborating any form of 'computer criticism' that could provide a richer frame for understanding computational arte-facts and their contexts.[16] At the core of such reluctance sits the bulk of our conceptions concerning the practice of programming, ideas that are embedded in strong cultural formations of thought and rationality. An example that throws light on both epistemological styles and their consequences for computation, the Logo program-ming environment for children – a pioneering project of its kind – was built upon the recognition that many computational environments, for the purpose of education, still preserve canonical dogmas, such as the fixation on outcome or result achieved by predetermined means. On the contrary, the Logo environment has shown that many children favour a style that contradicts the formal canonical one identified with planning and reasoning, opting for a more 'intuitive' mode. Both are conceptually valid.[17] The example of Logo is problematic in the sense of its limited domain of actual use, but the way in which it opened the possibility for different programming idioms to come to fruition and to be recognized as being idiomatic, with different perspectival weightings and affordances, is significant. Today, different programming methodologies, scripting environments and frameworks, and the increasing sense of coding and computation as part of popular cultures and interesting subcultures, open computation to a multiplication of conceptual and idiomatic registers.[18]

In fact, such conceptions of programming based on ratiocination have a long history in the development of the computational field itself and find their philosophical origin in a historic battle between rationalists and empiricists, from Descartes' figuration of reasoning as the base of existence, followed by Kant's denial of the contingency of true knowledge, to those contemporarily who, in their most useful formulations, find the rational folded into and entangled with the aleatory, intuitive and experiential in ways that defy the capacities of expectation of either model. Still, much of modern Western science has been influenced by rationalist mathematical modes of thought, and even more intensified by the successes of technological development, faith in the dependency of such rationality, and a corresponding ability to recognize a world which is increasingly reformatted into its own image.

The history of Western thought, however, is also a history of successive collapses of total formalizations.[19] Kurt Gödel's 'incompleteness theorem' that exposed the fissiparous faultiness of rationalism when turned upon itself is only an example, but a crucial one in the history of computing. The thesis opened the way for a new epistemological agenda where the idea of incompleteness would prevail, a decisive element in bringing the paradigm of interaction centre stage for the development of computing. Alan Turing famously took up Gödel's theorem and in 1936 published a paper 'On Computable Numbers, with an Application to the *Entscheidungsproblem*', showing that mathematics could not be completely modelled by computers. However, whilst they acknowledged the foundation of the Turing Machine in the tracing of limits to computability, computer scientists at large adopted it, providing a seductive model with which to address problems. Computer science took the transformation of 'inputs into outputs' as a defining characteristic of computation, a transformative process already known to the mathematical field and best described by formal algorithmic operations.[20]

Approaching the 1990s, computer science faced new challenges. With a new logic of ubiquity, from the world wide web to wireless devices, phones and other more cranky assemblages, new questions appeared. Logical-axiomatic transformations (as understood through

171

the 'inputs into outputs' of the Turing Machine) as the sole answer to computational problems – those problems to which computing was addressed and distinct, therefore, from 'computable' ones – would no longer suffice. By that time, many already felt the need to extend computation into new paradigms, as the novelty of machinic formations evolving out into diverse ecological conjunctions allowed the exploration of, for instance, physical effects rather than solely logical ones. Today, one result of this drive is the development of interactive-identity machines, simple transducers characterized by non-algorithmic behaviour that use the computing power available in the surrounding environment, replacing mathematical reasoning with empirical development.[21] Here, the new interactive paradigm appeared the most attractive, since it not only best explicated possible relations with 'real' environments that could not be completely pre-determined by a list of configured inputs, but also provided the best extension for the already achieved capabilities of the Turing Machine. The twist was that the 'incompleteness' now supplied by the interact-ing environment is a feature that is not under the machine's control or not integral to its axiomatic nature, but generated out of its points of (intensive and extensive) conjunctions with the world.

Engaging in a constant switching back and forth between the figure and ground of computation in the machine, and in the potential for computability within the environment, the new interactive ecolo-gies could not rely on formal computable algorithms. There was an increasing demand for the development of new dynamical models to new interactive algorithms,[22] extending to computation beyond calculation. Most importantly, interactive computing allowed the necessary resistance to the canonical style, rejecting computer sci-ence's military legacy, finally leaving space for a new epistemological orientation. Of course, it is not that suddenly a computer becomes something more than a technically describable object; rather, the computer was turned inside out, with its processes and affiliations routing themselves through non-computable processes producing new *moiré* patterns of resonance, interaction, and interference.

The Interactive Paradigm: A Cybernetic Revival

We can also trace the origins of interactive approaches to the Macy conferences held between 1946 and 1953 in New York, when a group of researchers met with the goal of discussing 'Circular Causal and Feedback Mechanisms in Biological and Social Systems'. Here, the term 'cybernetics' was taken on, following the title of mathematician Norbert Wiener's book on control and communication.[23] Two of the interdisciplinary researchers present – Wiener and neurophysiologist Warren McCulloch – inaugurated what later became characterized as the 'first-order' cybernetic movement. The research motto was the idea that the dynamic entities which maintain certain kinds of consistency over time, such as the human nervous system, can be characterized by internal feedback processes that maintain constant stability.

Part of the research agenda of cybernetics was an emphasis on interdisciplinary applicability through the creation of meta-categorical concepts, such as feedback, that crossed both living and non-living entities. Cybernetic approaches, based on powerful degrees of abstraction, were later applied to the development of new kinds of artificial intelligence, now retrospectively framed by a connectionist approach that emphasized structures of simpler but interconnected neural units instead of intelligence deriving from one main central processor.[24] This bottom-up approach was applied to both machinic computation and human cognition. Aspects of this approach are paralleled by what is often recalled as second-order cybernetics, epitomized in, but not limited to, the work of physicist and philosopher Heinz von Foerster and participants in the Biological Computing Lab at the University of Illinois. Whilst second-order cybernetics is characterized by finding ways in which feedback loops travel outside of the boundaries of an entity, affecting its behaviour in reflexive and non-determinable ways, von Foerster introduced the idea of subjective dynamic construction into the complex web of feedback loops within a given system. This abstract framework relocates the position of the observer or agent of a given system into its dynamics. If for first-order cybernetics the agent was decoupled, with second-order cybernetics this would no longer be possible. Such a position re-describes, with a different scale of reference, the relevance of situating computational artefacts as 'external scaffoldings',[25] where agent and environment are no longer fully separated but mutually articulating.

In more recent times, there has been a growing interest in using von Foerster's ideas in the field of robotics. Key factors have been the importance of environmental situatedness and non-representational embodiment as the driving forces in the development of intelligent behaviour. Additionally, second-order cybernetics opened the door for what later would be called a 'dynamic systems theory of cognition' and the 'enactive theory of perception'.[26] For both, cognition is a highly interactive process where agent and environment have important and active roles. Building on, but also questioning, earlier theories of environmental perception, such as those of James J. Gibson,[27] which are well known in design, a dynamic systems theory of cognition recognizes the importance not only of the relation between an agent and its environment, but also of the 'state-space' that relates such entities and the permutations of actions that compose them. 'Enactive perception' recognizes the role of embodiment in the process of cognition; the agent only perceives to the extent its perceptual system enables. For both approaches, cognitive processes are determined by agent–environment coupling dynamics.[28] Reality is no longer an established edifice; rather it is subject – but not reducible – to an individual's interpretation. In the case of research performed within ubiquitous computing and its dependence on artefacts that track, monitor and respond to a set of human activities, the idea of agent-based reality puts in question, once again, the idea of a predetermined computational entity.

The transformation of computation from calculation to interaction is also in direct relation to the development of some of the main ideas developed by von Foerster, Gordon Pask, Gregory Bateson and others associated with second-order cybernetics. Turning intelligence inside out, this model opposed the idea of simple internal representation, proposing instead one of external and distributed pragmatics working with affordances. Such conceptions have in turn influenced computation itself, recomposing the idea of programming as a bottom-up process, a move that returns to influence ideas about intelligence as something being sited in the 'head',[29] tending instead to view it as an emergent quality depending on high levels of interaction. Again, there are strong levels of filiation: the bottom-up model was first developed by cyberneticians such as Wiener, based on corresponding connectionist approaches to cognition. Second-order cybernetics challenged this view, by locating the agent in relation to the same system,[30] further promoting a 'constructivist epistemology' where the observer, perspectively and enactively, constructs her own experience and cognition becomes a continuous dynamic process.

At this point, what is relevant to acknowledge is that a new conceptual approach to the materiality of the world is also devised: firstly, by providing means of recognizing the position of both agent and environment in a complex dynamic ecology, where the extensions or limits of either are not clear cut, or are rendered effectively meaningless; secondly, by providing means of abstraction in which behaviours and patterns that cross categorically distinct entities can be recognized. Finally, it was one form of thinking, based strongly in practice, which opened up to hybrid insights into forms of life, providing a new methodological approach when researching the 'social' and the 'natural',[31] or rather, with equal apprehension of their inadequacy as terms, the 'natural' and the 'artefactual'. Concerning the design of computational artefacts, such an agenda presupposes the relative importance of both user and artefact, now appearing in the light of more tricky, multivalent relations, and it also presupposes that the user is as much responsible for, or at least implicated in – in multiple, non-predictable ways – the construction of their own arte-factual ecology. Such a constructive process calls for an approach that places computation in a new light, re-emphasizing the importance of a research agenda that marks the expansion of computation through distinct layers of interactivity. This entails a transformation, not only for computer science itself, but also in the conception of new computational artefacts and environments.

The implication of the user in the expanded computational environment is, however, not a story of simply unfolding opportunity. The history of cybernetics is one both of systems of control and of a mode of understanding and synthesizing systems of recursive self-organization. A society of extended interaction is certainly being put in place; the computer has spread out into the world; computation is enfolding itself into all layers of life; but in many cases this is as systems of control. Writing from an island whose society puts more faith in surveillance cameras than in the citizens they watch, we have no reason to welcome the spread, distributed or open arms of control. Instead, we might usefully look towards coupling an understanding of interaction with a critical and inventive politics. As an applied science, cybernetics became in part, like early strains of human-computer interaction, a means of integrating humans with machine systems or those of the poetry of management.[32] In the 1980s, one of the resulting figures, that of the cyborg, became the subject of wry critical celebration, most famously in the work of Donna Haraway.[33] The current wave of re-engagement with cybernetics tends to emphasize not so much its application in systems of control as its empirical work amongst epistemic questions with the production of experimental devices.[34]

From Cybernetics to Interactive Designs

Such epistemic questions have instigated the need to understand interactive technologies in their actual use, blurring the modern divide of the 'social, symbolic and subjective from the material, real, objec-

175

tive and factual',[35] avoiding any absolute bifurcation of interaction between users and artefacts and the relations between them. This has been the true contribution of the field of participatory design, one that opened the field of computation, finally setting up the interactive paradigm to reach out into the 'situated, interpretive and messy' aspects of human nature.[36] Forms of participatory design have long questioned modernity's formalism and rationality, as grown in the research edifices of the Second World War and beyond; participatory design has questioned computer science's simply formal approach and the rational structuring of cognition by incorporating user and environment, cultural, economical and political contexts. In this sense, participatory design makes possible, if it does not always deliver, a 'third and hybrid space'[37] between users and artefacts, inaugurating a dialogical plane for action. As in 'distributed cognition',[38] both user and artefact come to play determining roles in the mix of effects and interactions with the explicit recognition of the processes of thought in relation to design. For designers at large this is of substantial relevance, since new forms of computation are bound up with the encouragement of new forms of sustainability, development and experimentation. Such considerations are especially potent when we consider the contexts in which users and technologies are embedded, and the variable kinds of access different users have today to the panoply of computational artefacts, processes and services.[39]

In this same context, it seems pertinent to attempt to consider innovation. Here, the ideal still ostensibly driving most technological research agendas is dictated not so much by innovations any more, but instead by uses or even misuses.[40] For this same reason, participatory design philosophy and methods have been taken on by some companies and in the development of user-centred approaches to innovation.[41] Its principles have been applied, in different interpretations, in a number of ways and sites ranging from the development of industrial artefacts to that of software. However, these are not without their problems. Improvements that only travel inwards to a company will soon make users rightly cynical. The world of marketing is not innocent of simulating 'demand' in order to generate it, and interaction will inevitably face many kinds of shaping by interested parties and social and libidinal forces.[42] Nevertheless, distributed innovation as it articulates the reflexive extension of interaction is a potent feral force that proliferates on the outskirts of policies and regulations, amongst distinct communities of users/designers, and is also brought to the core of others. This same shift has provided a new distributed conception of innovation and knowledge, with a significant move to test and extend the ways in which development methodologies and principles derived from free software might produce effects in other domains of production and use, such as non-executable data. For reasons such as this, we use the term 'interactive designer' as much as 'interaction designer'.

As a counterattack to this, many new approaches to the development of regulations and copyright policies have tended to imprison the same users by relegating full control to corporations or owners of intellectual property. These regulations, and sometimes the closure of designed objects, tend to retard innovation by limiting the scales and kinds of access to technological and cultural artefacts and processes. The rise of new computational technologies tends, however, to set this back, essentially by providing information and innovation opportunities to communities that may extend beyond traditional geographical or economic constraints. The affordability, often at the cost of abusive forms of production, of computational gadgets and the ease with which people start to manipulate them, and thus perhaps break out of the role of simple user, is opening some space for a new era of technological innovators. Indeed, several researchers have suggested that a democratic approach to technological design might have a tendency towards increasing opportunities, or instigating new forms of economic development.[43] Approaches to ubiquitous computing that develop significant modes of interaction will necessarily also meet with the question of the way in which data of all kinds moves about, whether it is shared, sold, wrapped in protective seals, or treated as simply part of the wider ecology of materials.

Feral Computation and Design

It now seems pertinent to ask: what might design facilitate or enter into combination with in this process? Can design catalyse a process of material reshaping, further influencing those already described? First, we need to extend this same venture and consider relations between designer, the artefact, and systems it engages with that now might appear in a planned or unplanned manner. This is perhaps even more relevant when seeking feral qualities in the hardware domain. Here, the recent and widespread increase in interest in tinkering, making idiosyncratic technical objects, and the extension of this into a renewed, perhaps quasi-popular engagement with electronics, through platforms such as Arduino (see http://www.arduino.cc/) and others, provides a means of recognizing and working with a quite palpable hunger for a more difficult, unpredictable, customizable and intelligent interrelationship with electronic design more commonly used on the level of prototyping. Such moves provide interesting options not only for design curricula but also for those engaged in design beyond formal education, as useful information and experiences move in ways that build self-organizing practices, thus, in turn, establishing possibilities for a new generation of designers, and more broadly of designing practices. By such means, as machinic platforms, knowledge and skills, coupled with modes of thinking that provoke ubiquitous curiosity rather than calmness, certain principles of hackability are extended to a wider range of users, who in turn modify them. We can only envisage potential future uses when bits and pieces become more robust, or usefully weak enough to make interesting connections, and are globally widespread, opening paths for new modes of commodity distribution, hackability and self-production. Here, design is involved in a more complex web of experimental devising, moving beyond the provision of simplified solutions, engaging in the construction of a system that continuously reshapes the questions that were initially waiting to be answered.

The qualities of ferality can also be found in applications such as Squirrel. Designed by Shannon Spanhake of the California Institute for Telecommunications and Information Technology, this small device incorporates a battery, sensor chip, Bluetooth and its accompanying software Acorn. The device allows users to monitor and read levels of carbon monoxide in the air through their mobile phones.[44] Pollution monitoring, once only in the hands of small public and private groups of specialized research enterprises, is now opened up to users with the potential for hacking the politically enclosed debate. In a similar vein, Mexican artist-engineer Gilberto Esparza González shows us the possibility of designing parasitical robotic artefacts, simple life forms that feed on power generated by human societies. The parasites clgd (colgado) and dblt (diablito) live suspended on telephone cables and re-circulate their energy while interacting with the surrounding environment through the emission of unusual sounds. The ppndr-s, a redaction of the name *pepenadores*, are small robot parasites that live amongst accumulated remainders disposed of by humans, carrying out simple tasks such as removing, scattering and sweeping.[45] These artefacts live out of surpluses and engender a sense of the uncanny in urban situations; they are feral robots that couple with rickety media ecologies and the leakages and disarray of cities. Thinking of new forms of relation between natural processes and those that are deeply synthetic in a way that can open them up

178

to wider understanding, or at least more tractable difficulty, Haque Design & Research (www.haque.co.uk) presents Natural Fuse, an eco-physical network that employs the capacities within the environment, such as plant carbon-sinking, to create a recursive system where energy can only be derived from electricity networks if sufficient plant matter is present in the circuit to absorb the carbon produced by the energy used. In all these examples, hackability is taken into a new, speculative dimension. Hackability itself becomes feral and pertains no longer solely to the material and infrastructural domain, in which it is measured by the relative technical openness of a system, but also to a performative one, in turn proposing new user modes for appropriating and experimenting with a wider sphere of interests. Finally, acquiring alternative sets of dimensions, scales and sizes of intervention, these examples call upon us to reinvent what the city is and what the 'proper' way of allocating energy might be, and circulate the capacity to know in new ways, demanding in turn new kinds of agency.

Rather tending to contradict mainstream perspectives on the sites of technological innovation, this call has been heard from economically impoverished countries, where salvaged machines imported from the West, or sourced direct from fabrication in the East, have, due to material scarcity, been incorporated into a tradition of maintenance and redesign. By transforming technologies in their own terms, users come to generate a body of knowledge unforeseeable by the original designer. The story of Morris Mbetsa, a self-taught inventor from Mombasa, seems pertinent. Mbetsa invented Block & Track, an anti-theft device and vehicle tracking system based on mobile phone technology. The device uses a combination of voice, dual-tone multi-frequency (DTMF) signalling and short message service (SMS) text messaging technology to control a vehicle's electrical system, providing the user with the ability to activate or disable the ignition in real time.[46] Such ingenuity, in 'developing' countries, is not simply a means for survival but a crucial resource for educational, economical and cultural development, which shapes its own conditions of emergence.

Interaction, Society and New Distributed Systems

To shift to another scale, such reflections become even more relevant if we consider the pace at which computational artefacts have become simply accepted objects for many children, making ubiquitous or distributed forms of computing everyday experiences in ways that

179

test their stability. New forms of computational literacy suggest that the relation of users not only to technology, but also to knowledge production itself, will change in unforeseeable ways. Not disinterestedly, perhaps, Microsoft is amongst those keen to argue that developing forms of knowledge will increasingly require more and new forms of computational literacy,[47] for which new forms of critical and inventive intelligence will need to arise. There is a fundamental and pressing need for the design of research tools that might enable or constrain new forms of experimentation and knowledge production. Even though, for Microsoft's vision of the future, computational literacy will imply primarily mathematical thinking, it seems rather probable that computational literacy will also imply a form of concurrent thinking that is able to couple recognition and understanding of formal processes with their other experiential scales and dimensions.[48] Computation, in the light of such an interactive conception, will of course have implications for education, challenging it with the evidence of new modes of experimentation. Here, materials will need to be modular and flexible, in order to elicit a constructive approach to both content and knowledge development. Finally, interactivity will imply novel forms of enquiry, by providing programmable and flexible tools that encourage ingenuity and reflexivity.

To achieve these goals, much has to be done, specifically when reflecting on the question of the implementation of information technology in school curricula. Whereas much effort has been directed towards the distribution of computers amongst pupils and ensuring fast connections to the world wide web, little has been discovered concerning the actual forms in which information technology might develop and enhance useful learning models.[49] We once more return to 'feral' understandings of computation, cognition and design, and it seems that the same kinds of thinking might usefully be applied to education. The sphere of knowledge production, and therefore also partially, perhaps rather too partially, of education, is relevant to the question of interactive design in the expanded sense. Education's involvement in the production of knowledge practices and of intellectual, organizational and spatial subjectivation has accompanied, if implicitly, much of the debate concerning the understanding of computation (specifically, artificial intelligence and its figuration of the position and kinds of intelligence) and the studies of cognition sketched earlier in this chapter. Add to this the commonplace that there is nothing more political than education, and the models we choose in the development of knowledge will have implications for the development of design and of societies.

Now, if the capacities for thought are distributed between people, artefacts and the ecologies they are in, make and wreck, the question of learning becomes a crucial one in the imagination of what is computable as much as what is thinkable. The consideration of education and knowledge in society suggests that ubiquitous intelligence already forms an uneven and fissiparous challenge to the simple proliferation of ubiquitous computing on all levels of life, and will itself demand or instigate new social and organizational approaches. The interactive approach, in becoming feral, articulates not only computation but modes of social organization and learning, and alternative modes of collective innovation. Here, we recall a cybernetic approach to systems development:

> one of the key ideas the general theory embodies is the principle of recursion. This says that all viable systems contain viable systems and are contained within viable systems. Then if we have a model of any viable system, it must be recursive. That is to say, at whatever level of aggregation we start, then the whole model is rewritten in each element of the original model, and so on indefinitely.[50]

This would mean that a feral approach to technological development would entail less formalized approaches to society at large. It would at one scale perhaps imply the formation of cybernetically reflexive collectives, a recursive public composed of modular but ungridded elements, where distinct modes of subjectivation, technicality and organization cooperate in the devising of their own infrastructural logics.[51] Finally, design and cybernetics might find a common path: design with its emphasis on 'participatory' approaches, and cybernetics in its consideration for the development of complex systems where the system cannot be separated from acts of observation and involvement.

For designers, considering such a principle of recursion means accepting a major responsibility in the development of systems, and also the responsibility of constantly reflecting back into their own sphere of activity, accepting and testing the task of actually designing design, and in so doing accepting their rather more minor role. Doing so requires an acknowledgement that creations devised by distinct professions might actually slip out, escaping description by initial intentions.[52] This implies a deviation from formal and discipline-oriented professional approaches to a more multivalent view, encouraging design to become more than a purely sectional interest in the life of objects, and instead to consider and take part in the political, social and cultural implications of its activity.[53] Such a position imagines an expanded role for design as an activity, but also, conversely, suggests a recognition of the wild expansion of the scope of people, thoughts and things involved in the activity of design and the selection, development, deprecation and implementation of technological systems.

Some Closing Remarks

Throughout the present work we have moved rather too rapidly – but hopefully suggestively – between distinct fields of enquiry, from computation and cybernetics to design, all under the rubric of an interactive paradigm. We have attempted to argue that this paradigm, emerging from computation's unfolding into the world, has prompted conceptual developments leading to new questions and formulations. However, central to our theme is the fact that none of this would have been possible without accounting for the development of new artefactual, technical and ubiquitous realities, where distinct artefacts have gone feral, interweaving with the subjective, social and ecological fabrics of our cities, lives and societies. The idea of ubiquitous computing, and of its characteristic embeddedness and partial containment within diverse, multi-scalar settings of many different kinds, has suggested the exploration of human–computer relations in ways that can no longer be seen as simply calm; they are also partially wild, if they do not drive us so.

By transforming our understanding of what computation is and how it might be done – shifting from a view of computation as centralized, sequential and result-oriented or as calculation towards an understanding of computation as interaction[54] – we are able to alter preconceptions concerning the practice of programming and computing itself. This implies a shift from the view of a science that once took the transformation of inputs into outputs as essential to an emphasis on a process-oriented view of computation that extends beyond prescriptive, algorithmic understanding.[55] Due to its strong link to cognitive science such transformations have found wider implications for computation and beyond. For cognitive science particularly, this has meant the proliferation of new approaches to the study of the human mind. Starting from the premise that the idea of mind itself extends beyond the confinements of head and skull,[56] the importance of the organism's environment can be recognized as crucial in establishing the complexities of any cognitive unit that is considered. The relations

I establish with my surrounding world are as relevant in the study of my cognitive capacities as the workings of my brain. By considering the mind's extension beyond the single body of an organism, such an approach challenges the webs of rationality and formalism that can only be sustained when we consider the intellect as something separate from the world I am constantly immersed in. It does not mean, however, that such boundaries cannot themselves be effective when enforced or entrained by other, wider means. All such boundaries, in themselves, have meaning.

Such conceptual workings that transverse both computing and cognition are more readily understood by revisiting their filiations to a third approach: the works of second-order cybernetics and its study of complex systems, including both humans and machines, and a field of study and practical experiment epitomized by the introduction of the idea of subjective dynamic construction into the complex web of feedback loops within a given system. Such subjective construction cannot be accounted for without considering the characteristic embeddedness of any organism, entity or practice. Ultimately, this has led to the development of the recognition of human–computer relations being highly situated in such a way that their cultural, subjective and political dimensions cannot be ignored.

A proper conceptualization of the message that we have as a welcome hand-me-down from second-order cybernetics might finally open new approaches to the study of human–computer interaction at large. Essentially, it allows us to recognize that this same relation extends beyond the tight formal coupling once devised by behaviourist and formalist approaches to both cognition and computation. By considering the messy and informal aspects ('subjective construction') of human–computer interactions, previous Fordist models of design seem to become obsolete, and the trajectory led in part by the participatory approach sheds new light on the design of alternative ecologies of computation and interaction, where user, artefact and designer play roles that are shiftingly determinant rather than fixed.

If we initiated our discussion by speaking of ubiquity as key instigator of a new interactive paradigm, one that brought novel approaches to computing, cognition and design itself, we have attempted to finish by considering how ubiquity might embody this same feral quality. In this light the feral artefact is one that has been able to escape a domesticated and captive state. It is not a sedative, exuding calmness for an already understood, tracked and pre-empted subject whose needs and requests have been mapped out and whose life as such corresponds to that of a finite state machine. To design for such a feral context is to work with processes of subjectivation that are not simply described by input and output, no matter how far away they are from traditional sites of computation. Instead, such a design works with artefacts, processes, ecologies, people, computation and politics, in a way that is able to explore the multiple potentials of the fields of interaction, calculation, control and cognition. When computing escapes from being unable to recognize itself outside of the formalizable, becomes promiscuous, starts finding itself recomposed in combination with packs of other epistemic currents, it becomes feral. When design recognizes that its expertise is distributed amongst people, institutions, media and infrastructures, and in the dissensus, joy and confusion of contemporary lives and their technological avidity, and starts to find means of generating a rigour in the chaotic, it too starts to lose its domestication. In doing so, recursively, it promises to produce something that renders their complex artefactuality sensible and open – with all kinds of difficulty – to design: to think with things.

NOTES

1 Mark Weiser and John Seely Brown, 'The Coming Age of Calm Technology [1]', 1996, www.ubiq.com/hypertext/weiser/acmfuture2endnote.htm.
2 Ian MacColl, Matthew Chalmers, Yvonne Rogers and Hilary Smith, 'Seamful Ubiquity: Beyond Seamless Integration', *Equator Research* (2002), http://www.equator.ac.uk.
3 Steve J. Heims, *John von Neumann and Norbert Wiener: From Mathematics to the Technologies of Life and Death*, MIT Press, Cambridge, MA, 1980; Philip E. Agre, *Computation and Human Experience*, Cambridge University Press, Cambridge, 1997.
4 Lynn Andrea Stein, 'Challenging the Computational Metaphor: Implications for How We Think', *Cybernetics and Systems*, 30:6 (1999), 473–507, http://cogprints.org/545/5/CCM.pdf; Peter Wegner, 'The Paradigm Shift from Algorithms to Interaction', 1996, http://www.cs.brown.edu/people/pw/papers/ficacm.ps; Michael Murtaugh, 'Interaction', in Matthew Fuller (ed.), *Software Studies: A Lexicon*, MIT Press, Cambridge, MA, 2008.
5 Wegner, 'Paradigm Shift'; Peter Wegner and Dina Goldin, 'Computation Beyond Turing Machines', 2003, http://www.cse.uconn.edu/~dqg/papers/cacm02.rtf.

6   Jean-Pierre Dupuy, *The Mechanization of the Mind: On the Origins of Cognitive Science*, trans. M. B. DeBevoise, Princeton University Press, Princeton, 2000.

7   Heinz von Foerster and Bernhard Poerksen, *Understanding Systems: Conversations on Epistemology and Ethics*, Carl-Auer-Systeme-Verlag und Verlangsbuchhandlung, Heidelberg, 2002.

8   John Mark Bishop and S. J. Nasuto, 'Second Order Cybernetics and Enactive Perception', *Kybernetes*, 34:9/10 (2005), pp. 1309–20.

9   Gordon Pask, *Conversation Theory: Applications in Education and Epistemology*, Elsevier, Amsterdam, 1976; Humberto Maturana and Francisco Varela, *The Tree of Knowledge: The Biological Roots of Human Understanding*, Shambhala, Boston, 1992.

10 Norbert Wiener, *The Human Use of Human Beings*, Eyre and Spottiswoode, London, 1950.

11 Ron Eglash, 'Cultural Cybernetics: The Mutual Construction of People and Machines', 2000, http://www.rpi.edu/~eglash/eglash.htm.

12 Helen Sharp, Yvonne Rogers and Jenny Preece, *Interaction Design: Beyond Human–Computer Interaction*, Wiley, Chichester, 2007.

13 J. C. R. Licklider, 'Man–Computer Symbiosis', *IRE Transactions on Human Factors in Electronics*, March (1960), pp. 4–11.

14 Stein, 'Challenging the Computational Metaphor'.

15 Stein, 'Challenging the Computational Metaphor'.

16 Seymour Papert, 'Computer Criticism vs. Technocentric Thinking', 1990, http://www.papert.org/articles/ComputerCriticismVsTechnocentric.html.

17 Papert, 'Computer Criticism'.

18 Adrian Mackenzie, *Cutting Code: Software and Sociality*, Peter Lang, New York, 2006.

19 Morris Kline, *Mathematics: The Loss of Certainty*, Oxford University Press, Oxford, 1980.

20 Wegner and Goldin, 'Computation Beyond Turing Machines'.

21 Wegner, 'Paradigm Shift'.

22 Adrian Mackenzie, 'Intensive Movement in Wireless Digital Signal Processing: From Calculation to Envelopment', *Environment and Planning A*, 41 (2009), pp. 1294–1308.

23 Norbert Wiener, *Cybernetics: Or Control and Communication in the Animal and the Machine*, MIT Press, Cambridge, MA, 1948; Eglash, 'Cultural Cybernetics'.

24 Bishop and Nasuto, 'Second Order Cybernetics'.
25 Paul E. Griffiths and Karola Stotz, 'How the Mind Grows: A Developmental Perspective on the Biology of Cognition', *Synthese*, 122 (2000), pp. 29–51.
26 Bishop and Nasuto, 'Second Order Cybernetics'.
27 James J. Gibson, 'The Theory of Affordances', in Robert Shaw and John D. Bransford (eds.), *Perceiving, Acting, and Knowing: Toward an Ecological Psychology*, Lawrence Erlbaum, Hillsdale, 1977.
28 Bishop and Nasuto, 'Second Order Cybernetics'.
29 Alva Noë, 'Experience Without the Head', 2004, http://socrates.berkeley.edu/~noe/EWTH.pd.
30 Bishop and Nasuto, 'Second Order Cybernetics'.
31 Eglash, 'Cultural Cybernetics'.
32 Chris Hables Grey, *The Cyborg Handbook*, Routledge, London, 1995; Stafford Beer, *Platform for Change*, Wiley, London, 1975.
33 Donna Haraway, *Simians, Cyborgs and Women: The Reinvention of Nature*, Free Association Books, London, 1991.
34 Brian Holmes, 'Future Map, or How the Cyborgs Learned To Stop Worrying and Love Surveillance', 2007, http://brianholmes.wordpress.com/2007/09/09/future-map; Usman Haque, 'The Architectural Relevance of Gordon Pask', in Lucy Bullivant (ed.), *4dSocial: Interactive Design Environments*, Architectural Design, London, 2007.
35 Bruno Latour, 'A Cautious Prometheus? A Few Steps Toward a Philosophy of Design (with Special Attention to Peter Sloterdijk)', 2008, http://www.bruno-latour.fr/node/69.
36 Phoebe Sengers, Steve Harrison and Deborah Tatar, 'The Three Paradigms of HCI', 2007, http://people.cs.vt.edu/~srh/Downloads/HCIJournalTheThreeParadigmsofHCI.pdf.
37 Michael Muller, 'Participatory Design: The Third Space in HCI', in Julie A. Jacko and Andrew Sears (eds.), *Handbook of HCI*, Lawrence Erlbaum, Mahwah, 2003.
38 James Hollan, Edwin Hutchins and David Kirsh, 'Distributed Cognition: A New Foundation For Human–Computer Interaction Research', 1999, http://citeseerx.ist.psu.edu/viewdoc/summary?doi=10.1.1.33.6906; Edwin Hutchins, 'Distributed Cognition', 2000, http://eclectic.ss.uci.edu/~drwhite/Anthro179a/DistributedCognition.pdf.
39 Michael Crang, Tracey Crosbie and Stephen Graham, 'Variable Geometries of Connection: Urban Digital Divides and the Uses

of Information Technology', *Urban Studies*, 43:13 (2006), pp. 2551–70.

40 Steven Shapin, 'What Else is New? How Uses, Not Innovations, Drive Human Technology', *New Yorker*, 14 May 2007, http://www.newyorker.com/arts/critics/books/2007/05/14/070514crbo_books_shapin.

41 Eric von Hippel, *Democratizing Innovation*, MIT Press, Cambridge, MA, 2005.

42 Jean-François Lyotard, *Libidinal Economy*, trans. Iain Hamilton Grant, Athlone, London, 1993.

43 Von Hippel, *Democratizing Innovation*.

44 Doug Ramsey, 'Tracking Pollution and Social Movement: Love Fest for Calit2 Technologies at "Make Fest 2007"', 2007, http://www.calit2.net/newsroom/article.php?id=1080.

45 Gilberto Esparza González, 'Urban Parasites', 2007, www.parasitosurbanos.com/parasitos/proyecto.html.

46 AfriGadget, '18 Year Old Self-Taught Electronics "Genius" Invents Mobile Phone-Based Vehicle Anti-Theft System', 16 July 2008, www.afrigadget.com.

47 Microsoft Research, *Towards 2020 Science*, 2005, http://research.microsoft.com/en-us/um/cambridge/projects/towards2020science/downloads/t2020s_report.pdf.

48 Stein, 'Challenging'.

49 Peter Gärdenfors and Petter Johansson, 'Introduction to Cognition, and Communication Technology', in Peter Gärdenfors and Petter Johansson (eds.), *Cognition, Education, and Communication Technology*, Lawrence Erlbaum, Mahwah and London, 2005.

50 Stafford Beer, 'Fanfare for Effective Freedom', 1973, http://grace.evergreen.edu/~arunc/texts/cybernetics/Platform/platform.pdf.

51 Christopher M. Kelty, *Two Bits: The Cultural Significance of Free Software*, Duke University Press, Durham, NC, 2008.

52 Matthew Fuller and Usman Haque, *Urban Versioning System v1.0*, Architectural League of New York, New York, 2008.

53 John Wood, 'Metadesign', in John Wood, *Design for Micro-Utopias: Making the Unthinkable Possible*, Routledge, London, 2007.

54 Stein, 'Challenging'.

55 Peter Wegner, 'Computation Beyond Turing Machines', 2003, http://www.cs.brown.edu/~pw.

56 Tim van Gelder, 'What Might Cognition Be, If Not Computation?', *Journal of Philosophy*, 92:7 (1995), pp. 345–81; Andy Clark

and David J. Chalmers, 'The Extended Mind', 1998, http://
consc.net/papers/extended.html.

REFERENCES

AfriGadget, '18 Year Old Self-Taught Electronics "Genius" Invents Mobile
Phone-Based Vehicle Anti-Theft System', 16 July 2008, www.afrigadget.
com

Philip E. Agre, *Computation and Human Experience*, Cambridge University
Press, Cambridge, 1997.

Stafford Beer, 'Fanfare for Effective Freedom', 1973, http://grace.evergreen.
edu/~arunc/texts/cybernetics/Platform/platform.pdf

Stafford Beer, *Platform for Change*, Wiley, London, 1975.

John Mark Bishop and S. J. Nasuto, 'Second Order Cybernetics and Enactive
Perception', *Kybernetes*, 34:9/10 (2005), pp. 1309–20.

Andy Clark and David J. Chalmers, 'The Extended Mind', 1998, http://
consc.net/papers/extended.html

Michael Crang, Tracey Crosbie and Stephen Graham, 'Variable Geometries
of Connection: Urban Digital Divides and the Uses of Information Technology', *Urban Studies*, 43:13 (2006), pp. 2551–70.

Jean-Pierre Dupuy, *The Mechanization of the Mind: On the Origins of
Cognitive Science*, trans. M. B. DeBevoise, Princeton University Press,
Princeton, 2000.

Ron Eglash, 'Cultural Cybernetics: The Mutual Construction of People and
Machines', 2000, http://www.rpi.edu/~eglash/eglash.htm

Heinz von Foerster and Bernhard Poerksen, *Understanding Systems: Con-
versations on Epistemology and Ethics*, Carl-Auer-Systeme-Verlag und
Verlangsbuchhandlung, Heidelberg, 2002.

Matthew Fuller and Usman Haque, *Urban Versioning System v1.0*, Architectural League of New York, New York, 2008.

Peter Gärdenfors and Petter Johansson, 'Introduction to Cognition, and
Communication Technology', in Peter Gärdenfors and Petter Johansson
(eds.), *Cognition, Education, and Communication Technology*, Lawrence
Erlbaum, Mahwah and London, 2005.

Tim van Gelder, 'What Might Cognition Be, If Not Computation?', *Journal
of Philosophy*, 92:7 (1995), pp. 345–81.

James J. Gibson, 'The Theory of Affordances', in Robert Shaw and John D.
Bransford (eds.), *Perceiving, Acting, and Knowing: Toward an Ecological
Psychology*, Lawrence Erlbaum, Hillsdale, 1977.

Gilberto Esparza González, 'Urban Parasites', 2007, www.parasitosurbanos.
com/parasitos/proyecto.html

Paul E. Griffiths and Karola Stotz, 'How the Mind Grows: A Developmental
Perspective on the Biology of Cognition', *Synthese*, 122 (2000), pp.
29–51.

Chris Hables Grey, *The Cyborg Handbook*, Routledge, London, 1995.

Usman Haque, 'The Architectural Relevance of Gordon Pask', in Lucy Bullivant (ed.), *4dSocial: Interactive Design Environments*, Architectural Design, London, 2007.

Donna Haraway, *Simians, Cyborgs and Women: The Reinvention of Nature*, Free Association Books, London, 1991.

Steve J. Heims, *John von Neumann and Norbert Wiener: From Mathematics to the Technologies of Life and Death*, MIT Press, Cambridge, MA, 1980.

Eric von Hippel, *Democratizing Innovation*, MIT Press, Cambridge, MA, 2005.

James Hollan, Edwin Hutchins and David Kirsh, 'Distributed Cognition: A New Foundation For Human–Computer Interaction Research', 1999, http://citeseerx.ist.psu.edu/viewdoc/summary?doi=10.1.1.33.6906

Brian Holmes, 'Future Map, or How the Cyborgs Learned To Stop Worrying and Love Surveillance', 2007, http://brianholmes.wordpress.com/2007/09/09/future-map

Edwin Hutchins, 'Distributed Cognition', 2000, http://eclectic.ss.uci.edu/~drwhite/Anthro179a/DistributedCognition.pdf

Christopher M. Kelty, *Two Bits: The Cultural Significance of Free Software*, Duke University Press, Durham, NC, 2008.

Morris Kline, *Mathematics: The Loss of Certainty*, Oxford University Press, Oxford, 1980.

Bruno Latour, 'A Cautious Prometheus? A Few Steps Toward a Philosophy of Design (with Special Attention to Peter Sloterdijk)', 2008, http://www.bruno-latour.fr/node/69

J. C. R. Licklider, 'Man–Computer Symbiosis', *IRE Transactions on Human Factors in Electronics*, March (1960), pp. 4–11.

Jean-François Lyotard, *Libidinal Economy*, trans. Iain Hamilton Grant, Athlone, London, 1993.

Ian MacColl, Matthew Chalmers, Yvonne Rogers and Hilary Smith, 'Seamful Ubiquity: Beyond Seamless Integration', *Equator Research* (2002), http://www.equator.ac.uk

Adrian Mackenzie, *Cutting Code: Software and Sociality*, Peter Lang, New York, 2006.

Adrian Mackenzie, 'Intensive Movement in Wireless Digital Signal Processing: From Calculation to Envelopment', *Environment and Planning A*, 41 (2009), pp. 1294–1308.

Humberto Maturana and Francisco Varela, *The Tree of Knowledge: The Biological Roots of Human Understanding*, Shambhala, Boston, 1992.

Microsoft Research, *Towards 2020 Science*, 2005, http://research.microsoft.com/en-us/um/cambridge/projects/towards2020science/downloads/t2020s_report.pdf

Michael Muller, 'Participatory Design: The Third Space in HCI', in Julie A. Jacko and Andrew Sears (eds.), *Handbook of HCI*, Lawrence Erlbaum, Mahwah, 2003.

Michael Murtaugh, 'Interaction', in Matthew Fuller (ed.), *Software Studies: A Lexicon*, MIT Press, Cambridge, MA, 2008.

Alva Noë, 'Experience Without the Head', 2004, http://socrates.berkeley.edu/~noe/EWTH.pd

Seymour Papert, 'Computer Criticism vs. Technocentric Thinking', 1990, http://www.papert.org/articles/ComputerCriticismVsTechnocentric.html

Gordon Pask, *Conversation Theory: Applications in Education and Epistemology*, Elsevier, Amsterdam, 1976.

Doug Ramsey, 'Tracking Pollution and Social Movement: Love Fest for Calit2 Technologies at "Make Fest 2007"', 2007, http://www.calit2.net/newsroom/article.php?id=1080

Phoebe Sengers, Steve Harrison and Deborah Tatar, 'The Three Paradigms of HCI', 2007, http://people.cs.vt.edu/~srh/Downloads/HCIJournalThe ThreeParadigmsofHCI.pdf

Steven Shapin, 'What Else is New? How Uses, Not Innovations, Drive Human Technology', *New Yorker*, 14 May 2007, http://www.newyorker.com/arts/critics/books/2007/05/14/070514crbo_books_shapin

Helen Sharp, Yvonne Rogers and Jenny Preece, *Interaction Design: Beyond Human–Computer Interaction*, Wiley, Chichester, 2007.

Lynn Andrea Stein, 'Challenging the Computational Metaphor: Implications for How We Think', *Cybernetics and Systems*, 30:6 (1999), 473–507, http://cogprints.org/545/5/CCM.pdf

Peter Wegner, 'The Paradigm Shift from Algorithms to Interaction', 1996, http://www.cs.brown.edu/people/pw/papers/ficacm.ps

Peter Wegner, 'Computation Beyond Turing Machines', 2003, http://www.cs.brown.edu/~pw

Peter Wegner and Dina Goldin, 'Computation Beyond Turing Machines', 2003, http://www.cse.uconn.edu/~dqg/papers/cacm02.rtf

Mark Weiser and John Seely Brown, 'The Coming Age of Calm Technology [1]', 1996, www.ubiq.com/hypertext/weiser/acmfuture2endnote.htm

Norbert Wiener, *Cybernetics: Or Control and Communication in the Animal and the Machine*, MIT Press, Cambridge, MA, 1948.

Norbert Wiener, *The Human Use of Human Beings*, Eyre and Spottiswoode, London, 1950.

John Wood, 'Metadesign', in John Wood, *Design for Micro-Utopias: Making the Unthinkable Possible*, Routledge, London, 2007.

— 10 —

JUST FUN ENOUGH TO GO COMPLETELY MAD ABOUT: ON GAMES, PROCEDURES AND AMUSEMENT

As a child I could get quite seriously interested in computer games, believe their imperatives, become enraptured by the proprioceptive experience, and get that simultaneously annoyed and excited sense that this is all that matters, which probabilistically speaking ends in tantrums. This childhood of course lasted quite a bit longer than the biological one. Nowadays, however, since much of working life is full of things that are approximately like games, or have some of the same underlying machinic aspect, I have less enthusiasm, less need to be locked into a set of animated imperatives. (One can take form-filling, for instance as merely a different representational form of combative monsters in a first-person shooter, needing different moves and key combinations, which sometimes require painful processes of acquisition, to see them off.)

Perhaps responding to such a condition, there is a genre of games design for jaded souls: casual gaming. The term describes phenomena such as Candy Crush, games that you pull out whilst on the bus, games to enjoy, to fidget with. The games are trivial and essentially about a relationship between instant gratification and the potential build-up of something more pressing, the drive to win – potentially, really – with the machinic imperative lurking just underneath. They are something like a cigarette, a real electronic one. Games such as Clash of Clans that work heavily with operant conditioning techniques to keep the user itching for a little more, a little update, exemplify this condition of the phone or tablet operating as replacement for the cigarette.

But even these are too much hard work, too much like answering emails. My gaming experience now is more daydreamy in a way, something like being a back-seat driver who doesn't say much. I like to watch the screen whilst other people play Skyrim, GTA, Assassin's Creed, open world games that are quite 'filmic' but don't have the imperative that you care about the depth of the plot or the characters in the way that you are supposed to if you watch an actual film or television. The work of caring too much about plot is tedious, but films with cars zooming round and explosions happening can be quite good. Equally if you watch Ingmar Bergman films at two or four times the intended projection speed, the effect can be tolerably entertaining, and it is thus with games: you see a hidden layer of action, which is most importantly indifferent to you, in which you can be relieved of consequence.

In a sense, the experience is like watching contact improvisation dance, some relatively plotless avant-garde procedural in which the simple movement of the character around in a space changes the information that you see, and induces responses and trivial interactions from non-player characters. The scripts of non-player characters are always fascinating, the extent to which their text is loaded with supposed clues, prompts to further action, or effective instructions, or is the work of some chatbot generating something like a fragment of the hubbub of a Renaissance town or a quasi-Viking village. A relation to landscape can be like this too; I like to see entities moving about onscreen in a way that reveals terrain. But, as these are computer games, such terrain always involves something like a puzzle; there's an incipient Zelda in each of them; even in the most ostensibly open world, something is there to trigger some kind of action. You need to identify it, figure it out, carry out the correct operation with it; and it always requires only one kind of interaction, only one way of getting it right. This is the thing that I can't be bothered with. Such things are too much like trying to get the fill function right in a multi-field form in a writable PDF in which there is a hidden control for the number of characters. It's never that easy, or more accurately, that interesting. A good game in this sense is a bit like mushroom picking, where the experience of the space is highly nuanced and detailed, exciting, but not quite determinant, and in the main faintly pointless.

I like to watch someone play a game where they take a certain enjoyment in doing so very seriously, but lightly against the imperatives of the game; for instance, someone who just likes driving around luxury cars in GTA and takes a delight in moving from a Lamborghini to a Maserati for no particular reason, just to enjoy the abundance of them, and the fact that a Bugatti Veyron is as likely as a pickup truck.

There's a kind of sub-manic futility that is pleasant to be infected by that has something in common with many of the pleasures of contemporary life: stock car racing, dog shows; shelves of highly specialized kitchen gadgets that are hymns to the futility of order and efficiency but that still find themselves in a remainder shop and thus seem like a lament for a lost, imagined world where efficiency would be slightly different; fashion blogs; bumbling about, enthusiasms building up and dying out, crazes, buzzwords; hyper-concentrated knowledge of trivia; the fabulous jargons accreted in specialized fields of knowledge. Things that are complex enough to fill your attention, but that can be rinsed out of consciousness almost immediately, though with the chance of perhaps a few minutes of micro-nostalgia for them as the enthusiasm wanes, and one wonders whether such an affect is simply the half-life of a mediatic hormone working its way through the metabolism, rather than any special relation to the half-remembered thing. That is to say that the watching of the interlocking of different imperatives – those of the terrain and of the game – with the interests of the person is part of a wider condition of drifting, irritation, gratification, the micro-interest in some mechanical novelties become modes of life that games articulate extremely well.

This enthused, slightly buzzy, but dozy neutrality is a bit useless in the world of game studies, in which a first point of accreditation is to be a gamer who cares and who plays, ardently. There is a rite-of-passage aspect to such work, an authenticity test, at which I am unfortunately, as in the games themselves, an early loser. To some extent, the critiques of the intellectualization of games as experienced by non-gamers echo those of the non-committed: there is a certain Stalinist authenticity to proper gamers, whose enthusiasm is conversely marked by the bite of their bitterly apolitical nature – as evidenced in the Gamergate events. The idea that one doesn't have to do sufficient work of concentrated caring, as you might were you to watch a soap opera, a reality TV show or a film, is perhaps an affront to those who do *make the effort* to do the hard cognitive work. After all, there's an abundance of stuff going on – all the work of design going into non-player characters, spaces, objects; it's an insult not to use it well. But all that work aimed at making the thing a certain kind of 'real' sustains a state of partial, but not enrapturing, entertainment, like Victorian fairy paintings (such as those of Richard Dadd), which has a certain Cantorian infinity of detail-work that is fascinating and deranging at the same time.

What might be the case, however, is that this condition of exploring the game as a field of potentialities that is slightly tangential, but not entirely opposite, to the imperatives of the operation-reward structure of the game is crucial to the game as a form of culture. It may be, indeed, that the most successful and interesting games accommodate this dawdling and daydreamy condition. Here, a number of things can become interesting. One is that with a 'realistic' game the crassness of the model of the external world that the game provides (for obvious reasons of computational and labour limits), even in a narratively and structurally self-consistent game world, the repetitiveness and laboriousness of some of the routines required provide some of the conditions of experience of the game. Following this, in many artistic uses of computer games as environment, deliberately 'wrong' behaviours are explored as a means of reflecting on the way in which the game models life and the operation-reward structures built into it. Equally, there may be exploration of glitches, such as the spaces internal to characters, as in Jodi's work using Max Payne (2006) or Quake (entitled 'Untitled Game' (2001)) to open up visually and procedurally interesting nooks and crannies in a game – the way that unseen elements such as an invisible polygon formed around a character operate to govern collision-detection.[1]

There are other, less meticulous explorations of such a condition. In Skyrim 2, for instance, a horse crossing a bridge visually does something like wading through it, as if it were breasting a river. There is a relief from the kind of relentlessly effective if not entirely convincing operations of the apparatus. Bethesda games have a certain form here with bugs that also excite a crop of findings with each new release.

People get interested in such conjunctures, glitches, in a way related to that in which they might develop a sentimental attachment to certain minor processes in a word processor or the specific qualities of a config file. There is a sense of malleability here as if, in a Wittgensteinian language game, there were little pockets in which other language games crop up and maybe provide a wormhole through to another condition. The artistic exploration of these pockets, these interference patterns, is a means of attending to the multiple nesting of different ordering and representational mechanisms, and how these may at times jump scale, fold each other inside out.

Let's Play

A related sense of this overly passive enjoyment of things that are valorized for their high degree of interactivity is the massive field of Let's Play videos on YouTube and other such platforms. Here, gamers play a game, and provide a running commentary on it as they do so. The screen shows what they see as a player, and footage of their face in an inset. Part of the pleasure of these videos is a sense of playing alongside them.

Some Let's Plays tend towards the rather mechanical exercise of virtuosity, telling the viewer what they intend to do and then doing it. Others are more playful, involving meandering chit-chat about the world along with commentary on the game; and some of the most known players belong to this kind: figures such as Stampy or Pewdipie. The game may become the opportunity for banter, the highly valued witty but ostensibly inconsequential chat that has become a separately branded mode of speech in the present. Banter, through its ostensive meaninglessness, is of course where a lot of questions of orientation, of parody, of inversion and reinforcement of norms get played out, as a form of linguistic operation of games physics. In Let's Plays, it is usually accomplished by a degree of expertise in the game.

Such videos may also be watched for straightforwardly informational purposes alongside videos that show a viewer how to get past a particular stage in a game. What Let's Plays point towards is that video games have become a sufficiently embedded and complex part of culture that they are pluralistic, with different modes of belief, use and imaginary operating and co-existing whilst operating with the same, or overlapping, sets of resources. The tangential reading is, perhaps perplexingly, fully constitutive of this condition.

Game as Block

Alongside this movement of reading games at a tangent to their axiomatic form, we can say that there is also another mode of approaching the game: addressing it as a single, self-consistent artefact, rather than as a space to be explored. A number of techniques take this angle. Speedrunning is an approach in which the fastest route through every level of a game is memorized and programmatically enacted. It results in extraordinary feats, such as the completion of Sonic the Hedgehog in 2.5 hours. Alternative kinds of runs, such as those that result in finding all the resources and killing all the monsters, are also used.

Relatedly, there are feats of automatic completion of gameplay in displays of deep learning algorithms where the moiré effect of one batch of rule sets interacting with another produces the effect of intelligence, with artificial intelligence (AI) software over time learning to play.[2] A claim made here is that machine learning technology is able to evolve novel approaches to game play, signifying something that, given certain constraints, maps across to intelligence.

Thirdly, there are approaches that set out to map the entire state-space of a game. Jeremy Douglass' mapping of all permutations of a set of games and Jodi's rendering of the ZX Spectrum game Jet Set Willy both treat the game as a single computational object in this way, spatializing the results in large mapping diagrams.

Aside from these very efficient approaches, which gain traction on a game with their reasoned measures, it seems there is room for a Monsieur Hulot or Mr Bean character to inhabit games, with a bemused and affable, or confused and frustrated, persona of interaction. Such an entity would act not out of intelligence defined according to rational achievement of goals, but rather by the purloining of the figure of intelligence by other drives: curiosity, the generative powers of stupidity or clumsiness, the power of confusion as a form of interest. Misinterpretation here becomes a multiplier of meaning, misidentification of the world freeing the player up to accrete a non-unified identity.

This space of constitution in an awkward but fecund relation to the world is also a space in which economic value is generated out of entropy. We can think of the figure of the Bored at Work Network that became the basic platform of Buzzfeed,[3] or the way in which, according to Olga Goriunova, Udaff.com was constituted by the frustrations and genre inventions of office workers.[4] The zone of interpretation may be corralled into a form of regression analysis to the correct – judged as the most time-efficient or most high-scoring – line through a game, or it may be recognized as a space in which the game also multiplies its dimensions. Indeed, there is a certain pleasure in watching the way in which these two imperatives intersect.

Procedures

One of the ways of working such an aesthetics is to look at the debate around the procedurality of computational culture. The formation of this discussion in electronic literature and in games studies in debates around the term 'procedure' (Janet Murray,[5] Michael Mateas, Noah Wardrip Fruin, Espen Aarseth) anticipates some of the concerns around algorithms that appear more recently in the social sciences and elsewhere. Here, we can say that a certain enthusiasm in the social sciences for algorithms as an explanatory factor passes in some forums as a means of re-founding a revised social physics of a variant kind to that promulgated by Quetelet, a physics of mechanics, and its dream of policy that is coded and directly implementable, simply because algorithms are demonstrably operative. We are in an age where the atomistic and probabilistic thermodynamic physics of Ludwig Boltzmann and those that came after him comes to the fore as a grounds for the interpretation of the social. Here, it can be argued, an aesthetics is fundamental. It is necessary too not simply for the fine and rare formulations of mathematical process as they intersect with other scales of the world, but also for the lumpy, coagulated and thickly fleshy aspects and entities of the world and the way it is munged together in software systems.

In such a regard, the discussion of procedure in electronic literature and games provides a way of thinking such terms as 'experiential', as a something that is found most intensely in the middle of an ongoingness. One of the most precise of such formulations is that of 'process intensity' proposed by game designer Chris Crawford, who says:[6]

> It uses the ratio of operations per datum, which I call the crunch per bit ratio. I intend here that an operation is any process applied to a datum, such as an addition, subtraction, logical operation, or a simple Boolean inclusion or exclusion. A datum in this scheme can be a bit, a byte, a character, or a floating-point number; it is a small piece of information.

'Process' here is a synonym for the textural aspect of the algorithm – an effective procedure – in some respects, but also at another level for mathematical and logical forms, partially realized as algorithms, and also those in other states, as they operate in relation to hardware, as programs, or as ordered data. Crawford notes, for instance, that a table of data can be used to effect the operation of an algorithm/ procedure in memory-constrained computers, so the pertinent data structure also has its role in generating the nature of the experience of a game. As Ian Bogost writes in his noted discussion of process intensity in games, some such games may indeed allow for a kind of exploration, since they create a space in which multiple threads of programming are under way.[7] Indeed, he remarks, game assets themselves, in their visual or sonic unfolding, may be highly processual. A game can be said to emphasize the interaction of (multiple) processes to embody sustained complexity, as opposed to an approach that emphasizes data or the display of game assets. In this condition, the more a game acts as a place in which variation can be experienced and structurally and imminently operated on and in, the better it is.

This given, then, I want to look at two examples: games that exemplify certain aspects of the interrelation of both dawdling and process intensity. Here it should be noted that the two are neither entirely mutually exclusive nor fully overlapping. In some cases, dawdling may be immune from process intensity. In other cases it may be fully process intense, depending on the structure of the game, and what counts as an event within it.

Agar.io

Agar.io is a deceptively simple online game that involves moving a coloured dot around on a two-dimensional gridded plane of other, smaller or larger, variously coloured dots that are also moving. A user drags or pushes the dot around using a trackpad or mouse, or on a tablet or phone. The regime of accumulation that the games makes explicit is that larger dots eat smaller dots and thus become bigger. Each sprite is a target for others, and each must eat in order to militate against depletion. There are a few glosses on this, and niceties of tactics, such as the ability to spit out part of your dot to devour another, or the game's placement of obstacles called viruses on the playing space that break a larger dot up into numerous smaller ones, thus creating a certain kind of spatial tactics of accumulation.

To follow Crawford's model, Agar.io is relatively process intense. There are few graphic assets in the game and gameplay involves moving around, avoiding and eating. What can perhaps be added, then, is that a concomitant of process intensity is a certain ability to modulate such intensity by behaviour, to slacken it, to goof off, to dawdle – algorithmic dawdling that has the process as a coefficient, something that is constituent of it and that continues to unfold along with it, but to which it is not entirely reducible. Process intensity, then, is something that both models 'high-efficiency' gaming and provides a means of assaying the more dawdling mode of play. In such games, indeed, much of the processuality of the game is generated by the gamers and their interaction in the relatively simple space that it establishes. We should note, however, that each game would have its own conditions; dawdling play might be more or less process intense depending on the kinds of operations being carried out in the game.

To describe the game in simply algorithmic or procedural terms, assuming one brackets out those of the operating systems, browsers, networks and other structures that set it up, would be possible. Such an inventory would include:

- laying out the dots to be eaten
- movement, and inertia
- collision detection
- accumulation of the mass of a dot
- tracking of time online and other data around gameplay
- updating the information of all players in the same game-space.

To put it bluntly, this is a relatively small set of processes. The amount of data operated on is also concomitantly small. Much of the work of the game is achieved in frameworks and systems that are independent of it, within which it interoperates and which it relies upon. The game thrives on its simplicity and the way in which players are able to generate the active nature of the gameplay because of the way in which it can bring together a small cluster of processes amidst a larger-scale aggregate of procedures. Another way of saying this is that in this case, algorithmic processes are simply part of a wider mix, and critical attention brought to bear upon them needs to recognize the wider assemblages of which they are part.

In the case of Agar.io, due to the popularity of the program, there are newer services online making the use of bots available, so that players can establish presences in the game whilst doing something else. Services also exist for players to add further visual information to their dots, to skin them. Another reading, however, is to note how much can be done with simple sets of procedures. An algorithm is just one layer of description, but is key to the pleasures of the game in its relation to process.

Twitch Plays Pokemon

Twitch is a video-streaming service largely used by gamers to show live play of eSports. Using this system, Twitch Plays Pokemon is a series in which users work via a modification of the system to play an ancient GameBoy game en masse. The series is, at the point of writing, still ongoing, having moved through the series of games on GameBoy into those on NintendoDS. Using Twitch's existing video service, the project uses an internet relay chat (IRC) bot to read seven simple commands fed to the GameBoy emulator VisualBoyAdvance.

Given the nature of the game, there is a strong narrative element, different from Agar.io, but it is the way in which this is then taken up by the joint process of playing the game that is remarkable. The project started as a simple social experiment in online collaboration, that, whilst in progress, *went viral* and involved tens of thousands of players simultaneously. Having started on 13 February 2014, it took 16 days, 7 hours, 45 minutes and 30 seconds of continuous play to complete Pokemon Red, the first game in the series.[8] Compiling the seven different commands from tens of thousands of players at first meant that every command was taken in sequence as they were received. This meant that players would often contradict each other – often deliberately – and that the 'start' button, might also get pressed at any point.[9]

As the game progressed, another mode was introduced by its anonymous developer. This mode, 'Democracy', took a sample of inputs made within a certain timeframe and took the majority decision. The decision to enter this mode could be made by players voting during the course of the game. The original mode, now dubbed 'Anarchy', would be re-started every hour.

In the few days that this process was running for the first time, over one and a half million players took part round the clock. The game spawned numerous memes and social media discussions. It may also have incidentally proven the flexibility and robustness of the Twitch platform, which was sold to Amazon some time later.[10]

Adrian Mackenzie has written extensively on the way in which lags or mixed temporalities become a material force in online gaming environments. A player may, for instance, be able to use the delay present in a game server or the relaying of information by the network to shoot the avatar of another before the other knows they are even being shot at.[11] A whole infrastructure of international servers has grown up around ameliorating this problem. Lag is the ghost that haunts cloud computing and the endless roll-out of hyperbole about high-bandwidth internet. Lag is the experience of time not as universal measure but as highly specific undergoing of processing. Lag, operated differently by different protocols, is something that emerges out of the interplay of the material conditions of networks of computers running a stack of different software. Relayed in some software as buffering, where the buffer pre-empts the event of lag by pre-loading data, lag is more difficult to pre-empt in systems predicated upon liveness, such as games.

Twitch Plays Pokemon involved tens of thousands of players operating a black-and-white game with minimal command input, and with a wildly overflowing chatlog. It was hugely chaotic, but it also showed algorithmic processes to be something that people amuse themselves in experiencing. Lag here became a thickly operative part of the game, an entity that emerges out of the interaction of a multitude of parts. In this condition, simple moves may take hours to complete and may be sabotaged by players acting as trolls, or by simple lack of co-ordination of aims, understanding, timing, operating at multiple scales. Here, process intensity becomes a highly social factor, as process is bundled up and networked across the vast crowd of users. In the middle of the mayhem emerges a condition of rule sets as sociability – not one of efficiency, but of the relishing of muddle. Manic futility, the urge to throw oneself into a pointless process, the glorious abundance of nothing in particular becomes core here: we press buttons together in order to play a childish game on an emulator of out-of-date equipment, running under the faintly absurd mythos of a game running a hugely successful but slightly passé franchise, based on the idea of a game in a science fiction future, all of which is run across an advanced planetary communications network to afford maximum redundancy of interaction and the possibly maximal expenditure of processing power, labour and attention, in order to achieve a satisfactorily trivial task. In effect, we have the internet presenting itself as a gleeful parody of the regime of efficiency and collaboration and of digital abundance in which it is so often incorporated.

Ambience and Dosage

What can be proposed is that these means are ways of dealing with algorithmic culture as both ambience and dose; *ambience* because like, and as, the office workers bored at work, we are saturated with the temporalities, ordering and analyses of algorithmic processes. Many of these at the moment are exceptionally low-grade, background operations that provide a texture to contemporary forms of life. Others are highly focused, specific and singular operations. Others in turn are fundamental mechanisms of governance and ordering that make explicit and opaque operations of distinction that are enforced with the brutality of a border.

They operate as a *dose* in that they enable constitutive countermeasures of the break, addition, supplement, release in amongst the conditions of such forms of life. One sits in the waiting room of the UK Border Agency's Lunar House at Croydon waiting for a visa

201

interview playing a game, or doing friendship maintenance data-entry work, as a means of inhabiting the slow grind of sudden decision with other temporalities, other trivial and pointless operations, since their texture is more amenable to inhabitation and distraction than the operations of the life-size logic gate which one is inhabiting. There is such a condensation of procedure in such a place, such a heaviness of a logic, that to introduce a more minor one is to gain a certain release, even if only by the modulation of one irritation by another.

One way to read this is to suggest that self-constitution can be read as an act of mixing different temporalities, degrees of focus, procedural operations. This composition is collective as well as individuating, since such procedures are drawn from and imposed by numerous resources and contexts that operate across persons, organizations, economic regimes and conditions of information.

Each comes with its characteristic degree of echoing, modulation, interference of other patterns and processes. The interrelation of these procedures-as-forces is the context for and tonality of an ethos and an aesthetics of the creation of dispositions.

Dosage can be differentiated from the figure of the Pharmakon in the work of Derrida and Stiegler in that it doesn't consist of anything necessarily radically different from what it acts to 'cure'. We are simply talking of a different tempo, intensity or degree of triviality, of process. More fundamentally, the way in which this interaction of dose and ambience implies no substantial difference has some significance for a material politics of computing.

We can say also that ambience and dose operate at a range of scales. Their attraction for models of governmentality and those attempting to hold the condition of a society together, to perpetuate or intensify certain conditions, is related to, via various subterranean and explicit means, that of those attempting to hang together as a subject, in that ambience and dose provide an offer of the proper or imaginable ordering of things and a means by which they can seemingly be handled. More fundamentally, ambience and dose provide the challenge of imagining a composition that has a certain degree of self-consistency to it, at the same time as working on a provisional basis, one that can be thought on the basis of Unix-like systems of patches and pipes, or in terms of interacting chaotic locales, or a technocratic imaginary of order in a duel and a dance with entropy.

In such a state, moments of speed and of slackness, dawdling in conditions which may accelerate or ease down the texture of process intensity, passages of massing, snowballing, drifting, hiding, incoherence, inconsequentiality, collective engorgement in triviality or the minor pleasures of chasing, being chased, and being devoured, come to the fore. A veritable procedural paradise, approximately speaking.

NOTES

1 See, for an extensive discussion, Lisa Adang, *Untitled Project: A Cross-Disciplinary Investigation of Jodi's Untitled Game*, Rhizome Conservation Fellow Programme, Rhizome, New York, 2013.

2 Hado van Hasselt, Arthur Guez, and David Silver, 'Deep Reinforcement Learning with Double Q-Learning', 22 September 2015, https://arxiv.org/abs/1509.06461.

3 Jonah Peretti, the founder of Buzzfeed, proposed the idea of the Bored at Work Network as a form of surplus consciousness.

4 Olga Goriunova, *Art Platforms and Cultural Production on the Internet*, Routledge, London, 2012.

5 Janet Horowitz Murray, *Hamlet on the Holodeck: The Future of Narrative in Cyberspace*, Simon and Schuster, New York, 1997.

6 Chris Crawford, 'Process Intensity', *Journal of Computer Game Design*, 1:5 (1987).

7 Ian Bogost, 'Persuasive Games: Process Intensity and Social Experimentation', *Gama Sutra*, 23 May 2012.

8 *Know Your Meme*, 'Twitch Plays Pokemon', http://knowyourmeme.com/memes/events/twitch-plays-pokemon.

9 An article covering the early stages of the phenomenon: Andrew Cunningham, 'The Bizarre, Mind-Numbing Beauty of "Twitch Plays Pokémon"', 18 February 2014, http://arstechnica.com/gaming/2014/02/the-bizarre-mind-numbing-mesmerizing-beauty-of-twitch-plays-pokemon.

10 Kim Gittleson, 'Amazon Buys Video-Game Streaming Site Twitch', *BBC Online News*, 25 August 2014, http://www.bbc.co.uk/news/technology-28930781.

11 Adrian Mackenzie, *Transductions: Bodies and Machines at Speed*, Continuum, London, 2002.

REFERENCES

Lisa Adang, *Untitled Project: A Cross-Disciplinary Investigation of Jodi's Untitled Game*, Rhizome Conservation Fellow Programme, Rhizome, New York, 2013.

Ian Bogost, 'Persuasive Games: Process Intensity and Social Experimentation', *Gama Sutra*, 23 May 2012.

Chris Crawford, 'Process Intensity', *Journal of Computer Game Design*, vol.1, no.5 (1987).

Andrew Cunningham, 'The Bizarre, Mind-Numbing Beauty of "Twitch Plays Pokémon"', 18 February 2014, http://arstechnica.com/gaming/2014/02/the-bizarre-mind-numbing-mesmerizing-beauty-of-twitch-plays-pokemon

Kim Gittleson, 'Amazon Buys Video-Game Streaming Site Twitch', *BBC Online News*, 25 August 2014, http://www.bbc.co.uk/news/technology-28930781

Olga Goriunova, *Art Platforms and Cultural Production on the Internet*, Routledge, London, 2012.

Hado van Hasselt, Arthur Guez, and David Silver, 'Deep Reinforcement Learning with Double Q-Learning', 22 September 2015, https://arxiv.org/abs/1509.06461

Know Your Meme, 'Twitch Plays Pokemon', http://knowyourmeme.com/memes/events/twitch-plays-pokemon

Adrian Mackenzie, *Transductions: Bodies and Machines at Speed*, Continuum, London, 2002.

Janet Horowitz Murray, *Hamlet on the Holodeck: The Future of Narrative in Cyberspace*, Simon and Schuster, New York, 1997.

POWERS

— 11 —

BLACK SITES AND TRANSPARENCY LAYERS

Transparency is the quintessential contemporary virtue, one that applies to politicians, budgets, software and bureaucracy; to romantic relationships, the provenance of food and the decision-making of public assemblies. Transparency implies the possibility of accountability, and also the ease of transmission of things; that they are explainable, and can be rendered into accounts and systems that can be scrutinized. As well as being a quality to be elicited from and between things and in institutions, transparency may also be implemented *ab novo* by design. This is one of the ways in which software – as a culture founded in a state of reason; or failing that at least in a state of an implementable and self-consistent logic; or, where there are multiple patterns of interference between modes of logic that generate glitches or errors, founded, at least, on good intentions; or, where those are not available, on the need to give consumers something that they can understand and relish using – is particularly telling.

Transparency is thus always held slightly away from itself, or, to be sensed, must be motion-captured in a translation of one mode of transparency to another. Here, I want to propose a reading of the genealogy of software interfaces as they present notions and models for the knowing and active subject of computing, and then address in turn how the formulation of transparency bleeds out into the conditions that variant kinds of computational culture make of the world.

Transparency: what does it look like? Direct perception with no interference. Clarity and coherence of interconnection across all layers of an organization or an artefact. The sense of something being built from the roots up in a cogent and systematic manner that makes itself available for inspection and understanding at any scale; and that thus combines the compositional drives of honesty to materials and integrity of form with an openness of structure. In this equation, a transparent artefact is something that disappears when we understand it, but whose very transparency also improves us. This first part of the equation is a model of the transparent that is often ascribed to single-use artefacts. And it is in the latter part, the capacity for transformation, that transparency has been a key point of figuration for computer interfaces over their history as part of what Félix Guattari calls *collective equipment*, 'A multitude of intermediary operations, machines for initiation and semiotic facilitation that can capture the molecular energy of desire of human individuals and groups'.[1] Part of what complicates this position is the sheer flexibility of the collective equipment concerned.

Transparency may also be mechanical, a direct translation. This is where transparency also looks like a PowerPoint slide with three well-manicured bullet points following the proper laws of rhetoric as a falling ball follows the laws of physics. Another incarnation of transparency here is a data projector or beamer screening an empty slide, a white screen; transparency may also occur as the 'presenter view' of the same slide in a shot-reverse-shot showing four empty sub-panes, the clock time and time elapsed since the start of the slide show. Transparency is the reveal of the staging mechanism. In this case, transparency can alternatively be parsed in the following ways: as a hexadecimal code in HTML, #ffffff; as a descendant of James Clerk Maxwell's mathematical description of colour in RGB (red, green, blue) value, (255, 255, 255), to set colours on a screen; as process colour (four-colour CMYK; cyan, magenta, yellow, key), 0.00, 0.00, 0.00, for print; as a variant on the hexadecimal, the 'web safe colour' known as 'white colour'. Such parsing is also translation, from transparency to the colour white, which stands in for clarity and the lack of infusion with any other trace. Transparency, in this mode, is also a code for direct translation, a state of information processing in which there is an isomorphism between sender and receiver. Transparency is the clear channel uncomplicated by translation, but, on screen, one composed of equal parts of red, green and blue.

Metaphor as Transparency Layer

Transparency may also appear in the guise of a metaphor. In this mode, metaphor aids transparency by assisting translation via inference and association. Prior comprehension of a thing makes something new understandable via a mapping of one domain of reference

208

onto another. Transparency is not direct perception here, but a means by which the activation of an understanding of a function is arrived at. The metaphor guides thinking, but in some accounts is also seen to restrain it, in that the operation of the computer is perpetually being modelled on a prior form. Equally, via only partial mapping from one domain of reference onto another, a metaphor can mislead users, and worse, hold back the development of more fully transparent software.[2]

The classical formulation of a metaphor that aids such a transition between one domain of reference and another is that of the skeuomorph. Perhaps the epitome of a skeuomorphic interface is that of the Eimco Power Horse, a tractor made in North America from 1937 to 1942. The line-drive tractor was originally equipped with leather reins instead of a steering wheel. According to a tractor enthusiast, 'It would be an improvement over farming with horses, but it was dangerous.' 'When the farmer said "whoa!, it wouldn't "whoa". If he wasn't used to driving a gas tractor, he'd pull back on the reins to stop, like you would on a horse, and it'd put it in reverse.'[3] The mapping from one domain of reference – the use of reins to signal customary movements – was incomplete. Within a short time, cheaper tractors with steering wheels, by companies such as John Deere or Farmall, were available for less, knocking the Eimco out of business.

Such symbolic residues persist in computing in more ineffable ways such as that of the rough size of a piece of paper as a form factor for tablet computers and mobile phones. The translated familiarities become about proportions, aspect ratios, heft. Despite this, metaphor became a long-running approach within the graphic user interface (GUI), reaching a climax, or nadir, with Apple's iOS6, which featured a faux wooden bookshelf for eBooks, and an image of a reel-to-reel tape recorder to deal with podcasts. Felt, leather and wood were emulated as rendered surfaces in the 'Game Center' in order to give the impression of casino equipment.[4] These designs effectively ended metaphor as a technique by exaggerating it to the point of parody, or worse, of inefficiency. The amount of screen real estate given to establishing the metaphor rather than access to functions and information made the software clunky and irritating. The often highly nuanced thought that went into the earlier generations of Apple software can be seen from early on in the photo-documentations of programmer Bill Atkinson's parallel and interwoven work on the GUI, the system for rendering images to screen, and the grammar of the operating system, in which metaphor is thought through as a subtle indicator rather than an architecture of permanent over-explanation.[5] By comparison, later uses of metaphor collapsed under the weight of their own decoration.[6]

Transparency Layers

Metaphor creates a kind of transparency, but does so as one sort of *transparency layer*, a formation in which a certain systematization of visibility, access and control has dominance. The idea of the transparency layer draws on the formulation of the abstraction layer in computing. Abstraction layers include the means by which one scale of the computer addresses another, from operating system and applications, through to the kernel, assembler and firmware, down to the hardware. Abstraction layers are organized through this hierarchy, and may have numerous intermediating layers within them in particular cases. A variant kind of abstraction layer can also be found in programming languages, from higher-level languages that appear more humanly readable, to machine languages that address specific components and their particular characteristics of storage and control of data, and the primitive functions applied to it.

The essential thing about an abstraction layer is that it decouples general rules of operation from the underlying details, allowing abstractions at a higher level to ground and manipulate entities at a lower level of abstraction. Each abstraction layer is implemented and operates in relation to the formation of what is rendered as a detail, and what is formulated as general. Each different kind of abstraction layer has its own way of texturing relations amongst scales. Abstraction layers are different from part–whole relations. That is to say that each of their layers is ultimately as generalized as any other in the hierarchy. Whilst they might be logically equivalent, abstraction layers may also exhibit internal variation: each programming language may also be seen as an act of translation of what might be possible to be said in a parallel language. Assuming that all languages (even fun ones such as Emojicode, which uses the set of emojis in Unicode as symbols to program with[7]) are Turing complete, each one is a refractive translation of each other one. The specific differences in performance, texture and processability are significant; not to mention the material cultures of forums, integrated development environments (IDEs), text editors (with religious wars between users of Vim and Emacs), repositories, development methods, licences, training programmes, institutions, companies, and other factors that cluster around and run through them (without mentioning the pro-

210

found controversy over whether tabs or spaces are used to make indents when writing code). These aggregate, extend, invent and stabilize the nature of the collective equipment of computing, in ways that are due to the fundamentally polymorphous nature it owes to such a complete state.

In a certain sense, transparency layers operate by means of the reversal of the principle of abstraction; they move down from generality to particularity. But they are also more unruly, built less out of accumulations of primitives than out of principles that, like the skeuomorph, sometimes may not map into their intended domain: they may produce more transparency, or transparency of a certain kind, a parallax effect. Transparency layers may meld scales, cut diagonally across abstractions, sink through them shifting and gilding light like hot glass forming a lens. They may also give the illusion of doing so, of providing an insight that becomes impalpable. Transparency layers fold in ambiguity, each with its own concomitant texture of opacity, its means of slithering or swallowing light. Transparency layers may also be filters without any necessary input and output; they may be crystalline or viscid in texture, each with its own syntax of translation, parsing or plunging into another scale. This admixture of transparency and opacity may also be engineered. The blockchain technology of BitCoin that verifies a legitimate transaction at the same time as anonymizing it is one kind of such a combination that is explicit. Here, there is a calculus of reliability, of transparency as distributed transaction ledger, and of opacity. Transparency layers may be seen as an ergonomic shell-game of focusing attention as a resource, but they also provide part of the working materials of the programmer-heroes, such as Licklider, Sutherland, Engelbart and others, who invented much of the principle apparatus of contemporary computing. We are still in an ambivalent position on the surplus of vision of their work, both living through its aftermath, anticipating its coming or apotheosis, and recognizing that such single-author visions are now scheduled solely for the past. These architectures of invented, implemented or imagined transparencies, such as Ted Nelson's formulation of reversible hyperlinks (as distinct from the one-way links characteristic of the world wide web), haunt those that history has unidirectionally clicked on.[8]

The complexity and multi-functionality of the computer – the fact that it is at some level of description a universal machine – are what make design for it so difficult and so significant. It cannot be reduced to the clarity of the object with a small range of uses, such as a wine bottle, an axe or an intercontinental ballistic missile, each with the minimal implementation required for a purpose. Perhaps the closest to these ideals is the combination of Lisp and Unix, with their high degree of recursivity, modularity and an inherent encouragement for their user to learn, as the modality of transparency in operation.[9] It is this operation of learning that is key here: transparency becomes a modality of individuation characterized by an open-ended mastery that requires transformation, and in such a condition becomes something other than transparency. When such mastery is not at stake, or not available within the design of a system, transformation may be offloaded, secreted, operated at another scale as a processual surplus to be harvested.

Equally, either of these is a different model from the kind of transparency conjured in recognizable cause and effect, which in turn relies on the ability to conceal aspects of the transition from cause to effect in order to make legible; for instance, even something as simple as moving a cursor with a trackpad, or pressing a field on a screen to launch a function. Each formation of a transparency layer generates its own modes of opacity necessary for that transparency to function, a form of technical understatement or discretion. This is not to say that each syntax of transparency is essentially the same as any other, but rather to draw attention to the kinds of composition they elaborate, sustain and take part in, and to recognize the disavowals that certain modes of transparency make of the opacity that is their coefficient.

Flat Designs

After the era of metaphor we face a new manner of transparency, one that eschews reference to the past or prior media as a means of establishing the present. In this sense, interface design has finally become something contemporary, as something that is designed to exist by means of conventions, norms, architectures and understanding that are primarily brought together in the time of its own composition. That interface design becomes contemporary does not mean that it has not been so before in a history of advanced, experimental, visionary or artistic designs – both partially lauded and mainly submerged – but means that the interfaces aimed at a mass user base now largely take themselves to have no fundamental (rather than incidental) need for quasi-systematic metaphor. This might be indicative of something that used to be called progress. To say that interfaces are contemporary does not of course imply that they are adequate, but does imply that they can tell us something about the present.

The particular kind of contemporaneity that mass-user interfaces now address users with emerges, counterintuitively, in 2010 with the Zune Media Player (then in competition with the iPod Touch), in which the interface moves between a mode characterized by a grid of variously sized representations of media artwork, breaking with the then largely text-based interfaces of other music players, down through a directory hierarchy to 'oversize' representations and controls for the function of each file. Large, clear text, again sometimes oversized, leading to parts of words flowing over the edge of the screen, and minimal controls with transitions between modes and directory positions, are highly animated, dramatizing the touch-based interface. There is a tension between the structure of elements emphasizing clarity of position and the handling of functions and data, on the one hand, and the layered animations that give a sense of the responsiveness of the hardware, on the other. The two graphic modes are sometimes layered, sometimes discrete. The Zune inaugurates what has become known as flat design, since the emphasis is on clarity and ease of recognition within generally smaller screens where complex colour gradients, faux-3D and longer hierarchies of access to functions or data are flattened out into single colour, larger data representations (such as album covers) instead of icons, and shorter transitions between kinds of use. Although the Zune did not gain many users, the interface is influential and some of its characteristics spread rapidly into the wider Windows Design Language. Variations of the general flat approach influence design languages such as Google Polymer or Material Design[10] and the integrated design of Apple hardware and software.[11]

Each of these initiatives is driven by the imperative to simplify, remove and reduce clutter entailed by the constrained power and screen size of smartphones. This movement was most forcefully established by the operating system for the Windows Phone 7 in 2010, where brightly coloured asymmetrical animated tiles distinguished themselves from the grid of app icons characteristic of the iPhone. The operating system integrated social media and emphasized a minimal number of steps to execute tasks.[12] The movements of the interface shift from clicking points, dragging objects and interacting in a grammar of objects and verbs to a movement of swiping, touching, launching. One activates nouns, apps or objects of information, but the verbs are contained within the app's pre-set function.

Transparency here operates via a different refractive index, one in which, according to the *Interface Guidelines* for Apple iOS, designs are to 'Defer to content'[13] to allow the user transparent, direct access to their work, to their ideas, to themselves. There is a move from dealing with documents characteristic of the personal computer to using data and services established in the 'cloud' and the internet of things, often via a massive centralization that effectively reinstalls the master-computer slave-terminal configuration of mainframe-based networks of the 1960s. The characteristic functionalist tropes of the senses, procedures, objects and rationality being unified in one semantic force-field returns, but with animated, twinkling transitions between states. The pertaining mode of transparency operates by means of the idea of a direct handling of data-become-content. As devices become more autonomous, running processes independently of the user, often in relation to the delivery of information via internet services, apps jostle for user attention via notifications, which in turn begin to overflow and need differentiation, with platforms and operating systems aiming to keep users accessing information via them rather than via websites. In Windows 10 and other recent operating systems, data, such as social media, email and message notifications, stocks or weather, is pushed directly to the screen, where small entities give access to massive quantities: an effect of both quantities of data, and relational architectures.[14] Transparency configured as data-become-content is predicated on data being dynamic, locationally variable and of multiple kinds. Access to it must be tractable and immediate, but the move to the cloud means a further shift of relations: rather than the position of the personal computer, the user directly faces platform-based services that are constantly optimized to compete with other services (via the spread of functions) to introduce updates, and to capture potentially capitalizable data on the user's interactions as part of a population of representative and emergent types. The interface is collective equipment that establishes the organization of relation between computational forces and those manifesting as the user, and the user as a statistical container of a set of probabilities, but that also disarticulates and renders opaque many of the systems operating on the data that is yielded to the various services that the user opens their ports to.

Transparency layers also effect and are manifest in the design of hardware. Just as interface design revises its relationship to windows, scroll bars, buttons, frames and other standard components, a contemporary flat-screen television reformats its relationship to elements that previously used to be hard knobs, dials, switches and buttons.[15] Where, in a set from the last century, these elements would have been placed within a larger plastic, wooden or faux-wooden case, alongside speaker grilles and detailing or escutcheons to differentiate clusters of functions, they are now turned into software version of their functionality, or placed at the rear of the casing, in a monitor operating as a visual 'infinity pool'. The ambition of the contemporary screen is simply to be a luminous image that appears in the midst of a room without reference to a frame. Whilst the frame still exists for structural reasons, it is designed to recede visually, rather than being something that assists the image in distinguishing itself from the surroundings. (There is a recapitulation of the evacuation of plinths and frames in twentieth-century art.) In this condition of the mutability of screens, information moves across devices. Smartphones and smart televisions share the same interface and offer conjoined access points to data and functionality. Phones, televisions and monitors merge in terms of many of their visual and design characteristics. Other objects, such as tablets, emerge fully formed into the design language by exemplifying these changes, though not before shedding the apparatus of their ideational, yet unrealized, precursors such as the Dynabook.[16]

The condensing of information handling hardware into one uniform type is reflected in the way in which hardware components also aggregate, echoing Gilbert Simondon's description of the movement from abstract to concrete in technology.[17] The first iPhone had 'nearly thirty' interfaces between components. By late 2013, with the introduction of the unibody design (the phone casing milled from a single slice of metal), this number 'shrank to just five'.[18] Where the monitor intends to produce a slither of concentrated vision, with high resolution equating to high levels of perceptual intensity, here the aim of transparency layers is to produce the phone as a pure bloc of universal functionality; the ratio of perception to function, but not what is outside of either, equating to transparency.

Part of the transition to such a state is the movement to platform-based economies on the internet, where the concretization of devices is textured by a complex interplay between an imagined universality of the device; the apparent growth of differentiation in functions between apps; the consolidation of functions such as identification and location, as well as homogenized, exploratory and fast-replicated models of value-extraction shared across them; and the variegation of social roles and information needs that is in turn underwritten by a concomitant splintering and variation of formats, vocabularies, patterns of ownership, control and circulation, itself countered by illicit and informal modes of circulation. In the context of this multi-scalar texturing of interaction, software is often delegated the role of both embodying and facilitating each aspect of these conditions, and of delineating, securing and arranging its consistency.

API

In the era of the metaphor of the cloud, one of the key techniques for achieving this texture, and others, is the application programming interface (API). A structure by which programs establish transparency layers in and between themselves, the API is the interface for one program to make data available to other programs. This means that an API is an abstraction of the kinds of function or data that one program might make available to another, as well as the means by which this is done. Given the polymorphous nature of computing, APIs can be found in many forms: as libraries of software built into a language or system that can be called upon without needing a basic function to be coded from scratch; as classes establishing shared kinds of entity and process between objects in object-oriented programming; as systems that abstract processes and results from a cluster of languages into a single level of representation; as descriptions of objects that allow for them to be interacted with by entities external to their local system; and many other forms. The general class of API is thus a highly inventive field in which programs are written to mediate between programs, to disclose, enclose and encode information, to offer it up, and to translate and abstract it. APIs thus epitomize some of the complexity of software as culture and are at the core of the ways in which computational cultures speak to each other and fold out into the world.

Transparency layers differ from a standard configuration of objects and systems in science and technology studies. A key term here is 'black box'. According to Bruno Latour, 'The word black box is used by cyberneticians whenever a piece of machinery or a set of commands is too complex. In its place they draw a little box about which they need to know nothing but its input and output.'[19] The term arises from the increased use of electronics in aeronautics in the 1940s, and is incorporated into cybernetics vocabulary directly as a result of military surplus and surplus vocabulary entering labs in the decade following. The standard model of the black box is something so stabilized as to have no need for further thought applied to it and upon or with which further black boxes can be arrayed or stacked in a reliable manner. The black box is quintessentially modular. Latour notes a key aspect of the black box, one given in W. R.

216

Ashby's chapter on the topic in his *Introduction to Cybernetics*. What is generally missing from the understanding of the term acquired by science and technology studies (STS) is an important qualifier added by Ashby, when he describes the process of trying to figure out the operations of any such black box: 'By thus acting on the Box, and by allowing the Box to affect him [*sic*] and his recording apparatus, the experimenter is coupling himself to the Box, so that the two together form a system with feedback.'[20]

Part of the cybernetic understanding of black boxes as a term arises in relation to their critique of, but also partial dependence on, the legacy of behaviourism. The black box, as a stable modular entity, can be seen as the continuation of the abstraction of a biological or learned process found in constructions such as the Skinner Box. Stable or non-stable, the black box produces a structural coupling in interaction with the entities that work around and on it. This notion of a contagious aspect to feedback is a key condition of cybernetics as an enquiry into the epistemological conditions of technology.

That feedback processes induced by working with black boxes spill over so that both the operator and the operated affect each other is crucial to the way in which transparency layers also induce conditions of opacity. These feedback processes introduce an interplay between determinacy and indeterminacy in which variable conditions of transparency and opacity are established, played out and introduced. The difference between the figure of black boxes sustained in STS and black sites is that the former are built on a constitutive disavowal of this feedback and its formative relation to what is figured as the outside of the box. Understanding the black site, by contrast, is a process of working to recognize both the way in which this feedback entails reality-forming effects and how transparency layers and black sites are mutually interwoven. Their co-constitution is neither symmetrical nor based upon some notion of equilibrium in which quanta of each kind are distributed in a way that balances their proportional share. Rather, each mode of transparency produces a kind of opacity that is native to it, but that is not directly translatable into a transparency–opacity system of another kind.

Black Sites

The term 'black sites' came to the fore in the accounts of the CIA's secret rendition of people it considered to be suspects in relation to the West's feedback-riven 'war on terror', the invasions of Iraq, Libya,

Afghanistan and elsewhere. Territories that in the minds of military strategists were to be black boxed and dealt with in isolation produced contagious systems of feedback. In order to extract the truth of these conditions, certain individuals who were considered, whether by accident or from what passed as evidence, to be important to their determination, or who could be passed off as such, were extracted and held in secret prisons that became known as black sites. Within these operations, systems of interrogation, including torture, could be played out with impunity in order to establish a further notional idea of the black box: that input and output could be correctly correlated by means of punishment. Waterboarding, electrocutions, beatings, sleep deprivation and other means were, in the understanding of the West's finest agents and the psychologists who assisted them in the development of techniques, forms of input that were able to extract reliable intelligence as a form of output. In order for suspects to be rendered transparent they must be sealed off from the world, and, so the logic went, in order for the West to maintain its standing as an aggregate of societies in which transparency is a virtue, such places must be rendered obscure. Transparency depends on it. Black sites are thus things that fall off or out of the regime of openness, that slide between the occlusions of the layers of transparency, and that are also produced in the opacities that grammars of transparency rely upon. The particular qualities and intensities of the kinds of opacity that they produce, what aspects of life are drawn into them or that are established there, crystallize the texture of sociotechnical equipment. It must be said that there is no 'natural' relation between transparency and opacity, no zero-sum game in which a balance must always be played out, but, in the different formations of equipment, that there is a working through, a sealing-off, a disavowal, an opening up, a design, a means–ends calculation, a blundering, a settling for what is possible, an idea of progress, a pay-off, a non-optimal equilibrium, an information processing question, that plays a role of mediator.

Total Dashboard

This mediating interplay between transparency layers and black sites, what is sealed from inspection or is rendered unknowable, is a key aspect of the current political equipment, and one that is notably partially explicit, in certain ways, about the condition. One of the persuasive and interesting aspects of the theoretical bases of neoliberalism is its reading of the problem of information processing: that planned economies necessarily fail because they cannot take all necessary information into account. As Victor Serge's character Elkin, in exile and working in a state bureau under the strictures of the Stalinist 1930s, notes, 'I know how many fish are supposed to be caught in five years ... Alas nobody knows how many will be caught.'[21] Such a criticism, in different terms, is core to anarchist and liberal forms of opposition to centralization, but neoliberalism, in the work of Friedrich Hayek, produces a particular variant on the problem that sees it as a fundamental point of differentiation, partly due to the shift in register from the question of what is just to the question of what is technically best. It is this shift from politics to equipment, from liberty as ideology to its implementation as technology, that is especially acute in composing modalities of transparency in the present.

In the three-volume 1973–9 work, *Law, Legislation and Liberty*, Friedrich Hayek proposes self-organization as a form of spontaneous order natural to the market. The book extols the virtues of certain constructions of transparency; he proposes, for instance, that governments open administrative data sets.[22] The book argues that since there is an asymmetry of information, and a disequilibrium of values by which any information can be assessed, decisions as to the value of things must be made locally by the participants in the transaction; and it is the particular technical formulation of participants in markets and the means of their interaction and decision-making that are most interesting. In the earlier text 'The Uses of Knowledge in Society', one that attractively describes the hustle of the market, Hayek proposes that

> It is more than a metaphor to describe the price system as a kind of machinery for registering change, or a system of telecommunications which enables individual producers to watch merely the movement of a few pointers, as an engineer might watch the hands of a few dials, in order to adjust their activities to changes of which they may never know more than is reflected in the price movement.[23]

There is something hilarious in this vision of the economy as a system of dials and engineers, of observers watching a thin slit of reality and then, insofar as they are able, acting through it on the basis of their unique and inscrutable needs. To purchase, to sell, to wait, to watch, to track, to calculate: this is the grammar of interactions available in such a system, and its humour is palpable, except that, like any black box, it is a template whose systems, even or especially where they are imaginary, feedback wildly into those par-

219

ticipating in it, or amidst which it acts. Hayek's theme is something that he wrote on from the 1940s onwards: to promote the value-attribution capacities of local knowledge – a knowledge of specific time, place and needs in the individual – above any other modes of knowledge organization. Concomitant with that is a recognition of ignorance: that the individual can only ever know in terms of what might in another vocabulary be described as *situated* knowledge. To acknowledge that necessary ignorance is to make an argument for the liberal benefits of decentralization since, as a natural limit, it cannot be surpassed.

Opacity is figured here as the primary condition of information, the background against which it manifests as readings on a few dials, to be scanned fleetingly, or with sustained knowledge of particular fluxes of supply and demand, as a means of computing value. The market is described as a giant discombobulated machine (one that self-organizes in later work to appear as 'Catallaxy') that emerges from the interactions of the myriad black boxes that it entails. It is an image of the market that is susceptible to disturbance by machinic processes that tend to spread information, but it is also one that establishes something uncannily like a corporate dashboard as the condition of interface.

Whilst its proposition of money understood as pricing signals finally means we can rightfully subsume economics under media theory, a slightly mischievous reading might detect a concurrency with Whitehead's well-known proposition in the *Introduction to Mathematics* that 'Civilisation advances by extending the number of important operations which we can perform without thinking about them.'[24] A general economy of ignorance that increases gross levels of opacity entails a certain sort of progress, at least when measured by the inverse of what is thought.

Wittgenstein's battery of questions about beliefs, the shadows and tones of understanding and grounds for interpretation, may in turn be faced by those who ponder the catallectic dial.[25] Whilst under the conditions of Hayek's extended device, everything is a black box, with prices as inputs and outputs. Value generation, under such conditions of asymmetry of information, requires, and relies upon, multiple loci of indeterminacy to keep the great machine in motion – variable degrees of force within different components or sources of pressure. It is a means for negotiating and structuring volatility. As Claude Lefort reminds us in 'The Making of Machiavelli', the stakes of the co-ordinates by which such indeterminacies are arrived at are significant, since the prince asserts himself as such by sustaining the indetermination that is constitutive of the real.[26] The indetermination may be experienced as zany, stressful, anxiogenic, or able to produce magnificent conjunctions of worth, in which both an oil platform and an oil painting arrive at a conjoint place on separate dials. Wonder is aroused at the hidden capacities of what is rendered as the real. Amidst this oscillation and conjoining, separation and variation, there is a flickering backwards and forwards between axioms of determination and indetermination, and between modalities of determination and genesis. Amongst and engendering these movements are modalities of equipment.

Something rather like Hayek's system of dials turns up in the interfaces of systems such as Uber, Airbnb and other companies whose operation is via disintermediation; that is, by occupying the space of mediation between buyers and sellers. Participants in the system may view sections of each other's records, their locations, offers, ratings, number of transactions and other data, by a variable set of permissions structures. Their interactions are recorded, and a quasi-currency of ranking provides the enumeration for the dials. Certain forms of ranking are visible to all participants, while others are layered, modularized and structurally decoupled. Others are linked across to wider systems of record-keeping that serve to act as verification mechanisms for systems such as identity. In the model proposed by Google's Eric Schmidt and Jared Cohen,[27] larger incumbent institutions are dissolved as platforms aggregate and sort data between suppliers and users. There is a liberation from the constraints of hierarchically ordered institutions, or established forms of trade, but via the insertion of a new locus of a universal sorting mechanism that becomes a single, or at least super-dense, point of arbitrage of value. This sorting mechanism is in turn heavily modularized both at a technical level, following the model of the API, and at a financial one, using techniques of tax efficiency where companies are turned into networks of legal objects designed to minimize exposure to taxation, often spread across various countries, and de-risking, where costs are offloaded onto subcontractors who supply labour, vehicles, content and other resources.

Alongside their informational politics, the financialization strategies of these companies use the transparency of disintermediation as a means of 'going dark'. The refractive index of different modes of transparency and opacity is keyed into company and accounting structures. Interfaces act as multi-layered transactions, contracts, insurance schemes; as both the dial and the diagram of relations between entities that they at once put in place and render obscure.

221

A related mode, that of the black box inserted into circuits of information, allows for whistleblowers to circulate information. Where the WikiLeaks slogan 'we open governments' conjures a form of radical transparency, or of transparency taken as one form of ideal, it also entails the requirement for some shielding, what the design group Metahaven call 'Black Transparency'.[28] The calculus of transparency and opacity is not a condition of plurality, all of which kinds are equal, or at least mendaciously tradable, but a condition of ontogenesis in which many actions are impelled to be tactical.

Architectures

In architectural terms, there is nothing perhaps more telling of the strategic implementation of an asymmetry of transparency and opacity than the structure of drone warfare. When a screen-combatant in an air-conditioned container in Nevada works their shift they open the surfaces of Yemen, Afghanistan, Iraq, Libya, Syria and other places gifted with enhanced attention, to scrutiny and attack. In return, they are secluded from response. The attack surfaces available upon which to return fire remain in those theatres, and in those soft targets on the streets, in concert halls, mosques, marketplaces and cafés that are close to and far from the spaces allocated for the transparency regime of the drone. The interplay of transparency and opacity here indexes one as the answer to the other, in which the movement between states is one articulated as a gearing system of escalation.

An architectural vocabulary of containerized back-end, more mundane than strictly covert, fronted by a sophisticated apparatus of transparency, provides part of the diagram characteristic of computational capital, as much as it does of forms of procedural imperialism, and it is one recently played out in the architecture of Silicon Valley.

Long acclimatized to the use of 'whatever' buildings, from short-term leased office suites in generic low-rises, to the hero-garages where projects are cooked up in a sauce of sweat and insomnia, and to off-campus incubators where foetal companies are weened into the world, the architecture of the technology industry has until recently been merely a neutral, slightly scuzzy, backdrop against which the code played out. In a series of recent buildings commissioned by Facebook, Google and Apple, a shift is taking place that sees these companies both asserting their capacity to build in their own terms, and in each articulating those terms by means of an architecture that plays out variegated notions of transparency.

222

A precursor to this movement is the emphatic shift to modern architecture made by IBM in the 1950s and 1960s, one that ran through from the design of computer hardware to that of buildings. Indeed, one longstanding relation between computers and architecture, according to John Harwood, who writes its history, is inspired by the homology of terms established by the von Neumann architecture. Harwood goes on to show how IBM worked with modernist industrial designers and architects, such as Noyes, Breuer, Rand and the Eameses, to produce a sense of computing design as both spectacle and sober articulation of the workings of the machine. The large plate-glass windows of a display room on Madison Avenue, reworked in 1954 to show the bustle, mystique and power of computing as it was epitomized in the IBM 702;[29] or the pavilions and films for world's fairs that staged the cogency and importance of technological transformation; as much as the glass frontages to computers designed by Eliot Noyes that foregrounded the intricacy and beauty of the large circuits and components of these machines: all argued for their importance and the centrality of the company producing them.[30] Noyes' early work on hardware emphasized glass panels in cases. The International Style of architecture is the point of reference for the casing of computers such as the IBM 705 III or the IBM 305 RAMAC: these are the design principles of Mies van der Rohe's Farnsworth House reworked to display a materialization of Claude Shannon's translation of Boolean logic expressed in circuits. This conjunction of sobriety – the machine under the regime of the modern translation of the Calvinist curtainless window – with theatre is elaborated in part due to the requirement for an envelope around the machine that protects the working of components. Perhaps a more submerged reference is to the glass-fronted jukeboxes and amusement arcade machines these computers also resemble and whose transparent operation as automata is part of their charm. The Wurlitzer 1100 Jukebox, made in 1948, was advertised with the phrase 'Look at it! Listen to it! Probe into its innards and marvel at its engineering!',[31] and came fitted with illuminating and revolving coloured pilasters to boot. Something of this flavour was played out in the candy-coloured and translucent iMacs of the late 1990s, but the reflections, mutual interpenetration of spaces and sheets of brightness, fresh air and mobile, cleansing lightness that are held together like informational weather-fronts in recent headquarters buildings aim to address another scale.

This is a moment when Silicon Valley companies attempt to address the world, and to gird themselves, with an appropriate magnificence.

The new crop of headquarters buildings includes Facebook's 2015 building in Menlo Park, designed by Frank Gehry; Apple's, of 2016 built in Cupertino, designed by Norman Foster & Co.; and Google's new Mountain View campus, designed by Bjarke Ingels Group and Thomas Heatherwick Studio in 2016.

Facebook

Gehry's building revisits, in a slightly more guarded way, some of the style of his late-1970s work, the Santa Monica house built around an existing structure, by an accumulation of apparently rough, cheap materials with raw surfaces, arrayed in funky, almost accidental juxtaposition and an air of permanent construction. The house as building site, with chain-link fencing and corrugated barriers, is translated into the big box warehouse as collision space, one out-of-town store thrust into the other in a row. It is the aesthetics of the hero-garage extruded to the length of a multinational work-liner. Threaded around it are numerous cantilevered decks and walkways, steel staircases that veer in and out of the jaunty, sunshiny, big-windowed building. High ceilings allow for temporary structures, such as canteens and gathering spaces, careers.

On the opening day, a glass-walled chamber of a meeting room is filled with plastic ball-pool balls. Work is a playground. It is fast, quasi-hackable, the building's speed of assembly being an indicator of how fast the company can move on, to the next one, to be built on the other side of the freeway. Its state of unfinishedness is a three-dimensional press release to show how much more they can achieve. On the roof there is a nine-acre landscaped arrangement of paths, plants and decking. The layout of paths on the roof gardens looks uncannily like that set out by Archizoom in their 1970 competition proposal for the University of Florence, yet they are topologically distinct, with Facebook's being a relatively closed structure, like a social network analysis graph of one group of friends alone.[32] This is a space to work in a hammock or folksy Adirondack chair, to connect with yourself by direct message.

The place is built to encourage spontaneous encounters between people from different teams and specialisms moving around the internal and external balconies, walkways and stairs, and across the massive internal floors. Project teams cluster on mobile furniture, wires hang from the ceiling to power their large monitors and laptops. Developers and marketers slump on mid-century modern armchairs and are perked up by Aerons. The air is one of provision-

224

ality and has the tang of the freshly canned street art adorning some of the walls. When Zuckerberg stalks the premises, high-fiving and nodding, employees act furiously carefree. Transparency here is in the mode familiar from tech companies, expensively rough finishes belying sophisticated mediation of building codes and an attempt to self-social-engineer that is emphasized by its marked attempts to look effortless.

Apple

Developing the theme of meadows and trees as if riffing off Richard Brautigan's poem, 'All watched over by machines of loving grace', as merely a post-ironic list of ingredients for a successful campus rather than a declaration of foreboding, the pre-construction images of Apple's headquarters present a world of low trees, golden grasslands and paths to wander in. Personnel are on a pilgrimage or voyaging to a festival. On greener lawns, people in American blue-jeans sit on deckchairs or café chairs, lounge under a pergola covered in wisteria. Staffers serendipitously meet by the shrubbery. They hold their hands up to protect their eyes from the evening sun, as the shadows draw across the landscape engineering. And oh, in the background the sun is reflecting from one of the sheets of glass on the building's façade, a circular elevation four storeys high. The building is a circle of glass extruded down from the heavens to intensify light on earth. A number of the exterior panels are claimed to be the largest sheets of curved glass ever made.[33] The building is magnificently engineered, with components brought together with precision and attention to environmental impact. Inside the circle is more parkland, a stage, pathways, expertly curated arborial content.

What is notable about the people biding their time in the park is that none of them hold a phone or a tablet, wear bass-enhancing earbuds, flick their wrists at a watch, or tap at a laptop. The mock-up images of Apple's campus produced by Foster's office suggest a technology-free world of indolence surrounding this fortress of transparency. Inside the seven-mile circumference of the great vitrine of a headquarters, transparency is complemented by a superlative control over information flows. All staff are under the opaque exactitudes of non-disclosure agreements. Security clearances protecting siloed, perhaps competing, projects govern access control. This building takes the form of the glass atrium and extrudes it through a 360-degree rotation; an infinite atrium, with all the micro-politics of welcoming, displaying, enticing, waiting, intercepting and controlling that occurs in a building lobby scrolled through the structure and elaborated in electronic, legal and architectural hyper-dimensions. This fortress of transparency instantiates a style that, rather than operate a grammar by which they are held distinct, absolutely fuses transparency and opacity as identical qualities.

Google

What is impressive about the new buildings being drawn up and begun for Google is that the future arrives just as it has always been imagined. There is not one iota that seems to come from a future that has not already been had. The combination of the utopian architecture of the 1960s, biospheres, Buckminster Fuller and the blob architecture of the beginning of the century produces an architectural space-time matrix that collapses into a hyper-dense concentration of the inevitable. The campus folds volumes of air and light in, 'a single piece of super-transparent, ultra-light membrane'.[34] A series of glass tension-structures covers a modular architecture of recomposable storeys, of internal structure as furniture. And here is the novelty, not in the architectural vocabulary of glass membranes, but in the explicit way in which composition is expressed as power, but in a manner more natively computational: the building envelope works as an expression of *calculation power* expressed by the complexity of components set into relation by associative modelling, transcoding across forms, the elaboration of vector fields with multiple curvatures. Calculation power (partially exemplified in parametric design, claimed by its proponent Patrik Schumacher as the international style 'founded in advancing processes of post-Fordist restructuring, globalisation, market liberalisation and democratisation'[35]) substitutes the voluptuous use of complex geometry such as splines and nurbs for the classical symbols of Euclidian geometric power: columns, domes and walls. Masses of masonry become traces of numerical functions intensified across a myriad of particles. Gaskets, space-frames and meshes, with each component individually machined, flow in individuated arrays across space to cohere as canopies, whilst equally individuated crowds of skill-bearing employees mingle in the floors below.

In reciprocal mingling, beds of plants run across the boundaries of the canopies. As a Google blog says, 'With trees, landscaping, cafes, and bike paths weaving through these structures, we aim to blur the distinction between our buildings and nature.'[36] Unlike Serge's paucity of the programmability of fish, shoals of data array themselves in nets with a readiness that confirms the naturalness of the arrangement. In such an environment, according to the model images of the campus that are provided by Google, the trees are more verdant and shady, the grass is more bucolic, fed by streams. There is more of an informality to the planting, rope bridges threaded across waterways make the space more like a playground, small beds of vegetables make it like a market garden. The cafés and walkways that cluster around the canopies are open to the public, since the campus occupies so much of a space that would otherwise be a town. This is Center Parcs or the Eden Project reconstituted and generalized as workplace and holiday, a rendering of the form of contemporary power where the emperors themselves, rather than their clothes, are transparent.

Farm

The interplay between modes of opacity and transparency and their rendering in different modes of composition, at variable and fixed ranges of scales, and in their texturing of relations between the entities that they draw together and compose, provides a fundamental ground of organization for the present day.

Various forms of humanism suggest a model of a moment when humanity becomes transparent to itself in a hard-wrangled time of self-knowledge. For Marx, this moment would arise from communism, where the commodity form would no longer hide labour from itself. A more constructivist formulation suggests that different modalities, kinds and keennesses of transparency may be created by intercalating different textures, processes and matters of variable refractive indexes.

One project that plays in between these modes is the installation *Farm (Pryor Creek, Oklahoma)* by the Irish artist John Gerrard.[37] In order to produce this work, Gerrard first contacted Google to gain permission to photograph one of its server farms. Permission was refused, so a helicopter was hired, and around 30,000 frames of images were taken whilst it flew round the building. These images were then transposed into Unigine, a game engine that rendered the external characteristics of the building, to be projected onto the wall of a gallery. The installation consists of the slow progress of the rendering, and panning by a zooming process, around the model of the building. With barely a trace of glass, except for some light-vents in the flanks of an administration building, the server farm is a low construction, an extended concrete shed surrounded by large white tanks holding refrigerant gases, an array of steel towers and electrical supply equipment. The rural landscape of Pryor is transposed into a dully glowering desert in the installation. In both cases, the building effaces rather than celebrates transparency, but it is one of the architectures of opacity that subtends the crystal menageries being rendered around the Californian freeways.

All of these cases show that transparency cannot simply be implemented from a set of general principles as an absolute and addressable quality that can be invoked without translation. Transparency must be constructed, and in that movement refractions are induced. Each modality of transparency summons particular characteristics of composition to the fore. The field of human–computer interaction is a cluster of spaces for experimenting with the ideational forces of these modalities at the level of interface, but transparency layers run deep, into the relation of processors and languages, the relations of objects and processes in networks, and the figurations of entities in economies and cultural forms.

Following Gödel, computational logic is not wholly knowable to itself in its own terms, and thus folds outwards in order to maintain a point of reference. In so doing, it voraciously becomes part of the world, and, to stabilize its uncertainty, to give it some traction, starts to hold on to and work into other scales of existence, which it thus potentiates and recodes with the capacities for generality, construction and power characteristic of computing. The organizations, ideas and forces that are able to align themselves with this proliferation are able in turn to arrange it. They forge collective equipment at a time when technology simply is politics, is one of its primary grounds of constitution. The proliferation of calculation power entailed by computing entails an exponential quality that has similarities to the forces of desire, one that finds its forms in the myriad modes of connection, modelling, simulation, ordering, control, speculation, experiment, disintermediation, counting, recording, recoding, extrapolating, inventing and other kinds of movement in computational culture. Part of the stakes, then, of a theoretical, hackerly, political or aesthetic involvement in software is to catch this movement and to realign it, provide other moving points of reference, and other drives by which it might be refracted and intensified.

It is in amongst this condition that the formation of transparency layers occurs, in the movement between the generality of computation and what it tangles with and mutates and is mutated by; and in the way in which this condition is mediated and articulated by specific implementations, particular pieces of code, working methods,

228

the concatenations of libraries, languages, frameworks, companies, licences, protocols, objects; and in the ways in which these further concatenate relations of the means of ideation, eroticism, economy, sensation and the grinding machines of gender, class, race, nationality. One of the means to stabilize and align computational forces has been through the classic forms of bureaucracy, which provides its own customary diagrams and textures of opacity and transparency, its own means of elisions and accountabilities in negotiating the general and the particular. Transparency with certain modifications is one of the key bureaucratic ideals, as much as self-knowledge has been crucial to the ideals of humanism. Each of these has its vectors and textures of clarity, its characteristic blind-spots and the subjects that thrive in them. Their peculiar combination of transparency and opacity is what characterizes them and the calculus of possibility and indeterminacy that they establish.

That both the architecture and the operating systems of some of the key organizations of Silicon Valley are in this moment attempting to align themselves with a version of the contemporary, in a dual move that is surely aimed at more forcefully defining it; and that this movement is made by the elaboration of a rhetoric and a variable set of instantiations of transparency; must draw attention to the nature of the textures, grammars and processes such transparency entails. At the same time, the shifting dynamics of feedback around these immense glass boxes, the uncluttered interfaces and edgeless screens that they produce and the swirls of opacity that they disavow, effuse and rely upon, create conditions for reflection.

NOTES

1 Félix Guattari, *Lines of Flight: For Another World of Possibilities*, trans. Andrew Goffey, Bloomsbury, London, 2015, p. 11.
2 Donald Gentner and Jacob Nielsen, 'The Anti-Mac Interface', *Communications of the ACM*, 39:8 (August 1996), pp. 70–82.
3 Leslie C. McDaniel, 'Reining in the Power Horse Tractor', *Farm Collector*, August 1999, http://www.farmcollector.com/tractors/power-horse-tractor.aspx.
4 Scott Forstall was the Apple vice president who championed this approach.
5 Andy Hertzfeld, *Revolution in the Valley: The Insanely Great Story of How the Mac Was Made*, O'Reilly, Sebastapol, CA, 2011.

6 Such metaphor has its own counterpart in a typical interface produced under the graphic structures native to a language such as Visual Basic, in which a grey universe of fields, drop-down menus and other features presents the ability to operate on data with a high degree of detail, but incoherently. Here, the non-metaphorical becomes a metaphor for clarity.

7 The Emojicode project website is http://emojicode.org.

8 See the project documentation at Ted Nelson et al., *Xanadu*, http://www.xanadu.com.

9 John Lions, *A Commentary on the 6th Edition Unix Operating System*, University of New South Wales, Sydney, 1977; Harold Abelson, Gerald Jay Sussman and Julie Sussman, *Structure and Interpretation of Computer Programs*, 2nd edn, MIT Press, Cambridge, MA, 1996.

10 Google's Material Design, though 'flat', is remarkably insistent on its metaphorical debt to print and paper. Google, *Material Design*, http://www.google.com/design/spec/material-design/introduction.html

11 Leander Kahney, *Jony Ive: The Genius Behind Apple's Greatest Products*, Portfolio Penguin, London, 2014.

12 Nick Wingfield, 'The Critics Rave ... For Microsoft?', *New York Times*, 7 January 2012.

13 Apple, *iOS Human Interface Guidelines*, https://developer.apple.com/library/ios/documentation/UserExperience/Conceptual/MobileHIG.

14 Smart watches, echoing the jargon of watchmakers, add 'complications' to their faces.

15 Thanks to Dirk Paesmans of Jodi for a discussion of screens.

16 Alan Kay and Adele Goldberg, 'Personal Dynamic Media', in Noah Wardrip Fruin and Nick Montford, *New Media Reader*, MIT Press, Cambridge, MA, 2003.

17 Gilbert Simondon, *Du mode d'existence des objets techniques*, Editions Aubier, Paris, 2012.

18 Kahney, *Jony Ive*, p. 242.

19 Bruno Latour, *Science in Action: How To Follow Scientists and Engineers Through Society*, Harvard University Press, Cambridge, MA, 1988, pp. 2–3.

20 William Ross Ashby, *Introduction to Cybernetics*, Chapman & Hall, London, 1957, p. 87.

21 Victor Serge, *Midnight in the Century*, trans. Richard Greeman, New York Review Books, New York, 2015, p. 62

22 Friedrich Hayek, *Law, Legislation and Liberty*, 3 vols., Routledge & Kegan Paul, London and Henley, 1973–9.

23 Friedrich Hayek, 'The Uses of Knowledge in Society', *American Economic Review*, 35:4 (September 1945), pp. 519–30.

24 Alfred North Whitehead, *Introduction to Mathematics*, Thornton Butterworth, London, and Henry Holt, New York, 1911, p. 61.

25 Ludwig Wittgenstein, *On Certainty*, trans. G. E. M. Anscombe, Blackwell, Oxford, 1991.

26 Claude Lefort, *The Making of Machiavelli*, Northwestern University Press, Evanston, 2012.

27 Eric Schmidt and Jared Cohen, *A New Digital Age: Reshaping the Future of People, Nations and Businesses*, John Murray, London, 2014.

28 Metahaven, *Black Transparency: The Right To Know in the Age of Mass Surveillance*, Sternberg Press, Berlin, 2015.

29 This showroom was at the base of IBM world headquarters at the junction of Madison Avenue and Fifty-Seventh Street. Nathan Ensmenger, *The Computer Boys Take Over: Computers, Programmers, and the Politics of Technical Expertise*, MIT Press, Cambridge, MA, 2010.

30 The work of Noyes and of IBM's designers and consultant designers more generally is expertly brought together in John Harwood, *The Interface: IBM and the Transformation of Corporate Design 1945–1976*, University of Minnesota Press, Minneapolis, 2011.

31 Jukebox London http://www.jukeboxlondon.co.uk/index.php/gallery/a-1948-wurlitzer-model-1100-jukebox.

32 See a photograph of the maquette for this proposal in Catherine Rossi and Alex Coles (eds.), *EP. Vol. 1: The Italian Avant-Garde 1968–1976*, Sternberg Press, Berlin, 2013, pp. 152–3.

33 The glass company Sedak, which manufactures the panels, makes this claim at https://www.sedak.com/en/company/current/details/article/tim-cook-zu-gast-bei-sedak.

34 Phrase from Bjarke Ingels, speaking in a Google promotional video, 'Rethinking Office Space', https://googleblog.blogspot.co.uk/2015/02/rethinking-office-space.html.

35 Patrik Schumacher, 'The Historical Pertinence of Parametricism and the Prospect of a Free Market Urban Order', in Matthew Poole and Manuel Schvartzberg (eds.), *The Politics of Parametricism: Digital Technologies in Architecture*, Bloomsbury, London, 2015, p. 19.

36 David Radcliffe, 'Rethinking Office Space', *Google Official Blog*, 27 February 2015, https://googleblog.blogspot.co. uk/2015/02/rethinking-office-space.html.
37 Shown at the Thomas Dane gallery, St James, London, 2015.

REFERENCES

Harold Abelson, Gerald Jay Sussman and Julie Sussman, *Structure and Interpretation of Computer Programs*, 2nd edn, MIT Press, Cambridge, MA, 1996.
Apple, *iOS Human Interface Guidelines*, https://developer.apple.com/library/ios/documentation/UserExperience/Conceptual/MobileHIG
William Ross Ashby, *Introduction to Cybernetics*, Chapman & Hall, London, 1957.
Emojicode, http://emojicode.org
Nathan Ensmenger, *The Computer Boys Take Over: Computers, Programmers, and the Politics of Technical Expertise*, MIT Press, Cambridge, MA, 2010.
Donald Gentner and Jacob Nielsen, 'The Anti-Mac Interface', *Communications of the ACM*, 39:8 (August 1996), pp. 70–82.
Google, *Material Design*, http://www.google.com/design/spec/material-design/introduction.html
Google, 'Rethinking Office Space', https://googleblog.blogspot.co.uk/2015/02/rethinking-office-space.html
Félix Guattari, *Lines of Flight: For Another World of Possibilities*, trans. Andrew Goffey, Bloomsbury, London, 2015.
John Harwood, *The Interface: IBM and the Transformation of Corporate Design 1945–1976*, University of Minnesota Press, Minneapolis, 2011.
Friedrich Hayek, 'The Uses of Knowledge in Society', *American Economic Review*, 35:4 (September 1945), pp. 519–30.
Friedrich Hayek, *Law, Legislation and Liberty*, 3 vols., Routledge & Kegan Paul, London and Henley, 1973–9.
Andy Hertzfeld, *Revolution in the Valley: The Insanely Great Story of How the Mac Was Made*, O'Reilly, Sebastapol, CA, 2011.
Jukebox London, http://www.jukeboxlondon.co.uk/index.php/gallery/a-1948-wurlitzer-model-1100-jukebox
Leander Kahney, *Jony Ive: The Genius Behind Apple's Greatest Products*, Portfolio Penguin, London, 2014.
Alan Kay and Adele Goldberg, 'Personal Dynamic Media', in Noah Wardrip Fruin and Nick Montford, *New Media Reader*, MIT Press, Cambridge, MA, 2003.
Bruno Latour, *Science in Action: How To Follow Scientists and Engineers Through Society*, Harvard University Press, Cambridge, MA, 1988.

Claude Lefort, *The Making of Machiavelli*, Northwestern University Press, Evanston, 2012.

John Lions, *A Commentary on the 6th Edition Unix Operating System*, University of New South Wales, Sydney, 1977.

Leslie C. McDaniel, 'Reining in the Power Horse Tractor', *Farm Collector*, August 1999, http://www.farmcollector.com/tractors/power-horse-tractor.aspx

Metahaven, *Black Transparency: The Right To Know in the Age of Mass Surveillance*, Sternberg Press, Berlin, 2015.

Ted Nelson et al., *Xanadu*, http://www.xanadu.com

David Radcliffe, 'Rethinking Office Space', *Google Official Blog*, 27 February 2015, https://googleblog.blogspot.co.uk/2015/02/rethinking-office-space.html

Catherine Rossi and Alex Coles (eds.), *EP. Vol. 1: The Italian Avant-Garde 1968–1976*, Sternberg Press, Berlin, 2013.

Eric Schmidt and Jared Cohen, *A New Digital Age: Reshaping the Future of People, Nations and Businesses*, John Murray, London, 2014.

Patrik Schumacher, 'The Historical Pertinence of Parametricism and the Prospect of a Free Market Urban Order', in Matthew Poole and Manuel Schvartzberg (eds.), *The Politics of Parametricism: Digital Technologies in Architecture*, Bloomsbury, London, 2015.

Victor Serge, *Midnight in the Century*, trans. Richard Greeman, New York Review Books, New York, 2015.

Gilbert Simondon, *Du mode d'existence des objets techniques*, Editions Aubier, Paris, 2012.

Alfred North Whitehead, *Introduction to Mathematics*, Thornton Butterworth, London, and Henry Holt, New York, 1911.

Nick Wingfield, 'The Critics Rave ... For Microsoft?', *New York Times*, 7 January 2012.

Ludwig Wittgenstein, *On Certainty*, trans. G. E. M. Anscombe, Blackwell, Oxford, 1991.